Presidential Elections
in the
Television Age

Presidential Elections
in the
Television Age

1960–1992

E. D. Dover

PRAEGER

**Westport, Connecticut
London**

Library of Congress Cataloging-in-Publication Data

Dover, E. D.
    Presidential elections in the television age : 1960–1992 / E. D. Dover.
        p. cm.
    Includes bibliographical references and index.
    ISBN 0–275–94840–4 (alk. paper)
    1. Presidents—United States—Election—History—20th century.
2. Television in politics—United States. I. Title.
JK524.D68 1994
324.973′092—dc20   93–42803

British Library Cataloguing in Publication Data is available.

Copyright © 1994 by E. D. Dover

All rights reserved. No portion of this book may be reproduced, by any process or technique, without the express written consent of the publisher.

Library of Congress Catalog Card Number: 93–42803
ISBN: 0–275–94840–4

First published in 1994

Praeger Publishers, 88 Post Road West, Westport, CT 06881
An imprint of Greenwood Publishing Group, Inc.

Printed in the United States of America

∞™

The paper used in this book complies with the Permanent Paper Standard issued by the National Information Standards Organization (Z39.48—1984).

10 9 8 7 6 5 4 3 2

Contents

1 Presidential Elections in the Television Age	1
2 Elections with Strong Incumbents	23
3 Elections with Surrogate Incumbents	73
4 Elections with Weak Incumbents	121
5 Conclusions and Epilogue	171
Selected Bibliography	175
Index	183

PRESIDENTIAL ELECTIONS
in the
TELEVISION AGE

1

Presidential Elections in the Television Age

The American people have been holding presidential elections for more than two hundred years. We began during the initial weeks of 1789 by choosing George Washington as our first chief executive, and since then, his successors in years divisible by four. Washington won office unanimously, but over the ensuing two centuries presidential elections became highly competitive struggles for control of the executive branch of our national government.

In a sense every election is unique. The candidates, issues, events, and voters that dominate one election differ from those that dominate others. For example, on only five occasions in American history have the major candidates from one election encountered one another again. In three instances the loser of the preceding election defeated the incumbent (1800, 1828, 1892), while in the other two the incumbent defeated his earlier rival once again but did so in a substantially different context (1900, 1956). The leading issues of one year often lose salience with voters by the next, and new ones arise to replace them. Moreover, major events can alter the contexts of campaigns by forcing new, and often temporary, issues into the limelight. The Watergate scandal with its damaging effects upon Republicans played a leading role in the 1976 election but disappeared by 1980, while the Iranian hostage crisis hampered Jimmy Carter and the Democrats in this latter campaign but was a matter of little concern by 1984. The Vietnam War was important in three elections—1964, 1968, and 1972—but affected each differently. It was just beginning in 1964, was at its zenith in 1968, and was nearly over by 1972. Abortion became a far more important issue in 1992 than it had ever been before after a series of rulings by the U.S.

Supreme Court, including one during the campaign, upheld the efforts of some states to restrict access.

Finally, the composition of the electorate changes between campaigns. Many people—some young, some not so young—become voters, while others stop voting, voluntarily or by death. The new voters sometimes differ from those they replace, thus helping to strengthen or weaken the electoral strength of different communities, political parties, and ideologies. The ratification of the 26th amendment, which lowered the voting age from twenty-one to eighteen, added millions of new voters to the electorate between 1968 and 1972. The passage of the Voting Rights Act in 1965 helped remove many of the obstacles to full political participation by racial minorities and aided Jimmy Carter in winning the electoral votes of most southeastern states and the Presidency in 1976.

Despite these unique features, many elections bear striking resemblances to one another. The outcomes of the elections of 1972 and 1984 appear similar because the incumbents (Nixon, Reagan) won second terms by capturing the electoral votes of forty-nine states. The 1976 and 1980 elections also appear similar because the incumbents (Ford, Carter) failed to win reelection after encountering very divisive struggles within their own parties over renomination. Twentieth-century elections are similar because they follow a calendar that includes primary elections between February and June, nominating conventions in July and August, and a general election campaign from September to November. The presence of television is a recurring feature of more recent elections. Television is the medium from which most voters now learn much of what they know about the campaigns and the candidates. Televised news and advertising help create and reinforce mass perceptions of political realities. Finally, the nominees of the Democratic and Republican parties have been the two leading contenders in every presidential election since 1856. These and many other similarities are not random but instead occur with a certain regularity that political analysts observe and seek to explain.

ELECTION CATEGORIES AND TELEVISION

Older Categories

In "The Concept of a Normal Vote" (1966), Philip E. Converse postulates that the actual vote has two components: "(1) the normal or 'baseline' vote division to be expected from a group, other things being equal; and (2) the current deviation from that norm, which occurs as a function of the immediate circumstances of the specific election." The normal component derives from voters' long-standing partisan preferences. Many voters have an emotional commitment to a political party that often influences their electoral choices. The preferences tend to remain stable over many years, thus giving each party a base of support upon which it can rely for contesting elections. The party bases are not distributed randomly throughout the nation but instead are concentrated among specific groups of people who are distinguished from the general population by characteristics such as income, race, occupation, ideology, or national background. Moreover, each party's base tends to be concentrated within particular geographic locales. Since the distributions of particular groups vary widely among the states, it is quite usual for many states, over a series of elections, to vote for the nominees of one party at percentage levels that consistently exceed the national levels of support for that party. While most voters maintain their partisan preferences over much of their adult lives, certain influences unique to given elections can induce some to deviate from their partisanship and support the opposition. These short-term influences are rarely strong enough to induce most voters to abandon their partisanship permanently however. Most deviant voters resume support of their party once the influences subside.

Angus Campbell draws upon Converse's work and advances a set of categories for explaining the outcomes of presidential elections. Like his colleague Converse, he found that partisanship was the most important factor affecting voter choice. In "A Classification of Presidential Elections" (1966), he states that elections are either maintaining, deviating, or realigning. He derives these categories from variations in the interplay between the normal and deviation components of the vote. Maintaining elections occur when "the pattern of partisan attachments prevailing in the preceding period persists, and the majority party wins the Presidency." In such elections, short-term forces are relatively weak and fail to provide either party with an advantage. Campbell described most elections in the century prior to 1966 as maintaining, including those of 1948 and 1960. Deviating elections occur when "the basic division of party loyalties is not seriously disturbed, but the influence of short-term forces on the vote is such that it brings about the defeat of the majority party." The elections of 1952 and 1956 were deviating according to Campbell. Realigning elections occur when "popular feeling associated with politics is sufficiently intense that the basic partisan commitments of a portion of the electorate change, and a new party balance is created." Drawing upon V. O. Key's article "Toward a Theory of Critical Elections" (1955), Campbell designates the elections of 1896, which began a series of Republican victories, and 1932, when a series of Democratic triumphs started, as realigning. Other writers since Campbell consider the elections of 1828 and 1860, which marked the initial victories of Democrat Andrew Jackson and Republican Abraham Lincoln respectively, to be realigning.

Kevin Phillips writes that another realigning election occurred in 1968. In *The Emerging Republican Majority* (1969), Phillips contends that the Democratic Party majority that had dominated presidential elections since the

1930s had ended and that a new Republican majority, comprised of the supporters of Richard Nixon and George Wallace, would soon become a new majority. When one considers that the Republican Party had won only two of the nine elections between 1932 and 1964 but has taken five of the seven since 1968, Phillips' contentions appear quite compelling. There are some difficulties with Phillips' ideas however. While the Republican Party has won most presidential elections since 1968, it has failed to translate those triumphs into control of other political institutions, particularly Congress. The Democratic Party has maintained control of the House of Representatives continuously since 1954, and, except for a six-year period between 1980 and 1986, control of the Senate as well. Clubb, Flanigan, and Zingale (1980) point out that realignments are not limited to one institution but extend to the entire national government. The party that won the presidency in the realigning elections of 1828, 1860, 1896, and 1932 also won majority control of both chambers of Congress and then perpetuated its control of the Presidency and Congress for at least twelve years, that is, for three consecutive presidential terms. This control gave the majority party sufficient power and time to enact its program and to redefine the cleavages within the two-party system. This pattern has not occurred during the past quarter century. This fact demonstrates that the election of 1968, while perhaps marking the end of the Democratic Party's majority status, was not realigning.

While Campbell's categories are useful for explaining the outcomes of most nineteenth- and early twentieth-century presidential elections, they seem ill suited for explaining more recent ones. Quite frankly, there have been no maintaining, deviating, or realigning elections during the past three decades. The election of 1932 was the last involving a realignment of the entire political system. Moreover, in light of the fact that the Democratic Party has lost every presidential election since 1968 save two, it is unrealistic to depict the recent string of Republican victories as deviations from a normal Democratic majority that has existed since 1932. Finally, it is very difficult to view any recent election as maintaining. The unusually large fluctuations in levels of partisan support between elections since 1960 indicate the lack of a stable majority coalition that can be maintained over time.

The fluctuations have been so extensive that the vote distributions of any given election are not replicated in the next. In 1960 the Democratic nominee, Senator John F. Kennedy (Massachusetts), defeated the Republican candidate, Vice President Richard M. Nixon, by a popular vote margin of only two-tenths of one percent, which made that one of the closest elections in American history. In 1964, however, the Democratic incumbent, Lyndon B. Johnson, recorded one of the most lopsided victories ever, with 61 percent of the popular vote and forty-four states. This victory was so sweeping that some political observers proclaimed the Republican Party a permanent minority. The electoral volatility continued in 1968. Johnson suffered a serious erosion of support after 1964 and finally declined to seek reelection after strong opposition to his renomination emerged in the candidacies of Senators Eugene McCarthy (Minnesota) and Robert F. Kennedy (New York). The Democrats nominated Vice President Hubert H. Humphrey and lost the subsequent election to Nixon. The decline in Democratic fortunes since 1964 was substantial: Humphrey garnered less than 43 percent of the popular vote in the three-candidate election. Nixon's popular vote was only slightly higher than Humphrey's, although he did carry thirty-two states, while Governor George Wallace (Alabama) attained 14 percent and captured five states. The fluctuations continued over the next six elections. Nixon won a second term in 1972 with 61 percent of the popular vote and forty-nine states, a record number. Four years later, however, the Republicans lost power as Governor Jimmy Carter (Georgia) attained 51 percent of the vote. Carter acquired only 41 percent in his unsuccessful bid for a second term in 1980 in yet another three-candidate election, while Congressman John Anderson (Illinois) received 7 percent. Ronald Reagan expanded his 51 percent support from 1980 into 59 percent when he sought reelection in 1984 and, like Nixon, carried forty-nine states. George Bush extended the Republican winning streak to three in 1988 when he defeated Governor Michael Dukakis (Massachusetts) while acquiring 53 percent of the vote, but he failed to win a second term in 1992. Bush attained only 37 percent of the popular vote in this latter campaign that also involved three candidates. Governor Bill Clinton (Arkansas) became the first Democrat since Carter to win the Presidency, but he garnered only 43 percent of the vote. Ross Perot, with 19 percent, offered the strongest challenge to the two major parties since 1912 when Theodore Roosevelt was the nominee of the Progressive Party.

While the outcomes of elections since 1960 may appear unique and perhaps even random because of the aforementioned fluctuations, they do share many common patterns. They differ considerably from their predecessors in that they did not replicate those elections' relatively stable patterns of partisan support. More important, however, they differ from their predecessors because of the extensive influence of television in both personalizing campaigns and enhancing the powers of presidential incumbency. Nonetheless, while the size of the partisan vote has declined in recent elections, it has not disappeared entirely. Both parties continue to have bases of support that are concentrated among particular groups of people and certain geographic locales. Several states, including Minnesota, Hawaii, and Massachusetts, have voted Democratic in seven of the nine elections since 1960, while other states such as Virginia, Indiana, and Utah have voted Republican at least as frequently. The formula Converse advanced for dividing the actual vote into its normal and deviation components remains generally valid today, albeit the magnitude of the normal component has declined while that of the deviation has increased. Much of the increase in the deviation component derives from the influence of television.

The Influence of Television

Television affects elections by enhancing the personal characteristics of those individuals who are the subjects of its attention. This, in turn, increases the importance of short-term forces upon voter choice and diminishes the importance of partisanship. The organizations and reporters that produce television news programming (i.e., television news media) personalize events by illustrating them through the actions and words of individuals. In doing so, they direct attention to the key people involved in the events on which they report rather than to the institutional or contextual circumstances from which those events arise. With respect to elections, they depict candidates more as solitary aspirants for office than as leaders of governmental institutions or as spokesmen for political parties. The candidates reinforce these images through televised advertising when they seek to construct their own personalized constituencies. Such a combination of news and advertising encourages candidate-centered campaigns, as modern elections have come to be known, where candidates seek office as individuals and where voters rely more upon the personal characteristics of candidates than upon partisanship when making electoral choices. In such a context, presidential incumbency all too frequently proves to be the one characteristic that is most enhanced by this personalizing nature of television.

While television news media report on the happenings of many governmental institutions, they devote the lion's share of their political coverage to the Presidency. They make the Presidency the anchor point of their political reporting by defining most events from the perspective of how those events either originated with the President or of how they might affect his options and choices. To them, foreign and domestic difficulties are problems that should be viewed from the vantage point of the Presidency and can be solved only by the President. Television news media often create the morality play of movie westerns when they report about the Presidency. They depict the President as a solitary individual who is separate from the institutions of government, despite the fact that he is the nation's chief executive. They show him as a "Lone Ranger," an outsider who supposedly fights for popular justice against evil and corrupt institutions. Moreover, they depict governmental institutions, and Congress in particular, as obstacles the President must overcome to achieve this justice. They do not depict Congress as a co-equal partner in a political system that is characterized by a constitutionally mandated separation of powers structure.

This pattern of news reporting influences mass perceptions about the relative importance of the Presidency within the American political system. It encourages people to believe that the President is the personal leader of the nation and the dominant policy maker of government. It also encourages them to believe that the President is separate from the institutions of government and instead rules through the strength of personality and charisma. Finally, it provides the President with invaluable opportunities for manipulating the content of television news in hopes of enhancing mass perceptions of his political competency and in generating the widespread personal support that can secure his renomination and reelection.

Three incumbent Presidents since 1960—Lyndon Johnson, Richard Nixon, and Ronald Reagan—were successful at doing so and won reelection by vote margins rarely attained in American history. Three other incumbents—Gerald Ford, Jimmy Carter, and George Bush—were unsuccessful and joined the small list of incumbents who have been denied second terms. Three others—Dwight Eisenhower, Lyndon Johnson (1968), and Ronald Reagan—did not seek reelection, but their parties looked upon their Vice Presidents as personal surrogates and nominated them as the hoped-for successors. Voters rejected two of those Vice Presidents in the general election however. The leading determinants of the outcomes of these nine elections were voter evaluations of the personal qualities of the incumbents and of their individual performances in office. Voters evaluated three incumbents positively and reelected them, evaluated three negatively and rejected them, and had mixed views of the three who retired. These personally focused evaluations derived partly from changes that have taken place in political communication over the past several decades. Such evaluations are now so important in voter choice that it seems less appropriate to consider modern elections as battles between the Republican and Democratic parties than between the presidential party (the one in power) and the opposition (the one that is not). Throughout this work, I use the terms *presidential* and *opposition* to designate the two major parties involved in any given election.

Newer Categories

My purpose in writing this book is to present an alternative explanation and corresponding set of categories of recent presidential elections. The explanation and categories take the presence and effects of television, particularly news reporting, into account and consider how that presence has enhanced the importance of candidate-centered campaigns and incumbency while reducing the influence of partisanship. Although I concentrate much of my discussion upon the electoral changes that have been enhanced by television, I do not dispute Converse's formula for dividing the actual vote into its normal and deviation components, for they are still very much present. I do contend, however, that certain patterns that occur regularly in television news reporting, and which are often supplemented by candidate advertising, have helped to expand the magnitude of the short-term and increasingly personality-related deviation vote while helping to diminish the magnitude of the normal or partisan vote. Campbell based his categories of outcomes on the idea that partisanship was the leading determinant of voter choice while various short-term forces interacted with it. I base my categories of outcomes on the idea that televised incumbency has now become the leading determinant of voter choice while partisanship interacts with it.

When judged from the perspective that televised incumbency is the leading determinant of voter choice, elections since 1960 divide into three categories: (1) elections with strong incumbents, (2) elections with weak incumbents, and (3) elections with surrogate incumbents.

Elections with strong incumbents are those in which the President wins another term, for example, the elections of 1964, 1972, and 1984. These elections are characterized by the fact that the incumbent consolidates political power within his own party prior to the beginning of the election year. As a consequence, he enjoys widespread personal and political support and encounters minimal or no opposition for renomination. Television news media cannot show him actually consolidating power, so instead they illustrate the aftermath of that consolidation by directing attention to the President acting in the role in which he is governing the nation. The incumbent uses television, and television news media readily comply, to enhance mass perceptions of his personal and political competence by projecting images that he is acting "presidential." Voters see him as a statesman and national leader who is worthy of their support. Television news media serve as partners in the generation of consensus in support of the incumbent. The opposition party encounters quite the opposite conditions however. Certain institutional limitations in American government tend to inhibit this party from uniting behind one undisputed leader before an election campaign. Therefore, the party must undergo a lengthy campaign in order to select its standard bearer. It usually attracts a large number of relatively unknown aspirants who must spend many months engaging in what is often intense competition in order to win. Television news media direct much of their attention to controversies that divide the party and then personify those controversies in the candidacies of the leading aspirants. The effect of this pattern of coverage is to help prolong the campaign until the party's national convention and to make those aspirants appear more as politicians in search of power than as statesmen. Moreover, it conveys the implicit message that they are not qualified to lead the nation.

Elections with weak incumbents are those in which the President is defeated in his quest for another term, for example, the elections of 1976, 1980, and 1992. The most important factor that distinguishes these elections is that the incumbent is in political trouble at the outset of the campaign and as a result is challenged for renomination. The existence of the challenge, perhaps even more than the nature of the challenge itself, reflects the political weaknesses of the incumbent. The incumbent's challenger(s) often attacks him on ideological grounds and seeks to mobilize a faction of the party behind his candidacy. While any challenger of the incumbent is unlikely to win the nomination, he usually forces the incumbent into a divisive and prolonged battle that may well last until the national convention. This battle soon becomes the leading televised political news story of the first months of the election year and serves to deny the weak incumbent the opportunities that strong incumbents enjoy for manipulating news coverage and appearing "presidential." In contrast, the opposition party tends to resolve its nomination with relatively little disharmony and then presents a candidate to the voters who appears as a highly qualified replacement for the embattled incumbent. He is, in essence, a "presidential" appearing alternative. The opposition party usually attracts as many candidates in these years as it does in election years with strong incumbents, but it also attains far less negative televised news coverage of its campaign because of the presence of a battle within the presidential party. By paying little attention to his adversaries, television news media implicitly help the front-runner of the opposition party develop a consensus in support of his nomination. They are less willing to do this in years when the incumbent is unopposed for renomination.

Elections with surrogate incumbents occur when the President does not seek reelection, for example, the elections of 1960, 1968, and 1988. Despite the retirement of the President, incumbency nonetheless plays an important role. It encourages vice presidential succession to the nomination of the presidential party even in those years when the Vice President encounters strong rivals for the honor. The modern Vice President occupies a unique vantage point from which he can generally convince most of his fellow partisans that he is the one leading political surrogate of the retiring incumbent and that he should receive their support. While possession of the vice presidential office is useful for succeeding a retiring incumbent as a nominee, it does not necessarily lead to victory in the general election. The Vice President must expand his surrogate following beyond his own partisans in order to win the election and usually encounters some difficulty in doing so. The opposition party tends to undergo a nomination campaign that is likely to be shorter and less divisive than those during years with strong incumbents, and its nominee will appear to have an excellent chance of victory after the conclusion of the national convention. Many voters are particularly attracted by the theme of change when an incumbent retires and as a result are inclined to look favorably upon the nominee of the opposition party. Some of the support for this nominee is illusory, however, and is partly an artifact of television news coverage of the nomination campaign. The nominee must address some problems relating to his personal image that have the potential to cost him the general election. If he does not adequately address them, he may see his support decline as the final vote nears and he may very well lose the election.

In the three chapters that follow, I discuss the recurring patterns of television age elections that lead me to categorize the past nine as I have and to argue why these categories will likely remain applicable in future years. I also explain my reasoning for the generalizations mentioned above. My selection of the order of the chapters derives from the outcomes of the past three elections. Since the election of 1984 was an election with a strong incumbent, I begin by discussing that category of outcomes in Chapter 2. I follow in Chapter 3 by considering elections with surrogate incumbents including that of 1988, and devote Chapter 4 to a discussion of elections with weak incumbents. The most recent election, 1992, belongs to this latter category.

The Television Age

One issue that needs to be resolved is the time span of the television age, at least with respect to presidential elections: I consider it to have begun in 1960. Granted, television was present before then, as the networks had begun broadcasting national conventions in 1952. However, the 1960 election marks an important turning point in the role of television in presidential election campaigns. It stands out from its predecessors, and is similar to its successors, to the extent that candidates and voters began using television as their primary medium for sending and acquiring campaign-related information.

The 1960 election occurred after a decade of dramatic growth in the extent of ownership and usage of television. While ownership and usage had spread rapidly after the Second World War, more than a decade passed between the beginnings of network programming and its availability in most American households. Herbert Asher reports that only 51 percent of voters in the election of 1952 used television as a medium for acquiring political information. Far more voters used newspapers (79 percent) and radio (70 percent). In contrast, television usage surpassed that of all media in 1960, as 87 percent of voters reported using it as a source of information. This percentage has remained consistent since that time. Growth of this magnitude meant that presidential candidates would have to adapt their efforts to television in order to have any realistic hopes of success.

One can see evidence of this adaptation in the public careers of John Kennedy and Richard Nixon. Today many people consider Kennedy as the founder of the televised Presidency. Throughout his public career, Kennedy used television to bypass party leaders and to develop his own personal support instead. His successes encouraged the growth of candidate-

THE TELEVISION AGE

centered campaigns. Kennedy acquired invaluable public exposure at the Democratic National Convention in 1956 when he was defeated by Senator Estes Kefauver (Tennessee) for the vice presidential nomination. He used that exposure to develop a nationwide political following and a presidential candidacy. He expanded his initial support during the televised hearings in the late 1950s about corruption in the Teamsters union. During the 1960 campaign Kennedy relied upon television as a medium for winning several primary elections at the expense of Senator Hubert H. Humphrey (Minnesota), for persuading doubtful convention delegates that he could win the general election, for diffusing the religious issue about his Catholicism, for "defeating" Nixon in the famous debate in September, and finally for rallying Democratic voters who initially were wary of his limited age and experience.

Despite his loss to Kennedy, Nixon was actually quite effective at using television for advancing his own public career. He came very close to being the founder of the televised Presidency. Without his own previous use of television, Nixon would have been in no position to lose the election to Kennedy. He gained important public exposure through television during the late 1940s with his investigations into Communist spying when he was a member of the House Committee on Un-American Activities. This propelled him into national prominence and led to his selection as the Republican nominee for Vice President in 1952. Nixon used television in September of that year to save both his place on the ticket and his public career with his "Checkers" speech after controversies surfaced about his personal finances. He acquired many unique opportunities from television during his eight years as Vice President for generating personal support for his future candidacy, and he successfully exploited them. In 1960 Nixon became the first Vice President in more than a century, but hardly the last, to succeed an incumbent to the nomination of his party.

In contrast to Kennedy and Nixon, the candidates in the 1952 and 1956 elections, General Dwight D. Eisenhower and Governor Adlai E. Stevenson, Jr. (Illinois), gained little from television. Stevenson actually was somewhat awkward at using it. He was a reluctant candidate in 1952 and did not compete in any primary elections. He won the Democratic nomination only after receiving a last-minute endorsement from the retiring incumbent, Harry S. Truman. Eisenhower had gained much of his public following through his military leadership in Europe during and after the Second World War at a time when few Americans had access to television. As a presidential candidate, he emphasized his background at a time when the Korean War had reached an unpopular stalemate.

Finally, there is little evidence to indicate that television affected the outcomes of any elections before 1960. No candidate during the 1940s and 1950s relied upon television to gain his party's nomination or to compete in a general election campaign. There is also little evidence to suggest that either televised news reporting or advertising influenced the choices of many voters. The audience for television news was somewhat limited during this time. The landmark voter studies of the 1940s and 1950s, "Voting," "The People's Choice," and "The American Voter," concluded that television had only limited effects upon the electoral choices of most people. Instead, voters acquired much of their information about government and politics from sources other than television and relied more upon partisanship than television when making their decisions. They used television primarily as a medium for reinforcing their initial opinions. This, of course, changed remarkably after 1960.

NEWS, NOMINATIONS, AND TELEVISION

News Values

A necessary step before one can explain how television news media influence presidential elections is to explore the values and interests that they use for selecting and producing politically related news. In doing so, I direct attention to the choices of topics for political news, to the interests and motives behind those choices, and to how those choices affect election processes and outcomes.

Television and other news media tend to view themselves as objective, neutral observers of events who report their findings to their audiences. This viewpoint is limited, however, because news is far more intersubjective in nature than objective. With objectivity, one assumes that the truth or importance of events lies outside the mind of the observer and that all unbiased observers will arrive at the same conclusions. With intersubjectivity, which is shared subjectivity, one places the truth or importance of events in the shared values and beliefs of the community of observers. These values and beliefs may differ from those of persons outside the community. Community members develop a consensual view of reality from their shared values and beliefs, a paradigm as some call it. Such a view, in turn, guides the members in their choices of events for future observation and for explaining and ascribing meanings to the results of those observations. News is intersubjective in nature because it is produced by a community of people who employ shared sets of values for reporting about events, for ascribing meanings to those events, and for making choices about future reporting.

News producers frequently consider discrete actions that differ from the usual course of events to be newsworthy and therefore deserving of observation and reporting. It is newsworthy when an airliner crashes with substantial loss of life; it is not newsworthy when an airliner arrives at its destination on time without mishap. The former event is the exception; the latter the norm. News producers find scandals involving important politicians, controversies arising from court decisions, or congressional hearings that embarrass the President to be newsworthy. They rarely find the routine happenings of government and politics newsworthy. These perspectives differ from those of political scientists who tend to consider regularly occurring events, such as the normal vote, worthy of attention. For example, if 95 percent of congressional incumbents win reelection in a given year, news producers will direct their attention to the few who lose, while political scientists will seek to determine why so many were victorious.

Two aspects of news production are particularly significant with respect to television: the unique visual nature of that medium and the setting of news production in profit-seeking entities. Visual images are essential for television. Regardless of whether their messages involve news, comedy, sports, drama, or advertising, producers of television programming communicate with their audiences primarily through the use of visual images. The images enhance events in ways that are often unavailable to other media, including those media that rely upon the written word. Producers of television programming can direct attention to individuals and can highlight the personal characteristics of those individuals. While one can use print media to describe events and radio to transmit voices, one can use television to show, through the use of images and sound, the words and deeds of individuals. This allows producers of news to use television to personalize events. They can identify events with the choices and actions of individual actors rather than with institutions, and can suggest that the actual occurrence of the events would have been unlikely except for those individual actors. News producers can use television to convey emotional appeals from individual actors to audiences in ways that make those individual actors appear as if they are separate from the institutional or political contexts from which the reported events arise.

Consider, for example, the inaugural address of John F. Kennedy. Without televised news coverage of his address to a national audience numbering in the millions, Kennedy most certainly would have failed to generate the widespread personal and emotional support that he came to enjoy from the address. Rather than develop support from his actual words, however, Kennedy built his following primarily by using television to convey a very pleasing visual style and image of himself to his audience and coupled it with a strong sense of emotional excitement. People responded more to the persona than to the actual words of Kennedy.

The public response to Kennedy's address demonstrates an important and unique characteristic of television: two messages are transmitted simultaneously. One is conveyed through visual images, while the second is conducted through words. With respect to news, the message through words is the reporter's narrative that accompanies the visual images. It is not uncommon for the two messages to be unequal in strength, as in the case of Kennedy, or even contradictory.

One can see an example of the contradictory nature of these two kinds of messages in the successful attempts by Ronald Reagan's media advisors to manipulate television news for his political benefit and in the apparent unwillingness of many news producers to resist them. On many occasions, the visual messages that Reagan conveyed through television news did not correspond to the narratives of the reporters. Visually flattering images of Reagan often accompanied far more critical narratives. Michael Deaver speaks of his efforts at creating scenes for Reagan's public appearances that contradicted reporters' narratives. For example, he claims that he once had Reagan stand before a construction site and speak about new housing starts, while reporters described grim governmental statistics about a national decline in new starts. Deaver calculated that the positive visual images conveyed through television of both the new construction and of Reagan's optimism would remain in the minds of viewers far longer than the pessimistic forecasts and far more negative words of the reporters' narratives. One can see a related example in the experiences of Lesley Stahl, a television news reporter. She tells of how a representative of the Reagan administration telephoned her after her network broadcasted a story that she narrated about how Reagan's media advisors manipulated televised images of him for political purposes. The representative told Stahl that the pictures she used for describing their efforts would actually prove helpful in reelecting Reagan.

The content of television news is also affected by the structure of its production and delivery. It is produced and delivered by profit-seeking entities that derive their revenue primarily from the sale of commercial advertising. Throughout most of the years that are considered in this work, television news programming has been dominated by three major networks: the American Broadcasting Company (ABC), the Columbia Broadcasting System (CBS), and the National Broadcasting Company (NBC). A fourth network, the Cable News Network (CNN), joined the big three in the later 1970s. The three major networks broadcast many types of programming—sports, comedy, drama, movies, and news—which are available in virtually all American homes. Cable News Network broadcasts only news and reaches a smaller audience than the other three networks. The most significant parts of the three major networks' news programming are their daily reports during the early evening. Initially, the reports lasted fifteen minutes, but the networks expanded them to thirty minutes in 1963. The programs are anchored by one or more reporters who enjoy considerable public recognition and respect. Such was the case with Walter Cronkite of CBS for nearly two decades.

The three networks do not transmit their programming directly into individual homes. Instead, they convey it through affiliated stations which then retransmit it within specified locales. The networks do not own the affiliates but operate with them through contractual relations. Most affiliates broadcast the early evening network news reports in conjunction with their own news programming. They direct much of their programming to matters of local or regional interest but occasionally include reports of national or international events that they acquire from the networks. They also broadcast additional news programming in the late evening and, once again, usually include excerpts from network reports. Each network grants exclusive rights to one affiliate to broadcast its programming within a specified locale. In most cities, the three television stations with the largest viewer audiences are usually the affiliates of the three networks, and this helps attract even more viewers to network news reports. The fourth network, CNN, lacks local affiliates and thereby is at some disadvantage since it cannot link its programming with local reporting.

The networks and their affiliates are profit-seeking entities supported primarily by the sale of commercial advertising. The rates that they can charge for advertising time during particular programming are usually contingent upon the size and composition of the audiences they attract. In general, the formula is the larger the desired audience, the greater the revenue and profits. This need for large audiences influences producers of news in their choices of themes for reporting about government and politics. They often relate the newsworthiness of events to the size of the potential viewing audiences that they believe the reporting of those events can attract.

The networks and affiliates direct a considerable amount of their programming at people they perceive to be marginal viewers. Marginal viewers are those who are not regularly part of an audience but whom broadcasters believe can be attracted under certain circumstances. An example is someone with a moderate interest in sports who may watch a telecast only if the local team is involved. More avid fans would watch regardless of the teams. In order to attract larger numbers of marginal viewers and thereby generate even greater advertising revenues, networks often televise games between teams from different geographic regions or between teams that may be involved in championship races. With respect to televised news, the networks and their affiliates also direct their programming at marginal viewers. From their perspective, marginal viewers are less interested in news programming that emphasizes the complexity of problems and policies, the concentrations of political power, or the routine workings of institutions than in programming that transmits excitement, controversy, competition, and the actions of dynamic individuals.

The tendency of producers of televised news to direct attention to unusual events and individuals in order to increase their numbers of marginal viewers sometimes encourages the creation of unrealistic perspectives about American government and politics in the minds of members of the viewing audiences. Television news media believe that for unusual events to be newsworthy they must be fairly recent and must be undergoing enough rapid changes to make them susceptible to different visual images and narratives. Newsworthy events about government are often about economic, social, or foreign policy shortcomings, or involve personal scandals and controversies. The reporting of these matters encourages people whose major source of news is television to see governmental and political processes as little more than a series of never-ending, fast-breaking stories about solitary individuals who are preoccupied with one crisis after another to the exclusion of all else.

Finally, it is virtually impossible for television news media to observe events without affecting the course of those events. They are not separate and distinct from the events they observe, and their presence is not neutral. Instead, their presence and observations often alter the outcomes of events by enhancing or discouraging certain actions. This happens mainly because human actions are not deterministic, that is, having but one potential outcome, but probabilistic, with a variety of outcomes possible, some of which are more likely than others. The observation of events by television news media may change the context of events and alter the probabilities of the varieties of potential outcomes. The changed probabilities may then induce different outcomes. For example, politicians often change their words and deeds when reporters are present and they sometimes "play to the camera." They actively seek televised news coverage of their contrived actions simply because that coverage is so readily available. It is because of their capacity to alter the actual course of the events on which they report that television news media can affect the conduct and outcomes of presidential elections.

Network News Coverage of Nomination Campaigns

Television news media are particularly influential in nomination campaigns. These campaigns, in turn, affect the outcomes of general elections. The presence of television has contributed to far-reaching changes in the institutional sources of nominees for the two political parties over the past three decades and to alterations in the processes by which those nominees are selected. The presidential party nominated the incumbent in every election after 1952 if he sought reelection or the Vice President if the incumbent retired. This occurred even when the executive branch candidate encountered some challenges. The opposition party nominated either a former Vice President or a candidate with limited experiences in national leadership who campaigned as a political outsider. In contrast, neither party selected a leader of Congress as its standard bearer nor appears likely to do so in the foreseeable future.

The renomination of an incumbent by the presidential party is not unique to the television age, although the widespread support for some incumbents in general elections certainly is. The nomination of the Vice

President is a relatively new phenomenon however. The Republican Party's choice of Richard Nixon in 1960 marked the first time in more than a century that the presidential party selected the Vice President to succeed a retiring incumbent. The last time that happened was in 1836 when the Democrats picked Martin Van Buren to succeed Andrew Jackson. As an indication of the uniqueness of Nixon's nomination, there were eleven elections between 1840 and 1956 in which the presidential party selected a candidate who was not the incumbent. Nine of those candidates were either governors, generals, members of Congress, or former officeholders. Only two held office in the executive branch of the national government, and neither was the Vice President. The rather abrupt change to vice presidential succession in modern times derives partly from the fact that television has expanded the public visibility of Vice Presidents and has provided them with new advantages over their rivals. Several Vice Presidents used these advantages to develop personalized followings among their own partisans that proved large enough to enable them to win the nomination upon the retirement of the incumbent. The importance of the Vice Presidency as a stepping stone to a presidential nomination has grown so much in recent years that on two occasions (1968, 1984) the opposition party chose a former Vice President for the chief executive's position.

The influence of television is not limited to enhancing presidential and vice presidential incumbency. It also helps to undermine the electoral prospects of congressional leaders who seek the presidency. Through television news, congressional leaders often appear as defenders of an unpopular institution rather than as solitary champions of justice separate from government. Substantial numbers of people, through responses to public opinion surveys, consistently indicate their dislike of Congress. In one recent survey, respondents ranked "Congressman" as one of their five most disliked and disrespected occupations, placing it only slightly below drug dealers and organized crime bosses. Ironically, these same people usually approve of their own Congressman. This contradiction appears glaring but makes sense if one considers that members of Congress, like Presidents, attempt to develop public images where they appear as solitary champions of justice from outside of government, and they are often successful at doing so. It is the institution of Congress, not the individual members, that voters dislike. Part of this difficulty rests with the tendency of television news media to downplay the routine workings of government and to concentrate instead upon controversies and to then personalize and trivialize them. When television news media juxtapose a non-personalized appearing institution such as Congress against a popular and solitary appearing President, they implicitly encourage their viewers to regard Congress an an obstacle that stands in the way of effective solutions to national problems. Many voters quite simply do not understand the complexities of Congress and are often unaware of the roles played by its standing committees and subcommittees, procedural rules, behavioral norms, and party caucuses. They often fail to understand or appreciate the different roles that Congress and the President play in the separation of powers' constitutional order.

As an example, consider the public reaction to Oliver North when he appeared before a congressional committee investigating the Iran-Contra scandal. North created the illusion for television viewers that he was a solitary political outsider who could disregard the rules of institutions so that he could fight the nation's real or imagined enemies more effectively. The committee appeared as if it was the institution that had caused the problems North opposed. The setting of the hearing provided North with the visual context for generating this illusion.

Congressional leaders who seek the nomination of their party not only must face the popular dislike of Congress but often find that their institutional powers and the personal characteristics which enabled them to acquire those powers are not readily translated into delegate support. Several congressional leaders failed to secure nominations because they had little influence with the party activists who control them. In fact, every congressional leader who has sought a party nomination for President since 1960 has lost. Those Congressmen who did win—Kennedy, Goldwater, and McGovern—were junior members in both seniority and leadership. To become an effective congressional leader, one must possess the personal and political skills of conciliation, compromise, reciprocity, and deference and must be able to build coalitions and master procedural rules and strategy. These are not the skills of a political "Lone Ranger" and often clash with the popular images conveyed through television news that the preferred political leaders are solitary tribunes of the people who fight against corrupt institutions.

Television also affects nomination campaigns within the opposition party. It has already helped to undermine that party's institutional methods for selecting its nominees while enhancing their replacement with candidate-centered campaigns. The opposition party of today usually begins an election year without a standout leader who can serve as an immediate rallying point against the incumbent. Moreover, its most important congressional leaders rarely become successful presidential candidates. Other than former Vice Presidents, most candidates who seek the nomination of the opposition party have only limited experience as national leaders and most lack constituencies of their own. Finally, the methods that are now used for selecting the delegates who attend the national convention have the unfortunate side effect of minimizing the influence of party leaders while maximizing the influence of television over the selection of nominees. Before the presence of television, party leaders controlled the selection of both convention delegates and nominees. This is no longer the case. Nominations are now decided during the primary election period that runs between February and June, while the conventions serve mostly to ratify the results of the primaries.

Television news media can affect the contexts of these primary election periods and influence the meanings that voters ascribe to the efforts of the various candidates. They do this through their personal characterizations of the candidates and through their reporting and interpretation of political events. Their influence is particularly evident during the winnowing period. Winnowing is the reduction in the number of candidates from a relatively large number of aspirants to only a few leading contenders. It usually occurs shortly after the conclusion of the first caucuses and primaries of an election year, which is often during February and March. Television news media are integral components of the winnowing process in the sense that they attempt to reduce a large number of candidates to only two role-playing "semi-finalists" by limiting coverage to those two candidates. Moreover, they stereotype the two into predefined roles which they then use to guide future reporting. They depict the remaining candidates as losers and virtually cease reporting about them.

The more important of the two roles is front-runner. Television news media assign this role to the one candidate who appears to have the greatest chance of winning the nomination. After designating a front-runner, they define him as the central actor of the campaign and use him as the anchor point for reporting and evaluating political events. Events acquire meaning through their relationship to the front-runner. Television news media first create and then perpetuate a theme in which the predominant story of the campaign is the personal quest of the front-runner for the Presidency. Their model for this style of reporting is Theodore White's depiction of John F. Kennedy in *The Making of the President 1960*. White used Kennedy as the central actor in his description of the events of that year and defined candidates and events through their relationship to Kennedy. The West Virginia primary and the televised debates were significant to White because through them Kennedy overcame the personal and political obstacles that threatened to destroy his candidacy. Kennedy dispelled the problem that his religion might cost him the election when he won in West Virginia, and he cast aside lingering doubts about his leadership abilities by besting Nixon in the debates. White treated the other candidates, including Nixon, mostly as obstacles that Kennedy needed to overcome in order to advance to the White House. Kennedy overcame them, and White found the experience ennobling for him.

Television news media now use White's approach when reporting about contested nomination campaigns. They define a front-runner as early as possible and then stereotype him into the same role that White did with Kennedy. They depict him as the central actor of the campaign who happens to be engaged in a continuing effort to overcome a series of personal and political obstacles that stand between himself and the Presidency. If a front-runner overcomes the obstacles, as Kennedy did, he thereby proves his political virility and qualifications for holding office. If the obstacles overpower him, he fails the test and demonstrates that he lacks the "right stuff" to lead the nation.

The second role is leading adversary. Television news media depict this candidate as the antithesis of the front-runner and as a personification of the obstacles that the front-runner must overcome rather than as a candidate in his own right. They consider his actions and words important only in their relationship to the continuing story of the front-runner seeking the Presidency. White viewed Hubert H. Humphrey more as the Protestant antithesis of the Catholic Kennedy in the West Virginia primary than as a leading spokesman for the interests of some of the Democratic Party's more liberal constituencies.

The reduction in the number of candidates to the front-runner and his leading adversary occurs in some campaigns without the need for news media intervention. In other instances, however, no candidates readily emerge to assume one or both roles. Within these contexts, television news media often enhance the emergence of the two role-playing semi-finalists. They helped to create a front-runner for the Democratic nomination in 1976 and a leading adversary in 1984 by their extensive coverage of Jimmy Carter and Gary Hart after those two performed well in the Iowa precinct caucuses. Occasionally, most notably with George Wallace and Jesse Jackson in 1972 and 1984 respectively, television news media continue reporting about the efforts of a third candidate after the winnowing period. Nonetheless, they treat those candidates more as sideshows to the real action than as integral parts of the two-candidate battle for the nomination.

Television news media sometimes create self-fulfilling prophesies with this pattern of reporting. By depicting campaigns as two-candidate battles, they help to turn them into two-candidate battles. Political reporters often like to use an athletic metaphor, a horse race, to depict election campaigns. They see the campaign as an ongoing activity, a "race," in which the candidates, or "horses," strive, that is, "run," to reach the "finish line" before anyone else. As occurs in the announcing of actual horse races, political reporters tell their audiences about which candidates are leading and which ones are challenging. The metaphor fails after that however. The outcome of a horse race is not contingent upon the presence of the announcer. While televising both horse races and political campaigns, reporters often focus their cameras upon the leaders. Some of the runners in actual horse races come from far off the pace and win, as with Secretariat in the Kentucky Derby of 1973. The ability of horses to do so is not affected by the presence of television cameras. In contrast, early trailers in political campaigns rarely can come from behind the pace because they need television coverage in order to do so and cannot receive it because they are running behind the pace.

Television news media help to undermine the campaigns of these weaker candidates because they place them in a political catch-22 dilemma. Voters often have a limited awareness of these candidates at the outset of a campaign. The candidates must expand the voters' awareness of them but cannot do so unless they receive televised news coverage. They will receive such coverage only if they can demonstrate that they have voter support. Voters must be aware of them in order to advance that support however. These candidates tend to disappear from the campaigns (or from the races, as in the metaphor) about as quickly as they disappear from the television cameras. Candidates who, in the early stages of campaigns, fail to win enough support so that television news media will define them as either the front-runner or as the leading adversary soon disappear from television news coverage altogether. Moreover, they fail to register in the political consciousness of most voters and depart from the campaign before many television viewers become aware that they are even in it.

Finally, television news media perpetuate another theme during nomination campaigns that often affects the contexts and outcomes of general elections. After the conclusion of the winnowing period, they strive to reduce the total number of major candidates that remain between the two parties to only three. These three are the two "semi-finalists" for the nomination of one party—the front-runner and leading adversary—and the one candidate who has emerged as the front-runner for the nomination of the other party. This reduction to three major contenders is relatively easy in elections with strong incumbents since the presidential party has only one candidate. It is more difficult when both parties have contested nominations. Television news media enhance this reduction of candidates by directing far more of their election-related coverage to the events and personalities of one party while downplaying those of the other. This helps to perpetuate a battle between two role-playing candidates for the nomination of the one party while encouraging the rapid resolution of the nomination of the other party behind the early front-runner.

Television news media find no great need for the existence of two contested nominations. One appears to be sufficient for attracting and retaining the attention of marginal observers of politics. A campaign that involves four major contenders who are competing in two separate nomination "races" of two candidates each and that has two front-runners and two leading adversaries of those front-runners is far more difficult to report than a campaign that has only one contested nomination. A four-candidate, two-party nomination campaign simply provides far too many contrasting styles and images for television news media to illustrate in their daily coverage.

In all but one television age election, that of 1960, only three major contenders received any substantial television news coverage after the conclusion of the earliest caucuses and primaries. The three categories of elections differ from one another in the roles that these three contenders filled. In the elections with strong incumbents, two semi-finalists emerged, or were encouraged to emerge by television news media, for the nomination of the opposition party, while the incumbent was unchallenged for renomination. In the elections with weak incumbents, the President engaged in an intense battle for renomination with one major rival, and the inevitable nominee of the opposition party emerged very early during the campaign season, while television news media did not report about a leading adversary or even seek to create one. Neither party, presidential or opposition, had all of the two-candidate nomination battles in election years with surrogate incumbents. These battles occurred in both parties, but television news media encouraged them to occur in only one party in any given election. The television-enhanced winnowing and stereotyping of candidates affected the final outcomes of these more recent elections. Since 1964, the one party that had the misfortune to become involved in a two-candidate battle for its nomination, complete with a front-runner and his one leading adversary, lost the ensuing general election.

2

Elections with Strong Incumbents

Three elections since 1960 have concluded with the reelection of the incumbent. All three contain some striking similarities, including the fact that the incumbents recorded some of the most sweeping victories in the nation's history. To a great extent, these victories were highly personal and occurred after the incumbents had encountered little or no opposition for renomination, while their challengers had been unable to avoid highly divisive campaigns for their nominations. Television news media had responded to these circumstances by defining the roles and reporting about the actions of incumbents and challengers quite differently. This, in turn, affected the way that many people perceived and interpreted political events, evaluated the personalities and qualifications of the candidates, and eventually cast their votes. Finally, the voter alignments of each election deviated substantially from usual patterns but proved short-lived by not being replicated four years later. For these reasons, I depict these three as elections with strong incumbents. Here I describe the similarities of these past campaigns and outline a general scenario of elections that comprise this category. The past ones include those of 1964, when Lyndon Johnson defeated Senator Barry Goldwater (Arizona); 1972, when Richard Nixon won a second term over Senator George McGovern (South Dakota); and 1984, when Ronald Reagan was reelected at the expense of former Vice President Walter Mondale.

The incumbent Democrat, Lyndon Johnson, who became President after the assassination of John F. Kennedy on November 22, 1963, won the first of these elections with a margin of victory that was of historic significance. He acquired the largest percentage of the popular vote ever cast for a presidential candidate, 61.1 percent. This broke the old vote record of 60.8 percent achieved by Franklin D. Roosevelt in 1936. Johnson won the electoral votes of forty-four states, which was a near record number. At the time, that number was exceeded only by the forty-six states that Roosevelt had won. The 1972 election was just as lopsided. In this more recent instance, the incumbent Republican, Richard Nixon, scored a massive triumph over a Democratic challenger. In winning his second term, Nixon almost duplicated Johnson's percentage of the popular vote, 60.7, and carried nearly every state. Nixon won the electoral votes of a record forty-nine states and lost only Massachusetts and the District of Columbia.

A popular explanation of these outcomes, particularly right after they occurred, was that the unusual results derived primarily from the ideological excesses of the losing candidates. Goldwater lost supposedly because many voters, including substantial numbers of Republicans, rejected him because of their perceptions that he would seek many unpopular retrenchments in social welfare programs and would likely act dangerously and irresponsibly in foreign affairs, particularly with the use of nuclear weapons. Voters rejected McGovern supposedly because they believed that he would seek many unpopular expansions of social welfare programs and would conduct foreign affairs in ways that would threaten the best interests of the United States, particularly in relation to the Soviet Union and other communist nations. McGovern differed from Goldwater in that he was a far too liberal Democrat, while Goldwater was a far too conservative Republican. Goldwater's and McGovern's defeats carried an explicit political message: the American voting public did not want a President of immoderate views, and that only aspirants who did not stray far from the political center, such as the moderately liberal Johnson and the moderately conservative Nixon, could win the Presidency.

There are problems with explanations that attribute outcomes primarily to the ideological stands of the losers. They are limited because they fail to emphasize that Johnson and Nixon were incumbents and that television, as the most important communicative medium in presidential campaigns, often enhances the electoral advantages of incumbency. The outcome of the 1984 election illustrates the importance of these limitations and challenges these ideologically focused explanations. The Republican incumbent, Ronald Reagan, overwhelmed his Democratic opponent, former Vice President Walter Mondale, by popular and electoral vote margins that were similar to Nixon's earlier victory. Reagan acquired 58.8 percent of the popular vote, the fifth highest total for a victorious presidential candidate in the twentieth century. Reagan also captured forty-nine states, and his record 525 electoral votes exceeded Roosevelt's 523 votes of 1936. Reagan won all electoral votes except those from Minnesota and the District of Columbia.

Reagan was by no means an ideological centrist. He had been the leading spokesman for Republican conservatives since his election as governor of

California in 1966. He also had been the most conservative of the major contenders in each of his three campaigns for the Republican nomination prior to his 1984 effort for reelection (1968, 1976, 1980). Moreover, he advocated conservative policies throughout his first term as President. In contrast, Mondale was not as prominent a spokesman for the Democratic Party's liberals as McGovern had been. In fact, his views were somewhat less liberal than those of his two major rivals for the nomination, Senator Gary Hart (Colorado) and Reverend Jesse Jackson. Many voters indicated, through public opinion surveys, that their own views on major issues were actually closer to Mondale's than Reagan's.

A first-term incumbent President, ideology and party notwithstanding, had won another term in each of these three elections. Each incumbent had consolidated political power within his own party and had generated a widespread personal following prior to the onset of his campaign for reelection. Moreover, television news media had provided each incumbent with innumerable opportunities that had been unavailable to his challenger for developing a consensus in support of his reelection while simultaneously enhancing the generation of dissensus among the opposition. They directed more of their news attention to the Presidency than to other political institutions, to personalities rather than policies, and to campaign events that allowed for plenty of action, pictures, competition, and controversy. They tended to ignore topics that were related to the more subtle and less picturesque consolidation of power by the incumbents and the institutional limitations of American parties and government in producing leaders who can effectively oppose those incumbents. Moreover, they often depicted the incumbents as if they were performing in a presidential and statesmanlike manner, that is, as competent leaders guiding the nation and the free world. They also downplayed events that might have proven damaging to the incumbents. Finally, they directed most of their campaign-related coverage of the primary election season to the battles among the contenders for the nomination of the opposition party and frequently depicted those contenders as little more than aspirants for power rather than as statesmen. These patterns of news reporting helped engender widespread perceptions about the lack of qualifications of these contenders for holding office. The juxtapositions of contrasting images of competent appearing incumbents and unqualified appearing challengers helped set the stage for what eventually became three sweeping personal triumphs by strong incumbent Presidents.

PRESIDENTIAL PARTY NOMINATIONS

Overview

One should interpret the outcomes of the elections of 1964, 1972, and 1984 more as television-enhanced personal triumphs of strong incumbents than as voter rejections of ideologically immoderate challengers. If the opposition party had nominated someone other than Goldwater, McGovern, or Mondale, the final results would have been much the same. In fact, a majority of voters actually made their final choices several months before the general election campaigns even began. Most of them based those choices upon their perceptions that the personal and political qualifications of the incumbents were vastly superior to those of any potential challengers. Moreover, their choices were influenced by the fact that all three incumbents benefited from recurring biases that exist in the values that television news media use when reporting about presidential elections and about the Presidency itself. The incumbents successfully manipulated those biases into virtually insurmountable leads over all of the candidates who sought the nomination of the opposition party long before the summertime conclusions of the party national conventions. In particular, two recurring biases in televised news reporting stand out: the inherently favorable and consensus-enhancing coverage of the incumbents successfully performing in the role of President, and the inherently unfavorable and dissensus-enhancing coverage of the most divisive events and personalities in the nomination campaigns of the opposition party. I discuss the former in this section of the chapter and the latter in the next.

The most significant political fact in these three elections, and what set the stage for all that followed, was that the incumbents had consolidated political power within their own parties and among their own partisans well before the onset of these campaigns. As a consequence, each of them encountered minimal or no opposition for renomination. None attracted the opposition of a major political figure. Johnson was opposed in three primaries by George Wallace, and Nixon faced two little-known Congressmen in New Hampshire, but both incumbents easily dispatched these minor rivals. Reagan encountered no opposition whatsoever. This lack of opposition reflected the extent of the political strength of these incumbents: all three had effectively convinced the leading political figures of their own parties that they were quite simply unbeatable for renomination. Therefore they did not face any strong challenges. I draw support for this contention from the choices that appear to have been made by the possible rivals of these incumbents. Lyndon Johnson might well have faced a formidable challenge to his renomination in 1964 from Robert Kennedy. Kennedy declined to oppose Johnson at that time because he apparently realized that he could not win. He chose instead to run for a Senate seat in New York. Four years later, however, when Johnson was facing some very serious political troubles that threatened to end his tenure in office, Kennedy changed his mind and decided to challenge him for the nomination. If Johnson had appeared as vulnerable at the outset of 1964 as he later appeared in 1968, Kennedy might well have opposed him then.

Ronald Reagan appears to have made a similar choice with respect to the Republican nomination of 1972: he decided against opposing Richard Nixon when the latter sought a second term. This was the only election between 1968 and 1984 in which Reagan was not a candidate. This election also occurred during the very year that Nixon's political strength appeared to be at its zenith. Reagan acted quite differently in 1976, however, when he sought the nomination and opposed the vulnerable incumbent, Gerald Ford. Ford certainly appeared to be a far less formidable rival than Nixon. Robert Dole seems to have made a choice much like those of Kennedy and Reagan when he declined to seek the Republican nomination in 1984. He had been a candidate in 1980 and later became one in 1988, but he apparently knew that he could not defeat Reagan in this particular instance. Not only would candidacy be futile for Dole, it could very likely undermine any future presidential bid on his part and might also eliminate him from any party leadership position that he held or might aspire to hold.

The fact that each incumbent began his campaign for renomination without incurring any substantial opposition from among his own partisans reflected the existence of a united core constituency in support of his reelection. While the actual magnitudes of the popular followings of these incumbents were uncertain, the images that other political figures held of them possessing widespread support eventually became the realities of these election years and affected the actions of both candidates and news reporters accordingly. Television and other news media tend to direct most of their election-related coverage to those events that they envision as being related to the race, that is, to the numerous battles for voter support that take place among the various candidates. During the early months of a given election year, these media focus their attention upon the personalities, competition, action, and controversies that exist in the campaigns for the party nominations. A multicandidate campaign within the opposition party provides them with innumerable opportunities for coverage of these themes. An uncontested campaign within the presidential party does not.

Television news media often encounter some difficulties while reporting about the nomination campaigns of unopposed incumbents. They find little or no competition, action, or controversies about which to report. Moreover, the values they use for determining the newsworthiness of events lead them to disregard the routine exercises of political power. They cannot depict through action-related pictures what has already occurred through much more subtle means—the consolidation of political power by an incumbent prior to the onset of the election year. Since they judge the newsworthiness of events by the opportunities those events provide for action-related pictures, television news media often find the contrived appearances of unopposed incumbents at emotionally upbeat rallies as the most newsworthy events within the presidential party.

Several scholars, including Richard Neustadt, explain how individual Presidents can and have been successful at maximizing political power. They give particular attention to a President's bargaining abilities, sense for politics, timing, and interpersonal skills. The mastery of these and other comparable skills aids certain Presidents in acquiring power long before they actually seek reelection. Television news media cannot show this subtle acquisition actually happening, but they can illustrate its aftermath. They do so by depicting an unopposed incumbent in the act of governing rather than in the act of seeking office. Johnson, Nixon, and Reagan were unchallenged for renomination precisely because of their effective pre-election consolidation of political power. This prior consolidation is a necessary precondition for the existence of an uncontested campaign for renomination.

This pattern of reporting is not neutral with respect to either the contents or effects of news. Instead, it has the inherent content bias of depicting the incumbent in a relatively favorable light and the inherent effect bias of enhancing the development of a popular consensus in support of the reelection of that incumbent. It is favorable through comparison with the patterns of television news reporting that occur in two other electoral contexts. One of these takes place when an incumbent has not consolidated power within his own party before the onset of the election year and therefore must struggle to win renomination. These embattled incumbents tend to attain televised news coverage that is far less favorable than that of strong incumbents. As will be discussed in a later chapter, television news media do not normally illustrate an embattled incumbent engaging in the act of governing. Instead, they depict him in the act of fighting to consolidate power through the medium of a contested nomination campaign.

American Presidents fill two fundamental roles: head of state and head of government. The role of head of state can appear unifying and patriotic, while the role of head of government is often divisive and partisan. As a consequence of filling these dual roles, a President inherently fulfills the role of both statesman and politician at the same time. Most Presidents attempt to make the act of governing appear statesmanlike rather than political because of the greater popular support that they can hope to generate from such a role. Since television news media find controversial matters more worthy of their consideration than the routine and undisputed exercise of political power, they all too frequently help strong incumbents appear as statesmen rather than politicians after those incumbents have consolidated power.

The second context occurs within the campaigns for the nomination of the opposition party in the same years that strong incumbents seek reelection. Since none of the aspirants who seek the nomination of this party have enjoyed the same opportunities for consolidating power as the strong incumbents, they almost always must engage in prolonged and potentially divisive battles with other aspirants like themselves in order to win the right to run in the general election. Television news media respond by depicting these aspirants as divisive and partisan. As I illustrate in this and other chapters, the public imagery that candidates acquire in fulfilling this partisan role all too frequently proves to be a major handicap for them in winning office. There is an implicit message in the televised juxtapositions of statesmenlike incumbents and political challengers: the incumbents possess the skills that are required for national leadership, while the aspirants for the nomination of the opposition party do not. Contrasting images such as these, particularly if they are broadcasted repeatedly for months, condition viewers of televised politics to believe that wide differences may actually exist in the abilities of incumbents and challengers and that the incumbents are far more qualified for the Presidency.

Television news media even contribute to this implicit message through their election-year logos. They often use distinctive logos as signals to their viewers that they are about to broadcast a report related to the campaign. The logos contain such pictorial wording as "Campaign '92" or "Decision '92" and may even include the party symbols of the Democratic donkey and the Republican elephant. The news anchor adds to this signaling by beginning political reports with phrases such as "In politics today ..." or "The leading candidates ..." These words tell viewers that the focus of the news is shifting to another topic, to the continuing story of the battles among the candidates for the nomination of the opposition party. Earlier stories on this same news broadcast may very well have depicted the President in more favorable circumstances.

The successful manipulation of these biases by strong and unchallenged incumbents is an important aspect of the elections that I discuss in this chapter. One cannot fully appreciate this manipulation without first considering the extensive changes that occurred in the relationship between the Presidency and television news media during the campaign and administration of John F. Kennedy. Kennedy was unusually active and effective, compared to his predecessors, in his manipulation of television news media for enhancing his personal and electoral support. After attaining a number of media-related triumphs during his campaign of 1960, discussed earlier, Kennedy created the live, televised news conference upon taking office. These conferences have now become mainstays of presidential public relations efforts. As President, Kennedy courted television news indirectly, such as through the guided tour that his wife gave of the White House, and by circumstances such as the Cuban missile crisis. He generated a considerable amount of personal support while doing so. One of Kennedy's greatest assets was his ability to project a favorable personality and style through television. He created a public image by which he appeared as the personal leader of members of the television audience but also seemed separate from the institutions and problems of government. Some observers use the term *charisma* to describe this personalized style of leadership and followership. With respect to the Presidency, charismatic leadership involves the creation and enhancement of a direct relationship between the incumbent and the electorate that is conducted through the medium of television. It is also unmediated by any intervening institutions.

Television news media accepted these changes and now make the Presidency the anchor-point of their coverage of government and politics. They measure the importance of political actors and the significance of domestic and international events primarily through their relationship to the Presidency. They personalize the Presidency by directing much of their attention to the individual actions of the incumbent. They exaggerate the importance of a particular President by illustrating and describing his actions as if they are the most important events in government. While doing so, they help make the President appear as if he is actually separate from other political institutions, including his own party, and in some instances his own administration. This pattern of reporting provided the three strong incumbents of the television age with such invaluable opportunities for developing extensive personal support that they eventually translated into sweeping reelection triumphs.

The Rise of Lyndon Johnson

Lyndon Johnson was the first incumbent President of the television age to manipulate the biases of television news into enhancing his reelection prospects. Johnson began his tenure in office with fairly high respect from much of the electorate and particularly from his own Democratic Party. He retained much of it through the 1964 campaign. A substantial amount of his initial popularity derived from his association with Kennedy as both a running mate and as Vice President. Johnson then strengthened this initial standing by reassuring a nation that was distraught over Kennedy's death that he would provide a continuity of leadership. Finally, Johnson enhanced his own popularity even more during his first year in office with a number of significant foreign and domestic policy accomplishments.

Upon taking office, Johnson became the political heir to much of the Kennedy legacy, although he did have some competition for that honor from Attorney General Robert Kennedy. That competition, of course, grew as the years passed. Johnson was able to convince much of the American public that he was the legitimate heir of Kennedy for two reasons. First, much of mass media and the American public now look upon the television age Vice President as the leading political surrogate of the President. Moreover, many of the Vice President's own partisans actually see him as the probable successor of the incumbent. As I explain in the next chapter when I consider elections with surrogate incumbents, the presence of television has provided modern Vice Presidents with unique and invaluable opportunities for developing public images by which they appear as significant members of the presidential team. This presence has also provided them with a vantage point from which they are able to persuade their fellow partisans, as well as many other voters, that they are politically and personally qualified to advance to the Presidency upon the retirement of the incumbent. Johnson enjoyed the opportunities offered by this vantage point for three years prior to his becoming President, and he used them to supplement an already substantial public career. He had first gained national prominence during the 1950s as the majority leader of the Senate during a time when the Republicans controlled the Presidency. Johnson's political activities and related public exposure during these years enabled him to become one of the more prominent leaders of his party and provided him an opportunity to become one of the leading contenders for its presidential nomination in 1960. While certain political problems prevented him from winning the nomination that year, such as his Texas background and the difficulties that congressional leaders often encounter while attempting to translate their institutional power into delegate votes, Johnson did manage to finish in second place behind Kennedy at the national convention. He acquired more than 400 of the 1,500 votes that were cast at the convention, about half the number garnered by Kennedy. Moreover, he attained most of the votes from the southeastern states. This region was not particularly enthusiastic about Kennedy and was even suggesting at the time that it might support Nixon in the general election. Johnson helped strengthen the Democratic ticket and the Kennedy bid when he accepted the nomination for Vice President. This decision was invaluable to both Kennedy and Johnson since it kept the electoral votes of many southeastern states, Texas included, in the Democratic column. Without Johnson as his running mate, Kennedy would probably have lost the election.

While much has been said and written about the personal frustrations and political difficulties that Johnson often encountered during his three years as Vice President, one fact about that time stands out and eventually played a significant role in the 1964 election. A substantial number of voters considered Johnson to be an integral member of the Democratic administration and actually looked upon him as a surrogate and possible successor of Kennedy. The televising and personalizing of the Presidency is not limited merely to illustrating the actions of the occupant of the Oval Office; it extends to the first family and to leading members of the executive branch of government. Television news media often depict these people as if they are personal extensions of the Presidency. Such was the fate of Johnson during the Kennedy years. Television news media illustrated him as a presidential surrogate, just as they had done with Richard Nixon during the Eisenhower years and eventually would do with future Vice Presidents Hubert Humphrey and George Bush. Johnson was personally and politically linked with Kennedy in the perceptions of much of the television-viewing public.

The events that occurred immediately before and after Kennedy's assassination helped reinforce this perception. For example, Kennedy and Johnson made their joint political venture to Dallas in November 1963 in order to launch their bids for reelection. At the time, the upcoming campaign appeared very competitive with the outcome uncertain. The anger that greeted Kennedy and Johnson throughout much of the Southeast because of their advocacy and support of new civil rights legislation threatened the Democratic standard bearers with defeats in a number of states that they had won in 1960. It was quite possible that these potential losses could have been offset by important gains in other regions. The front-running Republican, Barry Goldwater, appeared to have limited appeal in the urban and industrialized states of the Northeast and Midwest. Nevertheless, the Democratic leaders could ill afford to lose Texas to Goldwater. The 1961 election of John Tower to succeed Johnson in the Senate was particularly troublesome for the Democrats since it provided yet another indication, and a powerful one at that, of the growing Republican appeal that was developing in both Texas and the Southeast. Kennedy and Johnson found their electoral troubles compounded by the fact that the Texas Democratic Party was divided into bitter factions. They believed that without the alleviation of this disunity, Texas might be lost. Hence they both went to Dallas in order to begin their mutual efforts for reelection.

The televised reporting of events related to the assassination provided Johnson with even more opportunities for generating personal support and consolidating political power. As President, Johnson employed a number of verbal, visual, and symbolic measures to reassure the nation that it was not without leadership. His swearing in ceremony aboard the President's airplane, for example, with Mrs. Kennedy in attendance, was a symbolic reassurance to the nation that he was the heir to the deceased President.

Johnson engaged in some additional symbolic actions in the weeks that followed that helped transform his image from one of surrogate to one of successor and heir. He claimed Kennedy's legislative program as his own during his first State of the Union Address in January. He then advanced much of that program through Congress, accomplishments that had eluded Kennedy. Johnson placed his own identity upon Kennedy's "New Frontier" goals by proclaiming that his agenda constituted a quest for a "Great Society." He called for a declaration of war on poverty and established the Office of Economic Opportunity, under the direction of Kennedy family member Sargent Shriver, to make that war a reality. He developed new support for an urban aid agenda, obtained additional funding for education and training, and sought the creation of the two health care programs that eventually became known as Medicare and Medicaid. Moreover, he was particularly effective in gaining congressional approval of the most comprehensive civil rights law of the twentieth century. Johnson signed this new act into law in a highly publicized ceremony at the White House shortly before the convening of the Democratic National Convention in August. With these actions, Johnson convinced many of his fellow partisans that he might very well become the most successful Democratic President since Roosevelt at securing enactment of domestic legislation. After achieving these initial successes and thereby breaking the stalemate that had existed between the Presidency and Congress during the Truman, Eisenhower, and Kennedy administrations, Johnson greatly expanded his political support among the same northern liberals who had been suspicious of him during his previous presidential bid in 1960. The most unified Democratic convention to meet since 1936 convened in August 1964 and nominated Lyndon Johnson for President. No Democratic convention has been as united since then.

Johnson did not lack opposition for the nomination but managed to dispatch it rather quickly and easily. Governor George Wallace (Alabama) ran against him in several northern primaries in order to demonstrate the strength of opposition to civil rights legislation. He did so in the hopes of generating a white backlash against the pending law. Johnson refused to face Wallace directly in any state primary but instead undermined his efforts by encouraging three political allies to run against the Alabama governor in their states as favorite son candidates. Wallace soon abandoned his candidacy after losing primaries in Wisconsin, Indiana, and Maryland. He did not oppose Johnson at the Democratic convention.

Johnson's apparent successes in the one policy area that would eventually prove his undoing, foreign affairs, provided him with additional opportunities during the 1964 nomination season for garnering even more public support. Throughout the campaign, Johnson attempted both to create and project the public image by which he came across as the "peace" candidate with respect to the Vietnam War. Such imagery was in stark contrast to Goldwater, who advocated a more militant solution to international dilemmas. Johnson pursued this image-building strategy as the intensity of the war expanded. He contrasted his position with that of Goldwater by emphasizing his opposition to an expanded American combat role while reiterating his support for the Kennedy policy of providing assistance to the South Vietnamese government. Nevertheless, Johnson eventually involved this nation in some significant armed engagements during August 1964 in what came to be known as the Gulf of Tonkin incident. While numerous critics have subsequently questioned Johnson's credibility and have even questioned his motivations in responding to the incident, his actions at the time seemed to be a measured and reasoned response. Certainly, television and other news media did not offer the critical assessments of his actions that were raised about the war during the latter years of his administration. Instead, their reporting actually enhanced the development of a strong consensus in favor of Johnson's actions and in support of his candidacy. The immediate effect of this reporting was to help Johnson win the election and provide him with the requisite support for justifying a further escalation of the war in early 1965.

Television news media implicitly helped Johnson by their often uncritical reporting of his domestic and foreign policy activities and by their willingness to illustrate him primarily in the role of chief executive rather than in the role of candidate. Johnson, in effect, attempted to use the "Rose Garden strategy," and television news media responded favorably. In such a strategy, the President stages events designed to gain televised news coverage of certain activities which allow voters to see him performing in the patriotic and unifying head of state role. He also uses this same news coverage to minimize whatever controversies might be related to his other role as head of government. Television news media helped Johnson in this endeavor by using events and pictures that linked statesmanship with the Presidency and controversies with the Republicans throughout most of 1964. This strategy appears to have worked. By the time Johnson accepted the Democratic nomination in late August and designated Hubert Humphrey as his running mate, he had opened up a large and virtually insurmountable lead over Goldwater that hinted at a sweeping landslide victory.

The Nixon Nomination of 1972

Richard Nixon became the second incumbent President of the television age to gain another term in office when he won reelection in 1972. The magnitude of his margin of victory was comparable to that of Johnson, although the circumstances that led to his triumph were considerably different. Unlike Johnson, he did not begin his tenure after an assassination, nor did he inherit the widespread respect of voters by serving as a leading surrogate of his immediate predecessor. Instead, he attained his victory through a combination of policy and political successes and, from what we have since learned, a number of illegal campaign activities. Nixon won his initial term in 1968 with one of the more limited electoral coalitions of this century. He attained only 43.4 percent of the popular vote in an election that included three major candidates, and he managed to defeat his major rival, Hubert Humphrey, by less than one percent of the vote. Moreover, the leading public opinion surveys of the time suggested that Humphrey was actually gaining on Nixon in the last weeks of the campaign and might have overtaken him if the election had occurred several days later than it did. Not only was his victory thereby limited, but Nixon's Republican Party failed to gain control of either house of Congress. Nixon became the first President of this century to take office while facing a Congress that was completely dominated by his partisan opposition.

These circumstances encouraged the Democrats to hope and the Republicans to fear that Nixon's victory was only a short-term consequence of the social and political turmoil of 1968. Indeed, that year had provided the nation with an unusual number of unsettling events that distinuguished it from most election years. As a nation, we witnessed the assassinations of two prominent political leaders, underwent an unusually high level of civil disturbances, and became even more divided and embittered over the direction of an unpopular war. The lack of a clear and definitive mandate for Nixon, as seen in the close election results, suggested that his administration might amount to little more than a transition between the turmoil of the late Johnson years and the next Democratic President. Certainly, many Democrats were optimistic about their prospects of ending Nixon's tenure after only four years. The large number of aspirants who sought the nomination in 1972 attests to the widespread nature of this belief.

In developing his reelection strategies, Nixon sought to construct the Republican electoral majority that Kevin Phillips had discussed and predicted in 1970. Nixon agreed with Phillips that the Democratic majority of the New Deal period was weakening and that the permanent replacement of that coalition by a new Republican one could be a promising endeavor. This new coalition would unite the traditional constituency of the Republican Party that favored economic individualism with a growing constituency that opposed the civil rights, antiwar, and countercultural social movements of the late 1960s. Many of these new Republicans would be attracted from the same social groups whose members had frequently supported Democrats in the past: industrial workers, white Southerners, and adherents of conservative religions. The magnitude of Nixon's reelection triumph suggested that the formation of such a long-term coalition might very well succeed. The aftermath of the Watergate scandal put a temporary end to this possibility however.

If an incumbent President is to be a strong candidate for reelection, it is essential that he first consolidate power within his own party and unite the elements of his core constituency. Nixon accomplished this task quite effectively. He united his traditional Republican followers with members of the new constituency that he sought to mobilize by changing the policies of the Johnson administration concerning Vietnam and race relations without causing any threatening divisions among these groups.

The Vietnam War posed an immediate dilemma for Nixon. It had contributed to the political demise of Lyndon Johnson and his vast array of new domestic programs by dividing the Democratic Party into two hostile factions and by leaving that party discredited in the eyes of many voters. If Nixon could not achieve a resolution to the war issue within a fairly short period of time that was politically acceptable to a majority of the American people, he could very well encounter the same fate as Johnson. In formulating a resolution, Nixon needed to avoid pursuing any actions that could divide his partisans into hostile groups favoring either further escalation or immediate withdrawal. The pursuit of one of these options could lead to a political reaction from the advocates of the other. Nixon strived for a middle course between these two by working for a gradual reduction in the number of American troops in the region and by providing for a corresponding expansion in the size and participation of the South Vietnamese military. His purpose was to reduce this nation's involvement in the war without appearing to have abandoned the cause. Moreover, there would not likely be a major reaction against his policy from within his own potential constituency. Nixon justified his policy of gradual disengagement by employing the verbal and symbolic phrase that he was seeking "peace with honor." The strategy worked in the sense that it allowed enough time for a negotiated solution to end the American phase of the half century conflict without compromising Nixon's chances for a second term. It also worked in the sense that the Democrats eventually appeared to favor only one option, immediate withdrawal, and seemed increasingly unwilling to defend American foreign interests.

The second dilemma that Nixon needed to alleviate was the racial or civil rights controversy. The traditional constituency of the Republican Party had generally supported most civil rights legislation and would not likely respond favorably to candidates who made open appeals to bigotry. In contrast, many of the same voters that Nixon sought to attract to his party were actually Democrats or former Democrats who were opposed to their party's growing emphasis on the interests of racial minorities. Once again, Nixon pursued a middle course between the views of two different components of his potential constituency without angering either side. He made clear that he was opposed to any form of racial discrimination, which had the political effect of muting liberal criticism and not angering the traditional Republican supporters of civil rights legislation, but he moved much slower than the Democrats in seeking legislative and legal remedies. This second aspect of his policy made Nixon far more acceptable to conservatives. He supplemented this with his public opposition to the use of school busing for purposes of racial desegregation and by his nominations and attempted appointments of conservative, often southern, candidates for the Supreme Court and for other judicial and law enforcement positions. By these actions he was sending a message to racial conservatives: he would be far less threatening to their interests than the Democrats.

Nixon's approaches to these dilemmas eventually had the effect of undermining any opportunities that potential opponents might have found for challenging his renomination. His two major rivals from the nomination campaign of 1968, Governors Nelson Rockefeller (New York) and Ronald Reagan (California), both decided to support his renomination, and each delivered a major address at the 1972 national convention. Reagan gave the keynote speech, while Rockefeller placed Nixon's name in nomination. Nixon faced only two minor challengers in the initial primary of 1972, Congressmen Paul McClosky (California) and John Ashbrook (Ohio). The former was more liberal than Nixon; the latter more conservative. Nixon had provided so little room for any challenges to his renomination that each man ended his futile effort shortly after suffering an overwhelming defeat in the primary.

Since he had now consolidated power within his own party, Nixon could spend the remainder of the nomination season creating imagery by which viewers of televised politics could observe him acting primarily in the head of state role. He used this opportunity to appear statesmanlike and presidential, while his numerous Democratic rivals had to spend their time competing against one another in a divisive battle for the nomination. One of Nixon's most significant televised successes during this early stage of the campaign year was his landmark trip to China. It provided him with a chance to distinguish himself from his potential challengers in the general election by directing public attention to his role as an effective world leader. The policy implications and political symbolism of the trip were staggering. There were distinct possibilities that the decades of ideological hostility that had marked the relationship between the United States and China could be coming to an end and that the balance of political and military power in Asia could be fundamentally altered. The long-standing perception that Asian-based communism posed serious threats to American interests and security, threats upon which Nixon had built much of his public career and which had led to the Vietnam War, could diminish or even disappear entirely as a result of Nixon's diplomatic accomplishments. Conservatives could not oppose these overtures because of Nixon's background as a communist hater and because of the fact that he controlled the Republican Party, while liberals were unable to claim any credit for an initiative that they generally supported. For all intents and purposes, Nixon effectively clinched another term of office through the extensive televised news coverage that accompanied the trip. Television news media enhanced Nixon's efforts in the sense that they illustrated him primarily in the role of a national statesman involved with the demands of world diplomacy rather than in the role of a politician soliciting votes.

Nixon continued with his televised political successes during the latter stages of the primary election season when he attended a summit conference with Soviet President Leonid Brezhnev in Moscow. He used this opportunity to sign SALT I, the first treaty between the superpowers designed to limit the size of their strategic nuclear weapons arsenals. As with his earlier journey to China, Nixon enjoyed the extensive televised news coverage of the ceremonial and symbolic activities of the Moscow trip that the head of state role creates during such meetings. The public relations payoffs of these diplomatic endeavors soon became apparent. Voter approval of Nixon's performance as President in general and of his conduct of foreign policy in particular increased to the point where Nixon now enjoyed the greatest support that he was to have at any time during his five and a half years in office.

As they previously had done with Johnson, television news media remained fairly uncritical of Nixon and of his policies throughout much of the primary election season. They seemed to be far more interested in reporting about the unending controversies that continued to keep the Democrats divided throughout much of the first half of 1972 than about raising any strong doubts about Nixon. They did not even attempt to develop a major story out of the growing scandal that eventually came to be known as Watergate, although the *Washington Post* did report about it extensively. The theme that guided much of the content of televised news coverage of Nixon throughout the campaign year was formulated early, particularly during the China trip. Television news media illustrated Nixon in the role of President governing the nation, while they depicted his Democratic rivals as politicians in search of votes. This theme even extended through the period of the party national conventions. Televised news coverage of the July Democratic convention showed a party in disarray, while the Republican conclave in August seemed to be a coronation of a successful President. By the time Nixon accepted renomination, his challenger had already been discredited. Moreover, Nixon had also opened up a large and virtually insurmountable lead over George McGovern that hinted at a sweeping landslide victory of the same magnitude as the earlier Johnson triumph.

The Reagan Nomination of 1984

Ronald Reagan was the third television age incumbent who attained reelection by means of a spectacular personal triumph. The scenario of his successful effort of 1984 was remarkably similar to the earlier ones of Johnson and Nixon; he consolidated power within his own party before the onset of the election, and television news media responded by illustrating him more as statesman than candidate. Reagan became President under circumstances that differed somewhat from those of the other incumbents. His political support upon taking office was weaker than Johnson's but stronger than Nixon's. Reagan attained office in 1980 by defeating a weak and unpopular incumbent in an election that involved three major candidates. His victory was far more definitive than Nixon's one percentage point triumph. He garnered a majority of the popular vote and defeated Jimmy Carter by nearly ten percentage points while winning the electoral votes of forty-four states. He also helped his party make some very substantial gains in Congress. The Republican Party took twelve Senate seats from the Democrats and acquired control of the chamber for the first time since 1954. Since more Democratic positions than Republican would be at stake in the upcoming elections of both 1982 and 1984, many observers assumed at the time that this new Republican control of the Senate would last for at least six years, as it eventually did. Finally, the Republicans gained thirty-five seats in the House of Representatives and reduced Democratic strength to its lowest total in that chamber in more than a decade.

As a consequence of the 1980 election, Reagan began his tenure in office with a stronger political base than Nixon and held out the promise of major legislative successes. He did not disappoint his backers. During his first year as President, Reagan defeated congressional Democrats in a number of highly publicized showdowns and attained some far-reaching changes in taxing and spending policies. These changes, in turn, contributed to significant economic growth during most of the ensuing decade and to Reagan's successful bid for a second term in 1984. There were some problems however: these triumphs contributed to a massive increase in the federal deficit and to the economic stagnation that eventually helped defeat Reagan's surrogate and successor, George Bush, in 1992.

One of Reagan's major legislative goals was to alter spending priorities by reducing domestic expenditures while increasing funding for military readiness and procurement. A second was to lower tax rates. With respect to domestic spending, Reagan sought to attain many of his reductions by consolidating a number of federal grants to state and local governments into larger block grants and to cut the funding of programs covered by the grants by about $40 billion. As a first step, he sent Congress several hundred proposed rescissions of budgetary authority. He also tried to increase funding for new weapons systems for both the nuclear and conventional components of the armed forces. He sought the acquisition of such nuclear weapons systems as the MX intercontinental missile, the B-1 bomber, and the Trident submarine. He also proposed increases in the size and readiness of all branches of the armed forces including the development of a six-hundred-ship Navy. These increases were politically popular in light of the recent embarrassments that the nation had endured because of the Iranian hostage crisis. An increase in the size of the military budget was not likely to avert any hostage problems in the future, as the Iran-Contra scandal demonstrated, but it did provide an economic stimulus and some psychological relief to people uncertain about a perceived threat from Islamic nations. Reagan did find some opportunities in which he could use this new military might to resolve international dilemmas. He enhanced his popular standing considerably after ordering an invasion of Grenada in order to oust a communist regime.

Reagan also advocated major revisions in the federal income tax. He advanced the idea of supply side economics in which government would take a leading role in stimulating economic growth by making substantial reductions in the tax rates of industry and upper income people. These producer sectors would respond by investing their new monies in jobs and technology. This would help increase production and alleviate the sluggish economic conditions that had marked much of the decade of the 1970s.

Reagan rallied the new Republican strength in Congress and attained each of these goals by the end of his first year in office. He gained his most significant victory when his supporters in the House of Representatives successfully amended a report from the Rules Committee and substituted a new one that called for an alternative procedure for voting on proposed domestic spending reductions. The Democratic leadership wanted to conduct specific votes on each of the more than six hundred proposed reductions. This would allow more time for opposition to develop against each reduction and would make the votes of individual members of Congress that much harder to come by. While most Congressmen support budgetary reductions in principle, they often encounter some difficulty in voting for specific ones. The intent of the Democratic leadership was to force the members to consider each reduction by itself. Reagan wanted all reductions voted on simultaneously and sought a rule to that effect. His supporters won by a vote of 217 to 212.

After this procedural victory, the way was open for Reagan to gain the enactment of the various components of his program. The Democratic oppositon increasingly failed to defeat him on any of the major votes that followed. In fact, many Democrats eventually supported much of Reagan's tax reduction plan. By the end of 1981, Reagan had achieved the legislative victories that set in motion the taxing and spending policies that would guide American government for the next twelve years.

Reagan also used these successes to consolidate power within his own party. His legislative accomplishments had been greater than those of most Republican Presidents of this century. He had attained nearly unanimous support from Republican members of both chambers of Congress through all of his battles with the Democrats and in doing so provided a strong definition of the national agenda of the party. In popular imagery, the Republican Party of the 1980s was the party of Reagan. In contrast, one cannot say that the Democratic Party of the late 1970s was necessarily the party of Jimmy Carter. With this requisite consolidation of power behind him, Reagan was now free to perform in the role of statesman rather than candidate, as he had been doing since his initial quest for the Republican nomination in 1968.

Reagan maintained a relatively high level of personal popularity throughout much of the early 1980s despite the onset of a fairly severe recession in 1982. He used the "bully pulpit" of the Presidency, with television as an added feature since the time of Theodore Roosevelt, to enhance his popularity and advance his ideological position that government was not the solution but the problem. He was exceptionally skillful at manipulating the symbolic dimensions of his office and the style and content of television news, as Michael Deaver and Lesley Stahl suggest.

Reagan used television as his forum for defending so-called traditional values, for denouncing the "evil empire" of the Soviet Union, and for projecting an optimistic feeling about the nation's past glories and dynamic future. In doing so, he staged a number of photo opportunities in which television news media could illustrate him as a statesmanlike leader.

The campaign for the Republican nomination of 1984 began and ended with Reagan as the only announced candidate. This lack of opposition reflected the extent of Reagan's prior consolidation of power and provided further proof of the fact that no challenger had any realistic chances of generating the support needed for a presidential bid. A fairly large number of potential candidates for the 1988 nomination began to emerge during this time however. They had one common goal: to convince their fellow Republicans that each of them was the party's best hope for extending Reaganism into a third and possibly a fourth term.

Reagan used the innumerable opportunities for favorable televised news coverage that tends to accompany uncontested campaigns and spent much of the primary election season appearing in staged events designed to illustrate him in the statesman role. Two of his most effective manipulations of televised news occurred with the coverage of his journey to France for the celebration of the fortieth anniversary of the Normandy landing during the Second World War and with the implicitly patriotic reporting that followed the vast number of American successes at the Los Angeles Olympics. The anniversary of the Allied invasion of June 6, 1944 occurred at a most opportune time for Reagan. The first week of June 1984 marked the conclusion of the primary election season. While Reagan was in Europe acting out the role of American statesman, the two leading candidates for the Democratic nomination, Walter Mondale and Gary Hart, engaged in a final set of bitterly contested primaries. Hart won the most important one, California, and thereby enhanced the Reagan reelection effort even more. Hart was too far behind Mondale in the delegate count to have any realistic chances of derailing the former Vice President's virtually certain nomination, but by winning California could perpetuate the campaign until the July meeting of the national convention. Hart's victory provided several more weeks for Reagan to continue acting in the unquestioned role of patriotic statesman.

Reagan also gained from the fact that American athletes garnered an unprecedented number of successes at the 1984 Olympic games. Many of these successes resulted because of the Soviet and communist bloc boycott. The two superpowers were engaging in mutual boycotts of each other's "games." The United States began the international snubs in 1980 when Jimmy Carter called for a Western bloc boycott of the Moscow games because of the Soviet invasion of Afghanistan. The Soviet Union responded by calling for a boycott of the Los Angeles games. The absence of many of the world's leading athletes from either of these meetings eventually led to a domination of most of the events by the host nation. The Soviet boycott had the unintended effect of enhancing Reagan's popular standing and reelection prospects in that it contributed to even more emotional support of his efforts to generate national pride. The televised emphasis upon patriotic imagery throughout the Olympics helped set the mood for Reagan's "It's Morning in America" reelection theme. Much of this coverage also occurred while the Democrats were still fighting bitterly among themselves.

As both Johnson and Nixon had done in their earlier campaigns, Reagan successfully manipulated televised news coverage of his party's national convention and projected favorable imagery of himself performing in the statesman role. Television news media readily cooperated as they all too frequently illustrated Reagan in upbeat, quasi-patriotic scenes that were devoid of controversy but which reinforced the theme that no problems existed that required difficult solutions. This consensus-building imagery was in marked contrast to the highly divisive scenes that had emanated from the convention of the opposing Democrats just one month earlier. The implicit message was there for all to see: the statesmanlike incumbent was vastly more qualified to lead the nation than his embattled challenger.

While television news media may very well have been aware of the manipulative efforts of Reagan's press corps, they nevertheless continued to broadcast these highly managed scenes. Moreover, they regularly disregarded information that might have proven damaging to Reagan. Foremost among the omitted information were any serious evaluations of the economic difficulties that loomed on the horizon because of the long-term effects of Reagan's taxing and spending policies. Instead, television news media directed their attention primarily to the positive and supportive picture-related campaign events at which Reagan so greatly excelled and thereby helped make his sweeping reelection triumph virtually inevitable.

OPPOSITION PARTY NOMINATIONS

Overview and the 1984 Democratic Campaign

The unchallenged candidacy of an incumbent President for renomination creates a serious and often insurmountable dilemma for the opposition party. The party becomes increasingly unable to compete effectively against the incumbent as the campaign year unfolds. As a result, it falls so far behind the incumbent in public esteem that it finally loses any chance whatsoever of winning the election. One reason for this dilemma is that the party almost always lacks a unifying leader at the start of the campaign who can immediately unite the party and then use that unity to challenge the promises and record of the incumbent. As discussed earlier, the American political system provides few opportunities for an opposition party to develop an undisputed leader without having to engage in a prolonged and potentially divisive nomination campaign. The party therefore loses valuable time while devoting most of the first half of the election year to finding a leader. During this same period of time, the incumbent manipulates television news and the trappings of his office and thereby creates a statesmanlike image and a massive personal following. By the time the opposition party concludes its nomination campaign and is finally ready to challenge the incumbent, its best opportunities may very well have passed.

A second problem is that the party may not yet have resolved the divisions that contributed to its defeat in the preceding election. In each of the three elections studied here, the opposition party had been driven from power four years earlier because of its failures to alleviate some of the major problems of the time and because of significant divisions that arose among its own members because of those failures. Those divisions had not subsided by the current campaigns. Instead, the two factions that had battled each other during the previous campaigns simply renewed their mutual and destructive quests for control of the party. The Republicans lost in both 1960 and 1964 partly because of their inability to alleviate a recession during the former campaign and because of disagreements among themselves during the latter over the role that the federal government should take in confronting the social and economic problems that encourage recessions. The Democrats lost power in both 1968 and 1980 partly because of foreign policy failures and because of their continuing divisions over the priority that should be given to domestic matters during a time of budgetary constraints. In each instance, they engaged in a highly divisive campaign in which the candidate who represented the administration was challenged by an adversary who was highly critical of the conduct of that administration. After the party's eventual defeat in both general elections, the two factions carried their own struggles for power right into the next nomination campaign.

Finally, recurring biases in televised news coverage of nomination campaigns adversely affect the prospects of the opposition party in years that have strong incumbents. As discussed earlier, television news media prefer that only one prolonged and competitive nomination campaign occur in any given election. Since such a campaign is possible only within the opposition party when the incumbent is unopposed, television news media direct virtually all of their election-related coverage to that one party during the nomination season. Moreover, they structure their reporting in ways that will encourage the outcome to remain unresolved for months. News reporting of this nature actually encourages these campaigns to be prolonged and divisive and helps undermine the personal credibility and electoral prospects of the opposition party's eventual nominees.

Television news media begin their dissensus-enhancing coverage by assigning the roles of front-runner, leading adversary, and loser to each candidate within the opposition party shortly after the conclusion of the first primaries and caucuses, if not earlier. They follow by depicting the leading adversary as the antithesis of the front-runner and treat him as the personification of the political obstacles that the front-runner must overcome. One can see examples of this pattern in the Democratic campaign of 1984. There were eight candidates who sought the nomination, with a front-runner readily available from the very beginning, former Vice President Walter Mondale. Mondale started his efforts by holding a fairly strong lead in public opinion surveys. About half of the respondents in a variety of surveys said they preferred him for the nomination. He announced his candidacy during the early weeks of 1983 and eventually received more endorsements from elected officials, party leaders, and liberal interest groups than any of his rivals. Mondale's successes at raising funds and building a campaign organization also outpaced those of the other candidates.

At the outset of the campaign, television and other news media divided Mondale's rivals into two groups. They placed five candidates who had joined the campaign during the first few months of 1983 into one group and two more recent entrants into a second one. The strongest member of the first group, at least in terms of support as measured by public opinion surveys, appeared to be Senator John Glenn (Ohio). The others were Senators Gary Hart (Colorado), Alan Cranston (California), Ernest Hollings (South Carolina), and former Governor Reubin Askew (Florida). Television news media soon depicted these five as if they were competing in two separate subcampaigns. The first subcampaign involved these so-called "second tier" candidates competing against one another for the right to become Mondale's one leading adversary. Television news media did not describe this early stage of the campaign as a battle among a large number of candidates of whom Mondale appeared to be the strongest, but instead depicted it as if it were akin to a set of playoffs for an athletic championship. Two Democrats eventually were to face each other for the "championship" of their party's electoral tournament and for the right to advance to the political "Super Bowl" where they would oppose Ronald Reagan in the general election. Mondale apparently had already qualified for a finalist position in this tournament. The other candidates were competing against one another to attain the remaining position. The second subcampaign involved the developing battle for the upcoming general election. Television news media were beginning to define this stage of the campaign as already involving only three major candidates; Reagan, Mondale, and the one other Democrat who would arise from the second tier contenders and compete against Mondale for the right to face Reagan in the general election.

The second group of Mondale's rivals consisted of two candidates who had entered the campaign toward the latter part of 1983, Reverend Jesse Jackson and former Senator George McGovern. Television and other news media did not consider that either had a realistic chance of winning the nomination. Instead, they considered that Jackson's appeal was limited mostly to blacks and that his main role would be as a spokesman for civil rights issues. They depicted McGovern's candidacy as quixotic, with his scant support confined to the more liberal elements of the Democratic constituency.

Three important electoral tests occurred during the first few weeks of the year. Two involved votes in single states and took place in February: the Iowa caucuses about mid-month and the New Hampshire primary one week later. The third involved primaries on the second Tuesday in March in five states: Alabama, Florida, Georgia, Massachusetts, and Rhode Island. The outcome of the Iowa caucuses seemed a foregone conclusion—political reporters expected a sweeping Mondale victory. Since there was little doubt about the identity of the Iowa winner, reporters speculated instead about the second place finisher. A second place finish would mean victory in the battle among the second tier contenders. There was virtually no possibility that television news media would depict the runner-up in Iowa as a loser. If they had described Mondale as the overwhelming winner and dismissed the others as losers, the campaign for the nomination might well have concluded right there.

With few exceptions, most aspirants for the nomination of the opposition party are not prominent national leaders at the beginning of the election year. Moreover, they also lack widespread personal constituencies and must therefore strive to create them. Since television news media direct much of their campaign-related reporting to personalities, events, and controversies rather than to questions of public policy, many of these candidates soon find that the already difficult task of generating constituencies becomes even more problematic. When a nomination campaign is presented to viewers of televised politics as a prolonged battle for strategic advantages among several little-known candidates, viewers often consider those candidates who fare poorly as losers unqualified for national leadership. A candidate who lacks a constituency can advance only one powerful argument to legitimate his efforts and persuade his own partisans that they should support him: he can win the election. His party should therefore nominate him since it prefers victory over all other goals. When the 1984 campaign began, all the Democratic aspirants except Mondale and Jackson lacked constituencies that they could rely on for future support if they failed in some of the early electoral tests. Many party and labor leaders supported Mondale, while a substantial number of blacks favored Jackson. The other candidates had such limited followings that they could not escape the media classification of "loser" if they failed to run well in Iowa.

The patterns of television news coverage and the nature of the campaign after Iowa differed considerably from what actually occurred in that state and indicate the power of television news media in helping to define and structure political reality. Mondale won the caucuses with about 48 percent of the vote, while Hart finished second with about 16 percent, one-third of Mondale's total. In fact, Hart barely finished ahead of McGovern who attained 13 percent. Mondale had defeated his opponents by wide margins, but his victory was not the major political news story that developed from the Iowa caucuses. The story was that Hart had finished second. Television news media changed the themes in their coverage of Hart shortly after the caucuses. They ceased depicting him as one of the many second tier long shots who was seeking the nomination and instead redefined him as one of the two major candidates. Moreover, they also redefined the campaign so that it became a struggle between the front-runner Mondale and his leading adversary Hart. They did not base their change of definition on any facts other than Hart's second place finish. Hart's support in other states was virtually nil after the Iowa vote, just as it had been before. Television news media had helped to create and then enhance mass perceptions that the campaign had actually become a battle between Mondale and Hart with the remaining candidates of no further consequence.

One should temper this discussion with the realization that the abilities of television news media to create campaign realities for their viewing audiences are limited. Quantities of news coverage are not the only reasons that differences exist in the relative strength of the contenders for a nomination. One cannot say that television news media were solely responsible for the fact that Mondale was the strongest Democratic candidate at the beginning of 1984, nor credit them with his victory in Iowa. Mondale's widespread public exposure during both his term as Vice President and his two prior campaigns for national office, along with extensive organizational efforts, account far more for his victory in Iowa than any television news coverage that he may have acquired during the campaign. Moreover, television news media did not cause Gary Hart to finish second and did not create the relatively poor showings of the other six candidates. Their greatest influence upon the campaign came afterwards. Television news media are most influential in defining the reality of a campaign and the status of the candidates after the earliest votes are cast. They assist in forcing the weaker candidates to withdraw and then help to redefine and stereotype those that remain. They helped redefine the campaign for the 1984 Democratic nomination and then stereotype the remaining candidates when they began reporting that the campaign had narrowed to a battle between front-runner Mondale and his one leading adversary, Hart, with the remaining candidates as losers.

The effects of this redefinition soon became evident in the New Hampshire primary. A variety of surveys that had been taken prior to the vote in

Iowa and the subsequent expansion in media coverage of Hart indicated that less than 10 percent of Democratic voters in New Hampshire supported the Colorado senator. Hart's support in the state expanded rapidly after the Iowa vote, however, and he defeated Mondale by a margin of 37 percent to 28. Mondale's tally actually was fairly similar to his standing in the earlier surveys. He did not lose support after Iowa, but he did not gain much either. Hart gained most of his expanded support from the followers of the remaining candidates whose campaigns failed after television news media started depicting them as losers. The two-candidate campaign between Mondale and Hart, which had not existed until television news media proclaimed that it did after the Iowa caucuses, became a reality during the New Hampshire primary.

The campaign changed rather dramatically after New Hampshire with television news media exerting some fairly strong influences upon the course of events. The extensive news coverage of Hart soon created the distinct possibility that the Colorado senator might outgrow his role of leading adversary and sweep all before him, including even Mondale. There were indications that Hart was on the verge of winning all five of the early March primaries. If so, he would have emerged as the new front-runner. The possibility that Hart might actually acquire this role might then have induced Mondale to conclude his candidacy and thereby resolve the nomination. Television news media had been unwilling to allow Mondale the opportunity to eliminate his opposition in Iowa since that would have left no "race" to report. A possible Hart sweep in early March would have accomplished the same result. Consequently they redefined the campaign once again, this time by raising doubts concerning Hart. The topics used to raise these doubts included several recent changes in Hart's name, signature, and birth date. Hart had shortened his name from Hartpence several years earlier, had made some noticeable and recent changes in his signature, and had once listed his birth date as a year later than it actually was. Television news media reported about these matters at a time when they needed to slow Hart's progress toward securing the nomination in order to perpetuate the campaign. They even gave extensive coverage to Mondale's comment that when he thought about Hart's platform he was reminded of a hamburger commercial that asked "where's the beef?"

This strategy seemed to work, and consequently Hart's support soon declined and then stabilized. Hart and Mondale divided the March primaries: Hart took three states—Florida, Massachusetts, and Rhode Island—and Mondale won in Alabama and Georgia. The lack of a definitive victory for either candidate now meant that the primary campaign would most likely be prolonged until the national convention in July. Except for Jackson, the remaining candidates had withdrawn by this time, and television news media continued to depict the Jackson effort as a sideshow to the real action.

For the next few months, the campaign conformed to the theme that had developed shortly after the vote in Iowa. Television news media used Mondale as the anchor point for their reporting and examined events and the actions of his rivals from the perspective of how they might affect his prospects. As John F. Kennedy had needed to overcome the obstacles of his religion and inexperience in Theodore White's saga of the 1960 campaign in order to reach the White House, Mondale needed to overcome some personal obstacles that could undermine his candidacy. After some attacks by Hart, television news media stereotyped Mondale as the candidate of the party establishment and treated him as an advocate of its "old ideas." This establishment allegedly was comprised of elected officials, party leaders, and the interest groups that tend to support Democratic candidates: civil rights, labor, and educational organizations.

Television news media continued depicting Hart as the antithesis of Mondale. While Mondale allegedly was the front-running establishment candidate, Hart, as his leading adversary, supposedly represented the Democratic insurgency that had opposed this establishment in several recent campaigns through the candidacies of Robert Kennedy, Eugene McCarthy, and George McGovern. Television news media helped to stereotype Hart into this adversarial outsider role just as they had encouraged their viewers to think of Mondale as the establishment candidate. They illustrated Hart as a charismatic rival of Mondale who stood for some enigmatic set of new ideas. While vaguely defined, these ideas were definitely not those of the party's leaders and allied interest groups. The televised contrasts between Mondale and Hart were also stereotypical. Television news media emphasized a few superficial controversies that allegedly distinguished the candidates, such as the nuclear freeze issue of that year. More importantly, however, they directed attention mainly to the battles over votes, delegates, money, and poll standings. In contrast, they placed very little emphasis upon matters that might have illustrated some common ground between the two constituencies.

In addition to redefining the campaign, television news media also helped enhance dissensus among the Democrats and eventually compromise the electability of both Hart and Mondale. The televising of a prolonged nomination campaign fought by two adversarial, role-playing contenders encourages voters to see them as personally flawed and lacking the qualities of leadership possessed by the incumbent they seek to replace. Voters observe the candidates primarily as contenders for power rather than as presidential-appearing statesmen. While partisan combat may be very appealing to some political activists and news media personnel, it is not particularly appealing to many voters. Far too many saw Mondale and Hart as overly involved in a continuing struggle for the nomination. Since most voters pay only scant attention to politics, most aspirants for the nomination of the opposition party have little support at the outset of an election year. Most voters develop their opinions about the candidates during the early months of the campaign. Hart, in particular, was relatively unknown at the beginning of 1984. Mondale also had his limitations since many voters identified him more as a former Vice President and surrogate for Jimmy Carter than as a leader in his own right. Both candidates needed to develop and then project strong images of their superior leadership qualities if they hoped to have any realistic chances of overcoming Reagan's immense television-enhanced popularity. Their prolonged and televised campaign made this task virtually impossible.

Neither candidate could acquire enough opportunities during the campaign whereby he could develop and project an image in which he appeared to have statesmanlike qualities comparable to Reagan. Instead, both candidates increasingly seemed to be extensions of the same combatants and factions that had compromised the electoral prospects of the Democratic Party four years earlier. Mondale looked as if he were offering a renewal of some of the more unpopular features of the Carter administration, while Hart appeared to be advancing the same questionable alternatives that had once come from Edward Kennedy. If one accepts the argument that Americans vote retrospectively, personal observations of the performances of Mondale and Hart should remind one of their negative evaluations of the leading combatants from the last Democratic campaign and should encourage a similar assessment of the candidates this time. Those who did not like Carter were encouraged to transfer their animosity to Mondale, while many of those who were wary of Kennedy were now quite uncertain about Hart.

One should again temper this discussion by realizing that television news media are not always the origins of the imagery that they sometimes use to stereotype candidates. Some of that imagery is in fact advanced by the candidates themselves. Television news media accept this imagery and then rebroadcast it so frequently that it eventually becomes stereotypical. Hart, and not television news media, was the architect of the charge that Mondale was the advocate of the old ideas of the Democratic establishment. Correspondingly, Mondale was the primary source of the accusations that Hart was superficial. Television news media readily accepted these charges and the characterizations that accompanied them and then used them to stereotype the candidates.

The media emphasis upon divisiveness and controversy among the Democrats continued both through and after that party's national convention. Even when the nomination was finally resolved, television media continued to direct news attention to various real or imagined controversies among the Democrats. One can see an example of this in the emphasis upon Mondale's decision to replace Charles Manatt as national party chairman. Television news media treated this matter, the significance of which was inconsequential to anyone except a small number of party leaders, as a controversy of major importance. Moreover, Mondale's image problems did not end with his nomination. The convention had barely concluded when television news media directed attention to yet another controversy, the troubled personal finances of the vice presidential candidate, Congresswoman Geraldine Ferraro (New York). While Ferraro was not guilty of any particular wrongdoing, the effect of this controversy was to make Mondale once again appear as an unqualified replacement for Reagan. This continuing and damaging news coverage of the Democratic campaign occurred partly because of the general lack of newsworthy events deriving from the uncontested nomination campaign of the presidential party. Without any such events, television news media responded by directing their attention to the one party that actually had a campaign, the opposition Democrats. This pattern helped damage Mondale's electoral prospects. He could not find enough opportunities during the nomination season to unify his own partisans, to convince voters that his party had resolved the differences that had cost it the last election, or to pose any serious or credible challenge to Reagan. By the time Mondale was finally ready for Reagan, the race was lost.

The Goldwater Nomination of 1964

The scenarios of the campaigns within the opposition parties in both 1964 and 1972, including the patterns of televised news coverage, were similar to those of 1984. The opposition party of 1964, in this instance the Republican Party, was attempting to regain power after having been driven from office only four years earlier. Television news media also repeatedly defined this campaign as a race between two role-playing candidates, a distinct front-runner and one leading adversary. This campaign also occurred within the context of an ideological and factional battle for party control. The Republicans had divided into moderate and conservative factions early in the twentieth century but had managed to unite during the Presidency of Dwight D. Eisenhower. They found continued unity difficult after their loss in the 1960 election however. The unity of the Eisenhower years lasted through the 1960 election campaign under the candidacy of Nixon, but it declined shortly thereafter. Following the retirement of Eisenhower and the temporary political demise of Nixon because of his electoral defeats, the Republicans were without an undisputed leader and were soon embroiled in bitter factional fighting over party control and the 1964 presidential nomination. Factions that had been relatively quiet during the Eisenhower years reemerged and contended for power.

Since the latter 1930s, several conservative aspirants for Republican presidential nominations had lost to more moderate contenders. Conservatives believed that they had a realistic chance of winning in 1964, however, and soon looked to Senator Barry Goldwater (Arizona) as their best hope. Goldwater was elected to the Senate in 1952 and spent much of his tenure in office serving as a leading spokesman for the conservative interests of the growing Republican population of the expanding areas of the Southeast and West. Their rivals, the moderates, initially looked to Governor Nelson Rockefeller (New York) as their strongest choice. Rockefeller was elected Governor of New York in 1958 and soon emerged as the most influential spokesman for the moderate Republican interests of the Northeast and Midwest. Goldwater and Rockefeller became the two leading contenders for the 1964 nomination shortly after Nixon's defeat for the governorship of California in 1962.

Television news media defined the campaign early in the year as limited to these two contenders, even though others were either seeking the nomination at the time or were planning to enter the battle at a later date. Among the others were the party's nominee for Vice President in 1960, Henry Cabot Lodge Jr., Senator Margaret Chase Smith (Maine), and Governors George Romney (Michigan) and William Scranton (Pennsylvania). Television news media proclaimed Goldwater as the front-runner from the very beginning, named Rockefeller as his one leading adversary, and depicted the others as marginal actors in the Goldwater-Rockefeller race. They eventually stereotyped each of the six candidates into these roles.

The New Hampshire primary, scheduled for the second Tuesday of March (the Iowa caucuses did not originate until 1972), was the first electoral event of the year. Goldwater and Rockefeller contested it but encountered some unexpected difficulties. Goldwater used this primary as an opportunity to emphasize his conservative ideology and his opposition to many of Lyndon Johnson's domestic policy proposals. In a sense, he was campaigning against the trends toward a more activist federal government that were the centerpiece of the Democratic Party's agenda. Rockefeller raised a number of strong objections to Goldwater's plans and suggested that the impact of some of them might be less than what many of the state's voters wanted. He argued that the implementation of voluntary participation in Social Security, as advocated by Goldwater, would lead to an eventual bankrupting of the program. While he managed to raise some important doubts about Goldwater and stall the Arizona Senator's drive toward the nomination, Rockefeller had a serious problem: adverse public reaction to his divorce and remarriage of two years earlier had caused a substantial number of Republicans to dismiss him completely as a potential President. The result of this increasingly bitter primary campaign was to lower the esteem that voters in both New Hampshire and the nation had of either man. New Hampshire voters did not seem particularly impressed with either candidate and eventually looked for an alternative. Their dissatisfaction was expressed in the form of two write-in campaigns conducted on behalf of Nixon and Lodge. Lodge won the primary with about 35 percent of the vote, while Nixon recorded nearly 20 percent for a fourth-place finish. Front-runner Goldwater and leading adversary Rockefeller finished second and third respectively and divided approximately 45 percent of the vote about evenly between themselves. Despite his excellent performance, however, Lodge was unwilling to resign as the Ambassador to South Vietnam in order to pursue a more active campaign. Consequently his successes seemed to be more of a reaction to the events of the New Hampshire campaign and did not serve to advance his hopes much beyond that state.

The one event that eventually proved to be crucial in deciding the outcome of the nomination was the California primary during the first week of June. Unlike the somewhat artificial depictions that television news media made at the beginning of the campaign in January, the California election was a two-candidate battle between Goldwater and Rockefeller. No other candidates, including write-ins, chose to compete in this primary. Despite his New Hampshire setback, Goldwater soon became the Republican front-runner by garnering very substantial support from conservative party leaders and activists throughout the Southeast and West. They packed local and state conventions and eventually seized control of the party apparatus in their states if they did not already control it. They also elected predominantly conservative delegations to attend the national convention scheduled for mid-July in San Francisco. Goldwater relied upon this support and opened up a sizable lead over Rockefeller, who had been unable to attain much backing from party members outside the Northeast. Rockefeller was looking more and more like a regional candidate whose major role would be to prevent Goldwater from winning a nomination he could not win himself. If this came about, it would open the door to the nomination of one of the other candidates. Despite these limitations, Rockefeller soon demonstrated that he remained a formidable contender when he defeated Lodge and Goldwater in the Oregon primary in mid-May. The immediate effect was to end any speculation about Lodge and to enliven Rockefeller's prospects in California.

The California primary that followed three weeks later was exceptionally competitive and provided television news media with many opportunities for broadcasting and thereby enhancing the divisions that existed among Republicans. The campaign also occurred while Lyndon Johnson was attaining some of his strongest legislative successes, including the final struggles that led to the passage of the civil rights act of that year. The results of the primary indicate the closeness of the divisions among Republicans: Goldwater won with 51 percent of the vote compared to 49 percent for Rockefeller.

While the outcome of the nomination was apparent after the California vote—Goldwater now had more than enough delegates to claim victory—the campaign and the television news coverage of the controversies that continued to be associated with it did not end. The California vote marked the end of the primary election season. Despite this fact, the nomination stage of the election year would not conclude until the Democratic convention met in late August. Johnson would use this opportunity to name his running mate and formally launch his campaign for the general election. Until that occurred, the campaign for the Republican nomination was the only electoral story available for television news media to report. Consequently, it retained that dominant position for two months following the California primary. During this time television news media directed considerable emphasis to the efforts that were being taken by a number of moderate Republicans, including both Rockefeller and former President Eisenhower, to stop the pending nomination of Goldwater. Rockefeller decided to remain in the race, although he had lost any chance of winning. Some moderate leaders instead wanted to find a new adversary to oppose Goldwater. Scranton soon became that candidate and replaced Rockefeller as the one leading adversary and antithesis of the front-runner.

The stop-Goldwater effort failed, but it did create some incidents before, during, and after the national convention that television news media found controversial and divisive enough for their attention. These included the battles that took place over the adoption of the party platform and the eventual walkout from the national convention of the New York delegation and the refusal of several moderates to endorse Goldwater. This walkout occurred supposedly because of the comments that Goldwater made in his acceptance speech when he said that "extremism in defense of liberty is no vice . . . moderation in the pursuit of justice is no virtue." Several days earlier, a number of moderate leaders, and Rockefeller in particular, attempted to add an amendment to the platform that called for the party to condemn all forms of political extremism. This amendment was aimed especially at Goldwater. Rockefeller and his allies had been charging for some time that Goldwater was an extreme candidate rather than one who hailed from the ideological mainstream. The amendment was rejected but not until hundreds of angry Goldwater supporters booed Rockefeller for several minutes when he attempted to speak in favor of the amendment. Of course, this outburst and Goldwater's response were televised for all to see and to be angered by the apparent unstatesmanlike behavior of the partisan rivals of Lyndon Johnson.

There were a number of similarities between the 1964 Republican campaign and the Democratic one of 1984. Two major role-playing contenders, the front-runner and his one leading adversary and antithesis, emerged or were encouraged to emerge by television news media very early in both campaign years. The candidates who eventually filled these roles were apparent at the beginning of the 1964 campaign, but media encouragement helped fill the adversary role with Hart in 1984. Each of the initial front-runners eventually won the nomination, but neither could force his adversary to abandon the struggle until the conclusion of the mid-summer national convention. Even if the front-runner had actually been able to eliminate the adversary from the competition, as Goldwater did with Rockefeller in the California primary, television news media would help create another one, as they did with Scranton. In addition, both Goldwater and Mondale were unable to end the televised reporting of controversies about their candidacies even after the conclusion of their national conventions. Since the incumbent had provided no controversy in his pursuit of renomination, television news media once again continued directing their attention to the events and personalities of the opposition party, even after its national convention.

The McGovern Nomination of 1972

These same patterns of news coverage, definition, and interpretation also occurred during the campaign for the Democratic nomination in 1972, but this time with an interesting twist. Television news media once again defined the campaign very early in the year as limited primarily to the two role-playing contenders of the front-runner and his one leading adversary and antithesis. They continued defining it in this manner until the conclusion of the national convention but altered their coverage by placing different candidates in these roles at various times during the year. The original front-runner eventually disappeared from the race. Shortly thereafter, the original leading adversary became the new front-runner and another leading adversary soon emerged to oppose him. This newest adversary withdrew several months later only to be replaced by yet another one. Finally, as was to occur with Jesse Jackson in 1984, television news media depicted a third candidate, George Wallace, as a sideshow to the main event.

The Democrats engaged in divisive and bitter factional fights during the last years of the Johnson administration and in doing so destroyed their chances of victory in the 1968 campaign. The factions originated in controversies related to the Vietnam War and became polarized behind the candidacies of Lyndon Johnson and Hubert Humphrey on one side and Eugene McCarthy and Robert Kennedy on the other. Like the other two elections discussed above, these divisions did not end with the election but continued into the next campaign as well. The factions renewed their differences shortly after Johnson left office in January 1969. Television news media also helped enhance these differences and thus encouraged dissensus within the party. They did not create the differences but helped to define and perpetuate them by associating them with some of the candidates who sought the nomination.

Although a number of candidates sought the nomination, television news media defined the race from the outset as primarily a battle between only two major contenders. The initial front-runner was Senator Edmund

Muskie (Maine), who had gained national attention as the Democratic nominee for Vice President in 1968. Muskie led all actual and potential candidates in public opinion surveys throughout both 1970 and 1971. He began 1972 with a fairly large lead in the polls and appeared headed toward an early capture of the nomination. As Mondale was to do in 1984, Muskie received the endorsements of many public officials and party leaders and endorsements from a number of the interest groups that aligned with the Democrats in most elections. He planned on making the New Hampshire primary his first electoral test of the year. Virtually all political observers expected him to win there by a substantial margin. As a result, many of his rivals decided to bypass that state and concentrate instead on the Florida primary scheduled for one week later. Those who chose Florida as their initial electoral effort of 1972 were Senators Hubert H. Humphrey (Minnesota) and Henry Jackson (Washington), former Governor George Wallace (Alabama), Mayor John Lindsay (New York City), Congresswoman Shirley Chisholm (New York), and former Governor Terry Sanford (North Carolina). Only Senator George McGovern (South Dakota) and three long-shot candidates opposed Muskie in New Hampshire.

Muskie won the primary as expected, but unexpectedly did so with less than 50 percent of the vote. Many news reporters initially had not believed that a contest actually existed in New Hampshire since they considered Muskie a certain winner. Since there was no Republican campaign to speak of, television news media did not want the Democratic Party to go without a contest of sorts. Without one readily available, political reporters helped to create one. They asked Muskie to designate the percentage of the vote that he would need before he could consider his effort as a success. Muskie was unwilling to accept a simple margin of one more vote than any other candidate, and several reporters eventually persuaded him to admit that he needed half of the total vote cast in order to claim victory. News media interests then judged the campaign by that standard. Such a standard was similar to the point spread in football games where bettors must select not only the winning team but also the margin of victory. The political equivalent of a point spread for a Muskie victory in New Hampshire was 50 percent of the vote. George McGovern, as Muskie's only major rival, stood between Muskie and the point spread.

Muskie won, or perhaps lost, the primary. He received more votes than any of his four rivals, but he did not attain the requisite 50 percent of the vote. He garnered approximately 48 percent of the vote, while McGovern finished in second place with about 37 percent. Television news media soon described Muskie's first place finish as a setback and McGovern's performance, objectively a loss, as a victory because it was better than expected. They had, after all, expected Muskie to equal or better the point spread. McGovern gained new respect from reporters because of his showing. He had prevented the front-runner from accomplishing his needed goal. He also benefited from his presence in New Hampshire. Television news media soon began depicting McGovern, by virtue of the fact that he was Muskie's only rival in the primary, as the leading adversary and antithesis of the front-runner. As with Hart in 1984, McGovern derived extensive publicity from his second place finish and used it to convince many of his own partisans that he actually was the one leading adversary of the front-runner Muskie.

After the conclusion of the two-candidate battle of New Hampshire, television news media redefined the campaign so that the remaining candidates received less coverage. These other candidates subsequently became less relevant and soon encountered some difficulty in defining themselves as viable contenders. Only two, Wallace and Humphrey, were able to continue with their efforts. Television news media depicted Wallace mainly as a sideshow to the actual campaign, but they eventually helped to transform Humphrey into the new leading adversary. The campaign itself changed somewhat after New Hampshire in the sense that the Florida primary immediately became the most important of the upcoming events. Wallace won this primary, and Humphrey finished second. Since they had already dismissed Wallace as an extremist candidate with limited appeal, television news media interpreted Humphrey's Florida showing as the best performance by any of the major candidates. Once again, they depicted a second place finish as a victory while downplaying the efforts of the winner. Humphrey did not achieve his first actual victory of 1972 until the Pennsylvania primary six weeks after the Florida vote. Humphrey was an exception to the catch-22 dilemma discussed earlier because he enjoyed some unusual advantages over the other candidates. He was a former Vice President and had been the Democratic nominee four years earlier. The other candidates whom television news media had not included in their illustration of the two-candidate campaign—Lindsay, Jackson, Chisholm, and Sanford—were not immune to this dilemma and soon ceased to be of any relevance to the final outcome.

Humphrey soon replaced Muskie as one of the two major role-playing candidates. Television news media depicted Muskie, after his so-called underwhelming victory in New Hampshire, as a front-runner who was incapable of locking up the nomination, forcing his rivals from the race, and unifying the Democratic Party. In reality, Muskie had been a candidate who lacked a constituency and whose only appeal was that he could win the election. Since he apparently could no longer make that claim, he ceased to have any rationale for continuing his efforts. Muskie declined from his first place "loss" in New Hampshire into a fourth place finish in Florida where he garnered less than 10 percent of the vote. He recorded yet another fourth place finish with a comparable percentage of the vote three weeks later in Wisconsin. Muskie withdrew from the competition at the end of

April after suffering two more overwhelming defeats. He lost the Pennsylvania primary to Humphrey and the one in Massachusetts to McGovern.

After Muskie's demise, McGovern emerged as the new front-runner, essentially by default. Since television news media had helped define the campaign as a two-candidate battle, the withdrawal of one candidate effectively placed the other in the position of front-runner. McGovern had benefited from his adversarial role in New Hampshire. While television news media had given his antiwar views some coverage, they had depicted McGovern less as the leader of the Democratic liberals than as the leading adversary and antithesis of the front-runner Muskie. Muskie was the candidate of the party establishment, much the same as Mondale would be in 1984. McGovern was the candidate of the opposition to that establishment, a role that would be played by Hart twelve years later. This depiction paid off in electoral benefits, however, as McGovern's standing in the polls grew rapidly after New Hampshire. One should realize, of course, that many of McGovern's earliest supporters were quite enthusiastic about his candidacy because of his strong opposition to the Vietnam War. After New Hampshire, however, McGovern expanded his following far beyond the members of this group. Public opinion surveys taken during the early months of the 1972 campaign indicated that many voters, including substantial numbers of McGovern's new supporters, were unaware of some of his views. This was by no means the fault of McGovern who certainly made his views known; it was more the fault of the processes by which people first learned about him. Television news media had initially depicted him as the leading adversary of Muskie in a campaign that they had illustrated as involving only two major candidates.

McGovern followed his New Hampshire media successes with an actual victory in the Wisconsin primary in early April that gave him the national lead in delegate votes. Television news media then proclaimed him as the new front-runner. McGovern's victory in the Massachusetts primary, three weeks after the Wisconsin election, gave added credence to this claim. The leading political story of the 1972 Democratic campaign now became that of George McGovern running for President, much as it had been the story of Edmund Muskie running for President only a few months earlier. McGovern also encountered the same dilemma Muskie had faced earlier: he needed to overcome the obstacles that stood in his way to the nomination. Hubert Humphrey personified these obstacles through his candidacy. By now, Humphrey had become the new leading adversary of the front-runner by virtue of Muskie's withdrawal and his own triumph in Pennsylvania. Television news media now depicted this newly redefined campaign in much the same manner as they had depicted the one between Muskie and McGovern: the front-runner was their anchor for political reporting, while the leading adversary was the obstacle that stood between the front-runner and the nomination.

The California primary once again served as the final electoral showdown between the two leading contenders and ended up very much like that of 1964. McGovern won with about 45 percent of the vote compared with Humphrey's 40 percent. Like Goldwater, McGovern's victory provided him with enough delegates to claim the nomination and virtually ended any chance that his leading adversary could attain the role of standard bearer. McGovern had already won more delegates throughout the nation than Humphrey even before the California vote. Despite what should have been a final ending of the campaign, the Democrats continued with their controversies and thereby provided television news media with even more opportunities for perpetuating their coverage of divisive issues. Some of McGovern's opponents sought to prevent him from winning the nomination by challenging the credentials of a number of his delegates. McGovern had far too large a lead to be denied, but the ensuing struggles over credentials and other matters compromised any chance that the national convention might serve as a forum for unifying the Democratic Party.

McGovern eventually won the nomination but did so at a terrible cost. He spent valuable time engaging in a number of divisive convention battles and even suffered some damaging public relations setbacks over the mental health background of Senator Thomas Eagleton (Missouri), who had been his initial running mate. These problems undermined the one political asset that McGovern needed in order to compete effectively in the general election—the perception that he was as qualified as the incumbent to lead the nation. The enhancement of dissensus that often results from televising a contested nomination campaign had encouraged far too many voters to believe that McGovern was unqualified for the Presidency. The stage was now set for Nixon's overwhelming victory.

PARTISAN ALIGNMENTS AND GENERAL ELECTIONS

The authors of the landmark voter studies cited earlier concluded that the long-term factor of voter partisanship, subject to the influences of certain short-term deviations unique to a particular year, best explains the outcomes of presidential elections. My argument is that the short-term influences of television-enhanced incumbency, subject to the lingering long-term effects of partisanship, better explains the outcomes of elections since 1960. These more recent elections, despite the influences of television, occurred within the context of the partisan divisions that have affected American politics for decades. Partisanship continues to exert important influences over the electoral choices of many voters. Individual voters do not enter campaigns as mental blank slates; rather, many of them tend to carry strong biases into campaigns that derive from their varieties of life experiences and values. While they may well receive substantial mediated information during an election campaign, they interpret much of that information from those biases. A Democrat and a Republican who acquire the same information often interpret it quite differently. One must appreciate the contributions that partisanship makes to voting behavior when studying the electoral effects of television. In this section I describe the outcomes of the three elections with strong incumbents and explain how they were affected by both the short-term effects of televised incumbency and by the long-standing distributions of partisanship.

Electoral Patterns

The general election campaigns and final outcomes in these three years were quite similar. Each incumbent led his challenger by about 20 percentage points in national public opinion surveys taken after the conclusion of the national conventions and never relinquished his lead. The magnitude of support that had developed for each candidate during the nomination season remained consistent through the remainder of the year. For all the speechmaking, activity, and media reporting that took place, these general election campaigns were virtually unnecessary. By mid-summer, most voters had rejected the challenger and had decided instead to support the incumbent for a second term of office.

I find support for this contention from surveys taken during these elections by the Gallup organization. The opposition party started the national convention season in each election by meeting in mid-July, while the presidential party followed with its conclave in August. The results of Gallup surveys taken between the conventions were similar to the eventual outcomes of each election. A survey taken in late July 1964, about one week after the conclusion of the Republican convention, indicated that Johnson led Goldwater by 36 percentage points. Johnson received the support of 62 percent of the respondents compared to 26 percent who backed Goldwater. A survey compiled at a comparable time in 1972, in late July shortly after the end of the opposition party's convention, showed that Nixon was ahead of McGovern by a margin of 56 percent to 37. Finally, a survey that Gallup released in the latter part of July 1984, shortly after the adjournment of the Democratic convention that had nominated Walter Mondale, indicated that Reagan was ahead of his rival by a margin of 53 percent to 41.

All three incumbents maintained these leads with little change through the remainders of these years. Johnson led Goldwater by 65 percent to 29 in early September, by 63 to 31 in mid-October, and by 64 to 29 in early November in what was the final survey of the year. Nixon increased his lead over McGovern to a margin of 64 percent to 30 after the conclusion of the Republican convention. He led by 61 to 33 in early October and by 62 to 38 in early November. Reagan also increased his lead after his party's convention. He led Mondale by 19 percentage points, 56 to 37, in mid-September, by 58 to 38 in mid-October, and concluded the campaign with a lead of 57 to 39 in early November. The election outcomes reflected these survey results. Johnson and Nixon each attained 61 percent of the popular vote, while Reagan garnered 59 percent. Johnson won forty-four states and the District of Columbia, while both Nixon and Reagan won forty-nine states. Johnson's only losses were Goldwater's home state of Arizona and five Southeastern states: Alabama, Mississippi, Georgia, Louisiana, and South Carolina. Nixon and Reagan each lost one state and the District of Columbia. Nixon lost to McGovern in Massachusetts, while Reagan failed to carry Mondale's home state of Minnesota.

Each incumbent campaigned for reelection by using the "Rose Garden strategy"—generating electoral support mainly by performing in the role of President. An incumbent President does not need to seek television news coverage; it seeks him. A strong incumbent can use this fact of political life and create televised imagery in which he appears to be spending much of his time governing the nation rather than campaigning. Television news media all too readily transmit this contrived imagery to their audiences and implicitly generate support for the incumbent. Since television news media tend to make the Presidency the focal point of their coverage of politics and government, a strong incumbent who has consolidated power within his own party can readily exploit this bias and thereby enhance his strength while subtly undermining that of his rivals.

These reporting biases sometimes help to create a major obstacle for the challenger however. To win the Presidency, a challenger needs to develop a favorable public image by which he appears as a qualified replacement for the incumbent. His best opportunities for developing such an image should be during the nomination campaign. He often loses them, however, because television news media tend to direct more attention to controversies concerning his pursuit of office than to matters relating to his ability to govern. The loss of these opportunities forces the challenger to direct even more attention to his personal abilities during the general election campaign. This need becomes virtually impossible for him to fulfill, however, because of the different coverage that television news media tend to provide about incumbents and challengers. If an incumbent is able to use the Rose Garden strategy effectively—and not all of them can—the challenger must by necessity appear confrontational in order to gain media attention. Moreover, he must also demonstrate that he has the same statesmanlike ability as the incumbent. If he appears confrontational, he runs the risk that voters will see him as acting political rather than statesmanlike. If he does not, he runs the opposite risk that he may lose control of his agenda and find that television news media, which thrive on controversy, may direct their attention to yet another one and thereby contribute to even more image problems to compound the ones that he has already.

There is an important contrast of images at work here. Television news media do not depict the incumbent and his challenger as equals. There is little question that the contrasting imagery in these elections, complete with all the trappings of power, favors the strong incumbent. As I discuss in the next chapter, these opportunities are not automatically granted to any incumbent. Several Presidents have failed to manipulate them into ways that helped provide them with second terms. The contrast of imagery between the strong incumbent and his challenger is important in light of the fact that many voters value statesmanship but not politics. Television news media all too frequently depict the strong incumbent as statesmanlike and as a defender of popular values and aspirations while depicting his embattled challenger as a politician who is engaged mostly in the search for votes and is perhaps quite ineffective at doing even that. This juxtaposition of contrasting images is often quite vivid and may well contribute to some very substantial electoral advantages for the incumbent. Consider, for example, the public relations bonanza that an incumbent who is effective at manipulating television biases can derive from an official visit to this nation by a foreign head of state. The televised scenes of the President meeting with the dignitary may reinforce popular impressions that he is competently governing the nation. Moreover, the challenger has no such opportunity to create comparable imagery. Even assuming that a foreign leader would meet with his host's political rival, the challenger must limit his actions in order to avoid creating any appearance of interfering in presidential policy making. The incumbent is under no such restrictions. Quite simply, the challenger cannot compete with the incumbent for favorable publicity from the visit of a foreign head of state. He also cannot escape from the damaging effects of his party's nomination campaign because of the implicit support that the personalizing biases in television news provide for strong incumbents.

For all intents and purposes, television news media become adjuncts of a strong incumbent's reelection efforts. They devote substantial air time to manufacturing consent by juxtaposing pictures and narratives about the actions of a competently appearing President governing the nation against pictures and narratives about the actions of a controversial and unqualified challenger. They apparently have succeeded in their efforts. Voters in all three elections indicated through surveys that they considered the qualification issue foremost in guiding their electoral choices and that they viewed the incumbent as far more impressive.

A related bias that also enhances the advantages of the strong incumbent is the emphasis that television news media place upon the state of the "horse race." Reporters all too frequently proclaim that the incumbent is "ahead," that the challenger is "trailing far behind," and that the incumbent is headed toward an almost certain victory. This carries an implicit approval for the impending triumph and aids the incumbent in generating support for his reelection bid. Television news media appear to accept the perspective of Theodore White that a presidential candidate can best demonstrate his ability to hold office by competing in and winning an election campaign. Candidates who possess the skills needed for winning must also possess the skills required for governing. Conversely, those who lack the ability to win also lack the ability to govern. This viewpoint has the practical effect of generating support for the incumbent's reelection effort. Television news media engage in a self-fulfilling prophecy when guided by this perspective. Since reporters who share this viewpoint tend to depict favorably candidates who succeed and unfavorably those who fail, they will almost inevitably depict a strong incumbent as a highly qualified, virile statesman and his rival as an ineffective politician.

Challengers' Problems

The nominee of the opposition party in an election with a strong incumbent must overcome three problems if he hopes to have any real chance of winning. His first problem is the political strength of the incumbent. As discussed earlier in this chapter, the incumbent is strong primarily because he has consolidated power within his own party and used that power, and the biases that occur regularly in television news coverage, to generate a widespread personal following among the electorate. The incumbent seeks to extend his party's and his own personal tenure in office for another term after what many voters perceive to have been a successful first term. In order to win in such a context, a challenger has to convince a majority of voters that a change from the policies of a strong, popular incumbent is necessary.

The second problem for the challenger is the negative public image of his own political party. It is not enough for a challenger simply to persuade voters that they should abandon the status quo represented by the popular incumbent; he must also convince them that he offers something more than a return to the unpopular policies of the previous administration. The opposition party in each of these elections had been driven from office four years earlier because of a widespread view that it could not resolve the more serious problems that the nation faced at the time. Walter Mondale's problem was that his Democratic Party had lost the previous election to Reagan partly because of high inflation at home and the Iranian hostage crisis abroad. Moreover, the Democrats had been divided during the 1980 nomination campaign over the candidacies of Jimmy Carter and Edward Kennedy and in the general election when many of their partisans voted for either Ronald Reagan or John Anderson. They did not have a particularly impressive record of recent accomplishments or unity upon which they could campaign in 1984. The Republicans understood Mondale's problems and employed the term "Carter-Mondale Administration" to depict the troubles that Reagan had been elected to resolve and to suggest that such troubles might return if the Democrats regained power. They also used the slogan "It's Morning in America" to summarize the idea that Reagan had made some positive changes during his first term that were in the nation's best interest. Mondale had to offer something more than a rerun of Carter's policies in order to win. His problems were compounded because far too many voters saw him as the surrogate of Carter since he was the former Vice President.

Goldwater and McGovern faced similar problems, although neither of them had been directly associated with a defeated administration. Each of them had actually campaigned for a change of direction by his party and had been opposed in his quest for the nomination by a number of officials from the previous administration. Goldwater campaigned against the so-called modern version of Republicanism associated with Eisenhower and Nixon. This modern version accepted, but sought to moderate, many of the social and economic changes that had originated during the Democratic administrations of the 1930s and 1940s. Instead, Goldwater wanted to lead the Republican Party in a crusade to destroy many of those programs. This eventually proved to be a serious political problem as many voters actually wanted such programs, particularly Social Security. Those voters saw Goldwater as the spokesman of a pre-Eisenhower version of the Republican Party, and they did not approve.

McGovern had campaigned against the Vietnam War in both his short-lived candidacy in 1968 and in his more successful one in 1972 and had indicated his opposition to the foreign policies of the Johnson and Nixon administrations. One would expect that such opposition would have made him immune from the popular dislike of Johnson. Unfortunately for McGovern, he was still a Democrat and inherited the legacy of his party for better or for worse. The contrast between the turmoil of the late Johnson years with the apparently intractable problem of resolving the war and the more tranquil 1970s with the Nixon administration's emphasis that "peace was at hand" created dilemmas for McGovern. He appeared to offer voters a return to the 1960s, which they did not want. The frequent televised scenes of his youthful supporters did little to alleviate this fear.

Finally, the televising of the nomination campaigns had left each challenger with a public image by which voters often thought of him as less qualified for the Presidency than the incumbent. As discussed above, the tendency of television news media to illustrate the aftermath of the incumbent's consolidation of power while emphasizing divisiveness among the opposition affects each party differently by enhancing consensus among the former and dissensus among the latter. This, in turn, helps create public images by which the nominees of the opposition party appear less qualified than the incumbent. Mondale had to spend many months defeating his antithesis, Hart; Goldwater had to repulse the efforts of one moderate spokesman after another; and McGovern could not stop other Democrats who sought to derail his candidacy until his nomination was finally recorded.

Goldwater, McGovern, and Mondale could not overcome these problems. Each failed to demonstrate that change from the policies of the popular incumbent was preferable, or that he offered voters anything more than a return to the policies of an unpopular administration that they had once voted out of office, or that he was even the personal or political equal of the incumbent he sought to replace. Meanwhile the incumbents used the Rose Garden strategy and spent much of their time appearing presidential in front of television cameras. They implicitly reassured voters, through a number of events contrived for television news coverage, that they would continue their successes of the previous term for another four years. The voters responded by providing them with three of the most sweeping electoral victories in American history.

State and Regional Partisanship

One should temper an appreciation of the electoral influences of televised incumbency with the realization that long-term partisan preferences also play a significant role in voter choice. It is to these influences that I now turn. The partisan alignments among today's electorate derive from both past influences and current attitudes. The strongest influences from the past, which originated before the presence of television, derive from the electoral coalitions that supported and opposed Franklin D. Roosevelt during the 1930s and 1940s. While Roosevelt attracted votes from a wide variety of sources during each of his four presidential bids, his strongest support came from liberals, lower income people, Catholics, Jews, trade unionists, residents of the larger cities, immigrants and their recent descendants, racial minorities, and white Southerners. In contrast, his support from conservatives, business owners, residents of suburbs and small towns, Midwesterners, and white Protestants was relatively limited. The voters who comprised the aforementioned categories were not distributed uniformly throughout the nation but were concentrated in particular states and geographic regions. Consequently some states and regions supported Roosevelt more than others.

While the popular vote in a presidential election is always important, the winner is determined by the electoral college, which is comprised of states rather than individual voters. Here I employ states as the unit of analysis for describing the past and current strengths of partisan coalitions. Since no two elections conclude with the same results, one must consider the outcomes of several elections in order to determine the approximate strength of each party in any particular state. While all states may exhibit wide fluctuations during any four-year election cycle in their support for either party, their deviations from nationwide partisan distributions are usually quite consistent from one election to the next. One can rely upon this consistency to determine the long-term strength of state partisanship. The states that are most supportive of a particular party in any given election are generally those that were most supportive in the preceding one. The few instances in which certain states violate this assertion either indicate the existence of temporary deviations unique to that election or are related to partisan realignments.

Indiana offers an example of such consistency. This state casts popular votes that are generally about 5 percentage points more Republican than the nation. Since Indiana is one of the first states to close its polls on election day, doing so at 6 P.M. eastern time, one can use this fact to make a fairly reliable forecast of national trends. If the Republican candidate carries Indiana by at least 10 points, he will win the election. If not, the Democrat will win. Richard Nixon carried Indiana by 12 points in 1968 and won the Presidency; George Bush captured the state by 6 points in 1992 and lost.

The realignment that led to the Democratic Party's acquisition of majority status during the time of Roosevelt actually unfolded over the ten-year period between 1928 and 1938. It began when the Democrats nominated Governor Alfred E. Smith (New York) for President in 1928. Smith's Roman Catholic religion served as an important, and often negative, voting issue for millions of people. While many Democratic Protestants temporarily deviated from their partisan backgrounds that year and voted for the Republican candidate, Herbert Hoover, many Catholics supported the Democratic Party for the first time in their lives by casting votes for their coreligionist Smith. The expanded Catholic support for the Democratic ticket was particularly noticeable in the Northeast. It helped Smith attain the electoral votes of the nation's two most Catholic states, Rhode Island and Massachusetts, and to finish relatively close to Hoover in a number of other states that had large Catholic populations. Despite Smith's defeat, the Democrats retained their new Catholic supporters in subsequent elections. These new voters, and the anger that was soon directed at Hoover because of the Great Depression, provided the Democrats with a unique opportunity to forge a new political majority. They seized control of the House of Representatives in 1930, captured both the Presidency and the Senate in 1932, expanded their number of congressional seats in 1934, and recorded the most one-sided victory thus far in a twentieth-century presidential election in 1936 with a sweeping 46-state reelection triumph by Roosevelt. However, the Democratic ascendancy ended in 1938 when the Republican Party made some rather substantial and what proved to be long-term gains in the congressional elections of that year.

Roosevelt's final two reelection victories, 1940 and 1944, reflect the nation's partisan divisions at the end of this realignment period. Roosevelt won each election with a popular vote margin of approximately 10 percentage points and with the electoral votes of about forty states. These margins were somewhat smaller than the ones he had attained in his first two victories. The Southeast consistently was his strongest region, while the Midwest consistently was his weakest. For analytical purposes, I consider the Southeast to be comprised of the states of Virginia, North Carolina, South Carolina, Georgia, Florida, Kentucky, Tennessee, Alabama, Mississippi, Arkansas, Louisiana, Oklahoma, and Texas. Roosevelt garnered a higher percentage of the popular vote in each of these states in the elections of both 1940 and 1944 than he recorded nationwide. His support, averaged for both elections, ranged from 56 percent in Kentucky to 95 percent in Mississippi.

Roosevelt also ran strongly in the Northeast and West. He carried every northeastern state except Maine and Vermont and every western state except Colorado and Wyoming (which he won in 1940) in both elections. I consider the Northeast to consist of the District of Columbia and the twelve states of Maine, New Hampshire, Vermont, Massachusetts, Rhode Island, Connecticut, New York, New Jersey, Pennsylvania, Delaware, Maryland, and West Virginia. The District was unable to participate in presidential elections until 1964. The thirteen western states are Montana, Wyoming, Colorado, New Mexico, Arizona, Nevada, Utah, Idaho, Washington, Oregon, California, Alaska, and Hawaii. The election of 1960 marked the first time that Alaska and Hawaii voted.

In contrast to his successes in the aforementioned regions, Roosevelt did not fare particularly well in the Midwest. He managed to carry only three states—Illinois, Minnesota, and Missouri—in both of his two final election triumphs and won only three others—Ohio (1940), Wisconsin (1940), and Michigan (1944)—once each. The remaining midwestern states—Indiana, Iowa, North Dakota, South Dakota, Nebraska, and Kansas—voted Republican in both 1940 and 1944.

The Democratic coalition of the Roosevelt years had weakened by the beginning of the television age in 1960. The decline was most noticeable among the western states but was also present in some parts of the Southeast. Democratic candidates generally ran quite well in the West until Eisenhower won office in 1952. They attained the electoral votes of a majority of the western states in seven of the ten elections that preceded Eisenhower's victory. These successes include the two victories of Woodow Wilson (1912, 1916); Roosevelt's four triumphs (1932, 1936, 1940, 1944); and Harry Truman's win in 1948. The three elections during the Republican-dominated 1920s (1920, 1924, 1928) were the only instances in which the Democrats failed to win a majority of the electoral votes of the West between 1912 and 1952. This Democratic regional dominance collapsed in 1952 when Eisenhower carried every western state, and it has not returned to this day. The election of 1964, in which Lyndon Johnson carried every western state except Arizona, and that of 1992, when Bill Clinton won all but five of the region's smaller states, mark the only occasions during the past four decades when the Democratic Party has won the West.

The western realignment was not limited simply to the permanent movement of the region into the Republican column however. It was accompanied by a reordering of the strength of state-level voter preferences for the two parties. The movement toward the Republican Party was far greater in some states than in others. The states that had been among the most Democratic in the region before 1952, those located in the southern Rockies, ceased to be so afterwards and became the most Republican of western states. These include Arizona, Nevada, and Utah, states that had been sparsely populated until after the conclusion of the Second World War. These states often supported Democratic candidates during the middle decades of the twentieth century because many of their residents were former southeasterners who continued to be guided by their long-standing Democratic preferences. Substantial migration from other regions of the nation, and particularly from the Midwest, expanded the population of these states considerably after the war. Many of the new residents were Republicans, and they eventually helped turn these states into strongholds for that party.

Spearman's rho correlations provide statistical support for the existence of this realignment. I ranked the states by the percentages of the popular vote that they cast for the Democratic candidate in any given election. I used only one rank to depict the partisan strength of individual states during the late Roosevelt years which I attained by averaging the results of the elections of 1940 and 1944. The correlation between the final Roosevelt elections and that of 1952 is only .16, and it is not statistically significant. The correlations between the final Roosevelt elections and those subsequent to 1952 are even lower. The highest is with 1960, .05, while the lowest, (-.19), occurs with both 1984 and 1988. In contrast, there are strong correlations between the election of 1952 and those of the television age. They range from a low of .66 for 1960 to a high of .91 for 1972. The correlation between the elections of 1952 and 1992 is very strong, .90.

The rank ordering of state partisanship has been fairly consistent in the Midwest and Northeast since the early 1940s. Every midwestern state has consistently voted less Republican than Indiana in virtually all elections since Roosevelt's time (Illinois, Iowa, Michigan, Minnesota, Missouri, Ohio, Wisconsin), or more so (Kansas, Nebraska, North Dakota, South Dakota). Minnesota is generally the most Democratic midwestern state in any given election as it usually casts a vote that is approximately 8 percentage points more Democratic than the nation. Nebraska is the least Democratic state in the region and tends to support the nominees of that party at a level that is about 11 percentage points below national trends.

The various Democratic candidates, Roosevelt through Clinton, generally ran stronger in six northeastern states than they did nationally (Maryland, Massachusetts, New York, Pennsylvania, Rhode Island, and West Virginia), weaker in three states (New Hampshire, New Jersey, and Vermont), and were very close to their national averages in three others, (Connecticut, Delaware, and Maine). The District of Columbia always votes Democratic, and it does so by a margin that is far above the national average. All six states that comprise the aforementioned first group have voted for the Democratic nominee in at least five of the nine television age elections, while every state in either the second or third groups has voted Republican in a majority of these same elections. For example, Jimmy Carter carried seven northeastern states in 1976 including all six in the first group and Delaware from the third, while Michael Dukakis carried Massachusetts, New York, Rhode Island, and West Virginia from the first group and attained about 48 percent of the popular vote in the other two states, Maryland and Pennsylvania. While Clinton won every northeastern state in 1992, he ran particularly strong in seven. His strongest states in the region were the six from the first group and Vermont from the second.

There was a realignment among some of the southeastern states in 1964, and it bore many similarities to the one of 1952 among the western states. In 1964 the Southeast changed from being the nation's most Democratic region in presidential elections to its least; moreover, those individual states that traditionally had been the region's strongest supporters of Democratic candidates became its weakest. Although its presidential candidates repeatedly garnered smaller percentages of both the popular and electoral votes in the Southeast after Roosevelt, the Democratic Party remained the majority party in the region. In fact, the underlying structure of the Roosevelt coalition was still very much in place, albeit by reduced numbers, in 1960. The correlation between the final Roosevelt elections and 1960 is .82. Republican strength increased throughout the Southeast after the 1940s, but the party actually became competitive in only those states that had been the least Democratic during Roosevelt's time. The Republican Party's four strongest southeastern states in the final Roosevelt elections were Kentucky, Oklahoma, Tennessee, and Virginia in that order. With the exception of Kentucky, these states joined with the western states and Florida and began voting regularly for Republican presidential candidates in 1952. All four states and Florida voted for Eisenhower in 1956 and for Nixon in both 1960 and 1968, and deviated temporarily to the Democrats only in the election of 1964.

The remaining southeastern states, with the exception of Texas, deserted the Democrats in 1964 or in 1968 or in both elections and were among the nation's most Republican states in 1972, 1984, 1988, and even in 1992. Six states (Alabama, Arkansas, Georgia, Louisiana, Mississippi, and South Carolina) were the most Democratic southeastern states between the conclusion of Reconstruction in 1876 and the election of 1960. These were the only southeastern states that voted for Smith in 1928, and all of them except for Mississippi voted for Kennedy. One can see the existence of a regional realignment in the fact that each of these six states either voted for Goldwater in 1964 or for Wallace in 1968 or for both candidates and were the only states in the nation other than Arizona to support either of those two candidates. The correlations between the final Roosevelt elections and those that have taken place since 1964 support the contention that a realignment occurred in the Southeast that year. The correlations are all very small and fail to reach statistical significance. The one between the Roosevelt elections and 1984 is only (-.01). Conversely, the correlations between the election of 1964 and the two that followed it are fairly strong: .74 between 1964 and 1968; .75 between 1964 and 1972.

This realignment seemed to disappear in 1976 with the victory of the southeastern candidate Jimmy Carter, but it returned shortly after Carter passed from the political scene. The correlation between the elections of 1964 and 1976 is virtually nonexistent, (-.05), while the one between 1964 and 1988 is statistically significant, .62. The realignment seemed to disappear once again in 1992 when another southeasterner, Bill Clinton, headed the Democratic ticket. The correlation between the election of 1964 and 1992 is only .08. Despite the fact that they garnered the electoral votes of many southeastern states that had been voting Republican, Carter and Clinton did not restore the Roosevelt coalition in the region. Instead, they appear to have offered something new. One can find support for this contention in the weak correlations that exist between the final Roosevelt elections and these two most recent Democratic victories: .25 and .03 for 1976 and 1992 respectively.

The regional realignments of 1952 and 1964 left the nation with a normal Republican majority in presidential elections. Virtually all of the southeastern and western states have voted Republican in a majority of the nine elections of the television age, a strong departure from the patterns of the Roosevelt years. The only exception to this pattern has been Hawaii, which has voted Democratic on seven occasions. The Midwest has continued with the Republican preferences that it exhibited during the 1940s, although Democratic candidates occasionally have been competitive in some states. The Northeast is the only region that has cast a majority of its electoral votes for Democratic candidates since 1960.

The outcomes of the three elections that have been the subject of this chapter were decided by the interaction of the effects of televised incumbency with the patterns of regional partisanship discussed above. In one respect, each incumbent consolidated power among his own partisans before the onset of the election year and then used that power to manipulate the short-term consensus-enhancing biases that can occur in televised news coverage of a strong President and his opposition. This combination of power consolidation and media bias provided each incumbent with some invaluable opportunities for constructing a personal following that supported his reelection and which vastly exceeded the usual appeal of his own party. In a second respect, each incumbent superimposed this personal following upon the patterns of partisanship that existed at the time and won reelection by a margin rarely attained in American national elections.

Conclusions

The elections discussed in this chapter, those with strong incumbents, share several characteristics that were not present in other elections of the television age. Moreover, these characteristics will very likely recur in one or more future elections. The most important by far is the extensive political strength of the incumbent President and the effects that such strength has upon the actions of the two political parties and television news media. Prior to the beginning of the campaign year, the incumbent President enjoys a number of far-reaching policy and public relations successes that he manipulates into widespread popular support and uses to consolidate political power within his own party.

Television news media tend to respond to an incumbent's consolidation of power by illustrating its aftermath rather than its acquisition and, as a consequence, become part of the process of building a consensus in support of that incumbent's bid for reelection. They do this through two implicit patterns of news definition and production. First, they illustrate the actions of the incumbent in many highly flattering visual scenes that help him appear "presidential" and statesmanlike. The incumbent seeks reelection through the use of the Rose Garden strategy, and television news media tend to aid him in his efforts: the incumbent runs for office mainly by performing in his role as President while television news media direct attention to virtually all of his actions. An incumbent can use the preoccupation that television news media have with the Presidency to dominate news about public policy, to create imagery by which he seems to be achieving great success in resolving major foreign and domestic problems, and to undertake many events that are specifically made for television and that give him maximum amounts of pictorial exposure to viewing audiences. Not only do television news media willingly broadcast such self-serving imagery, but they tend to be very uncritical of strong incumbents while doing so. This favorable imagery tells the television audiences that the incumbent is a very qualified and effective leader and that he is deserving of another term in office. It also helps generate a consensus in support of reelection. An important factor that contributes to the existence of this consensus-building imagery is that the incumbent's pre-election consolidation of power eliminated the possibility that he might encounter strong opposition for renomination. Potential rivals understood that such challenges would be fruitless and therefore did not undertake them. The lack of challenges freed the incumbent from the need to engage in a renomination campaign and permitted him instead to pursue the Rose Garden strategy with all the opportunities that it offers for media manipulation.

The second pattern involves the televised enhancement of dissensus within the opposition party and the subsequent loss of public esteem by that party's nominee. There are some very important institutional factors in American politics and government that tend to limit the opportunities an opposition party has for developing a predominant leader and unifying national spokesman before a presidential election year. The opposition party usually begins an election year without a strong leader while attracting many aspirants who wish to fill that role. As a result, the party must undergo a campaign that will probably last for many months and which may very well become highly divisive before it resolves this leadership void. Moreover, the party may also have some antagonistic factions that several of these aspirants may seek to mobilize in their individual quests for the nomination. Television news media love to report about controversy and competition. The existence of a prolonged and divisive battle among party factions for control of a presidential nomination certainly conforms to this preference. Television news media frequently seek to personify social and political struggles in the words and deeds of the leading individual actors. With respect to divisive campaigns for party nominations, they often attempt to personify the different factions through the efforts of the leading aspirants. This pattern of reporting helps make those aspirants appear more as politicians in quest of power than as statesmen qualified for the Presidency. It also helps make the incumbent appear far more qualified than the challengers who seek to replace him.

The opposition party also tends to suffer electoral consequences from the television news media preference for placing the various candidates into previously defined roles and then stereotyping them in those roles. The major role is that of front-runner. Television news media seem to believe that a nomination campaign within the opposition party must have a front-runner who can serve as their anchor point for the description and interpretation of political events. The front-runner is the central actor in the unfolding drama that becomes the campaign. Television news media seek to make the major continuing news story of a campaign that of the front-runner—Mondale, Goldwater, McGovern, and so on—seeking the Presidency. The campaign is thus personalized. It is no longer simply a battle among many faceless aspirants; it is now the personal quest of a personally identified contender. In the televised morality play that follows, the front-runner must overcome the many personal obstacles that stand between himself and national power. If he can do so, as John F. Kennedy did in Theodore White's saga of the 1960 campaign, he thereby proves himself worthy to hold the nation's highest office. If he cannot, as happened in these campaigns, then he is not qualified for office and deserves to lose the election. The existence of a front-runner is not a given. Sometimes, as with Mondale, one candidate is obviously stronger than the others at the outset of the campaign, and television news media will respond by proclaiming him to be the front-runner. When no such candidate exists, television news media create one by relying upon a few indicators of early political support, such as endorsements, poll standings, money, or the first actual votes, and then proclaim the candidate who appears to have attained more of these as the front-runner.

The second stereotypical role is that of the leading adversary of the front-runner. Other than the front-runner, this candidate is the only remaining viable contender for the nomination. Television news media depict him as the antithesis of the front-runner and as the personification of all the personal and political obstacles that stand between the front-runner and the nomination. This last adversary has only a very limited relationship to the morality play other than the fact that he fills this role of antithesis and thereby perpetuates the campaign. Without him, the campaign would be over and the front-runner would be the new party spokesman. The front-runner, of course, cannot defeat this leading adversary and drive him from the campaign until the national convention. In some years, a leading adversary of the front-runner already exists at the outset, as with Rockefeller, while at other times television news media seek to create one, as with Hart. Finally, television news media stereotype the other candidates into the role of loser by reporting about their electoral failings and thereby enhance their early departure from the campaign. This stereotyping of candidates thus helps create the context in which two candidates who fill predefined roles and who may seek to mobilize certain antagonistic party factions in their quests for the nomination can engage in a prolonged and divisive campaign that television news media can then simplify into a personal battle for power between two individuals. It also helps to enhance dissensus within the party and undermine the party's chances of successfully challenging the strong incumbent.

For all intents and purposes, these elections are over by the conclusion of the national party conventions, if not before. The incumbent, with the help of television, by this time has generated a strong consensus that supports his reelection. His challenger, the front-runner discussed above, has been discredited as a potential President by the dissensus-enhancing televising of his nomination campaign. He quite simply cannot overcome the effects of these two mutually supportive patterns in television news coverage. In this category of television age elections discussed in this chapter, the incumbent first consolidates political power before the beginning of the campaign and then gains from the biases that exist in television news coverage of presidential election campaigns and the Presidency itself and scores a sweeping personal victory. He does so, however, without necessarily disturbing the underlying patterns of partisanship that soon resurface in future elections.

3

Elections with Surrogate Incumbents

The second category of television age elections are those in which the incumbent is not a candidate for another term. There have been three such elections: 1960, 1968, and most recently, 1988. These three share a number of patterns that appear to be unique to the last three decades but which also seem likely to recur in future years when the incumbent does not seek to extend his tenure in office. The patterns seem to be enhanced, and in some instances actually created, by the presence of television and the biases and preferences that occur regularly in televised news coverage of presidential elections and the Presidency itself that I discussed in previous chapters. Three patterns particularly stand out.

The most important of these has been the consistent selection of a candidate whose political base was in the executive branch of the national government, and who was the Vice President in each instance, as the nominee of the presidential party. These nominations were not coincidental but were instead institutional developments unique to the television age. The modern Vice Presidency has developed into an office of substantially greater political power and public visibility than before and tends to attract far more capable occupants as a consequence. This development has been enhanced by the corresponding expansion of the political power and public visibility of the Presidency. These changes have provided television age Vice Presidents with the most favorable strategic position from which to seek the nomination of the presidential party when the incumbent retires. Each of the three Vice Presidents who was nominated as the successor of a retiring incumbent successfully manipulated these new advantages of his office and convinced a fairly large number of his own partisans that he was the one leading surrogate and rightful heir of the incumbent and that he deserved their support. For this reason, I use the term elections with surrogate incumbents to depict the campaigns of the aforementioned years. The nominations were not automatic however. Each of the three Vice Presidents encountered some opposition from rivals whose public careers and bases of political power rested with institutions other than the executive branch of the national government. Nonetheless, all three possessed certain clear and distinct advantages that appear to have derived from recent changes in the relative power and corresponding television news coverage of the various institutions of politics and government. Moreover, all three used them effectively in defeating their intra-party opponents.

The ambiguous nature of the challenge that tends to come from the opposition party constitutes a second pattern. This party had some fairly good reasons for being optimistic and pessimistic at the same time about its prospects in each of these elections. The optimism derived from the electoral context: the incumbent was retiring and no other potential nominee of the presidential party, including the Vice President, appeared capable of duplicating that incumbent's previous electoral successes. Despite this optimism, the opposition party faced a dilemma that cast a shadow upon these hopes. It lacked an undisputed leader around whom it could unite immediately and thereby offer alternatives to the policies and personalities that had dominated national politics for the previous eight years. Instead, the party was threatened with the prospect that it might well have to undergo yet another prolonged and divisive campaign for its nomination that could destroy its chances for victory. Some important institutional limitations of American government, discussed earlier, do not allow sufficient opportunities for an opposition party to develop unifying leaders before the onset of a presidential election. Consequently, these three nomination campaigns appeared very likely to attract several relatively unknown candidates who might then intensify some of the existing factional divisions within their party and thereby compromise any hopes of victory. Fortunately for the opposition, however, this dilemma failed to materialize. In each instance, the party united behind an appealing candidate who held out the promise of victory. These apparently anomalous results were also not accidental but seem to be recurring patterns in elections with surrogate incumbents that are enhanced by televised news coverage of nomination campaigns.

The third pattern common to these elections is that neither of the two major party candidates appears to enjoy an inherent advantage that derives from his unique vantage point of surrogate or challenger. This differs from those elections that have strong or weak incumbents in which the divisiveness of one party's nomination campaign and related television news coverage tends to enhance the opportunities of the other party's nominee to develop an insurmountable lead by the conclusion of the national conventions. Instead, both candidates in elections with surrogate incumbents have certain unique advantages and particular dilemmas that they must manipulate or overcome in order to win the election. How well they do so inevitably determines whether they win or lose. Each of these three elections was very competitive, with the lead, as measured in public opinion surveys, changing at least once during the election year. The Vice President has the dilemma that he often cannot expand his support much beyond that of his own partisans. The challenger tends to have the problem that his public image is often so vaguely defined after his nomination that he runs the risk of losing support during the final weeks of the general election campaign as skeptical voters become increasingly doubtful about his promises and personal abilities. Two Vice Presidents, Nixon (1960) and Humphrey, were unable to overcome their dilemmas and consequently lost their bids to succeed the incumbent, while a third, Bush, attained his victory only after his opponent, Dukakis, ran a campaign that many observers regarded as unusually inept. These outcomes suggest that the Vice Presidency may be a mixed blessing as a stepping-stone to the Presidency. It provides invaluable opportunities for its occupants to win nominations and unite their own partisans, but it all too frequently prevents those same occupants from offering the political changes that voters often want when an incumbent President retires. Moreover, some voters do not necessarily see the Vice President as the surrogate of the incumbent and respond by voting for the challenger.

Conversely, the challengers sometimes find that the Vice Presidency can actually be very damaging to their own prospects. While voters frequently indicate that they do prefer some political change, many of them are often quite reluctant to vote for those candidates who might bring it about. In response, they find the Vice President a safe replacement for the incumbent as they become increasingly doubtful about the challengers. Kennedy and Nixon (1968) eventually won their elections but did so by narrow margins that were diminishing in the final days of their campaigns. Dukakis had actually led Bush during the summer months of 1988 but saw his lead disappear by September. The fact that any of these elections could have ended differently suggests that neither the surrogate nor the challenger necessarily has an inherent advantage and that the final results of the elections that comprise this category derive from short-term factors that are related to the campaigns.

PRESIDENTIAL PARTY NOMINATIONS

Overview

The nomination campaigns within the presidential party in these three elections have one overriding fact in common: the successful candidates were the sitting Vice Presidents—Richard Nixon (1960), Hubert Humphrey

(1968), and George Bush (1988). The selections of these men as the would-be successors of retiring incumbents were not coincidental but were instead manifestations of the televising of both the modern Presidency and of its related election campaigns. This televising influenced nominations by providing new and very significant political advantages for these Vice Presidents that were not available to other candidates. The advantages, in turn, enhanced the personal visibility of the Vice Presidents and helped them develop public images by which each of them appeared as the one leading political surrogate and heir apparent of the retiring incumbent. Consequently these Vice Presidents became the early front-runners for their respective nominations and eventually secured them, even when confronted with some formidable obstacles and powerful rivals. The presence of television has helped transform the modern Vice Presidency into the most important strategic position from which to seek the nomination of the presidential party when the incumbent does not seek another term.

Succession to a presidential nomination by a sitting Vice President has not been a matter of course in American history. Instead, it is a phenomenon limited primarily to the television age. The Democratic Party nominated Vice President Martin Van Buren to be the successor of the retiring incumbent Andrew Jackson in 1836, and Van Buren won the subsequent general election. Despite Van Buren's victory, vice presidential succession to a presidential nomination soon proved to be most unusual. Neither party chose the Vice President as its standard bearer after Van Buren until the Republicans designated Nixon. While some of Nixon's predecessors succeeded to the Presidency upon the death of the incumbent, most found their office to be a one-way ticket to political oblivion. Considering that both Nixon and Humphrey lost their respective general elections, Bush was actually the first Vice President since Van Buren to be elected as the successor of a retiring incumbent.

The nomination of Nixon marked a major turning point in the political significance of the Vice Presidency as a stepping-stone to a future presidential candidacy. Since his time, many Vice Presidents have either won nominations or have become Presidents by other means. One can find support for this contention in the outcomes of the nomination campaigns of the past three decades. Nine of the eighteen major party nominations between 1960 and 1992 were won by a current or former Vice President. Three—Nixon (1960), Humphrey (1968), and Bush (1988)—went to the current occupants of the office, while four went to incumbent Presidents who sought second terms but who had once been Vice Presidents: Johnson (1968), Nixon (1972), Ford (1976), and Bush (1992). Finally, two nominations of the opposition party went to former Vice Presidents: Nixon (1968) and Mondale (1984).

This increased significance of the position derives to a great extent from both the expanded roles that are now played by the Presidency and its affiliated offices and from the televising of those offices that has resulted from that expansion. Modern Presidents have assigned increasingly important political and policy responsibilities to their Vice Presidents as both the power of the executive branch of the national government and the personalizing of the Presidency have grown. These changes, in turn, have helped transform the Vice Presidency into a more significant and thereby newsworthy position. Moreover, these changes have also encouraged presidential candidates to select running mates who have greater political and communicative skills than previous ones. One can hardly imagine a modern Vice President becoming intoxicated at the inauguration as Andrew Johnson did in 1865. These more qualified Vice Presidents thereby become even stronger contenders for the Presidency. The demands for quality that result from the presence of television virtually guarantee that modern Vice Presidents will possess the political skills required for winning the nomination of the presidential party upon the retirement of the incumbent. Moreover, television provides these Vice Presidents with invaluable opportunities for exploiting its emotion-conveying and personalizing nature. It helps them generate personal and political followings by illustrating them as leading members of the presidential team and as important surrogates of the incumbent. A Vice President's public image is very much interrelated with that of the President, and its strength often varies in tandem with that of the chief executive. Since a President's prestige is strongest among his fellow partisans, a Vice President often finds that the political advantages of his office are most useful when he seeks his party's nomination.

One can see the increased public visibility of the Vice Presidency and the need for candidates to be far more qualified than in the past by observing the selections of candidates for the position and the related television news coverage that accompanies them. Since most presidential nominations are now decided during the primary election season rather than at national conventions, television and other news media often find that convention events are of limited news value and usually repetitious of the themes of earlier coverage. Media respond to these changed circumstances by giving extraordinary attention to minor political events and controversies that politicians exploit in hopes of gaining attention at a time when news coverage and public interest are unusually high but significant events are often few and far between. The existence of this news vacuum allows for the selection of the Vice President, while already important, to become even more interesting as a topic for news reporting. The naming of a running mate by a soon to be nominated presidential candidate is now one of the most important political events in the last days before a national convention or within the first few days of the convention itself. The individual who gains the nod thus becomes the recipient of extensive media attention, scrutiny, comment, and quite possibly controversy. This news focus translates into expanded voter familiarity with the possible Vice President and frequently into greater personal respect and support for him from many components of the electorate but particularly from among the presidential nominee's most ardent followers. A vice presidential nominee gains much of his increased support from among those followers through the personalizing and emotion-conveying medium of television. This provides him with opportunities for accomplishing much more than simply becoming known to millions of voters. He can begin developing personal and emotional bonds with the activist core and primary election voters of his own party.

Television news coverage of the convention and of the campaign that follows provides a vice presidential candidate with even more opportunities for generating the personal followings and emotional commitments from the party faithful that will eventually prove crucial to his future quest for the Presidency. He makes his acceptance speech before the convention and before a national television audience shortly before the presidential nominee delivers his and then takes part in a traditional and upbeat display of party unity. These events make him appear to be a leading member of the campaign team and provide a symbolic and visual message that is politically and emotionally pleasing to his fellow partisans. The scenes and pictures of these events create a powerful impression among his partisans that he is indeed the leading surrogate for the presidential nominee. In 1987 *Newsweek* magazine described George Bush as a wimp and many Democrats readily agreed, but Bush was by no means a wimp in the eyes of the activist core and primary election voters of the Republican Party who had enthusiastically supported him as Ronald Reagan's running mate and leading surrogate in the elections of both 1980 and 1984.

Vice presidential candidates receive additional news coverage from television media during general election campaigns that provide them with even more opportunities for developing personal and emotional bonds with their party's activist core. They spend much of their time appearing in rallies that are designed to complement the travel schedule of the presidential nominee and to generate enthusiasm among the party faithful. While national television coverage of these appearances is often scant because of the tendency of the networks to direct their limited news time to the presidential contenders, vice presidential candidates frequently enjoy important local television news attention. An appearance by a vice presidential candidate in any media market usually results in coverage of his efforts by local television news organizations. These smaller media tend to be less critical of candidates and public officials than the national press corps and sometimes enhance, often favorably and certainly implicitly, the theme that the Vice President is acting as the leading surrogate for the presidential nominee and that he speaks for him. This, of course, once again helps the vice presidential candidate develop strong personal and emotional bonds with the party faithful from a variety of specific locales. In addition, vice presidential nominees have used the nationally televised

During his tenure as Vice President, Nixon had many more opportunities for public visibility that derived from both the expanded role of his office and from the presence of television. He used them first to create and then to project the public image that he was Eisenhower's leading political surrogate. He was consistently in the forefront of Republican spokesmen throughout these years, deriving opportunities from such diverse incidents as his assumption of executive responsibilities during Eisenhower's various illnesses, his far-reaching campaign efforts on behalf of Republican candidates, his sharp and highly partisan attacks on the Democratic leadership of Congress, and his various trips abroad including his debate with Soviet leader Nikita Khrushchev.

When he began his quest for the Republican nomination of 1960, Nixon was seeking the designation of a party that was facing the possibility of a return to minority status. In a manner of speaking, Eisenhower was the savior of the modern Republican Party. The party had been the majority for many decades prior to 1932 but fell from power that year because of the Great Depression and the existence of widespread perceptions that Herbert Hoover offered few, if any, answers to the crisis. The Republicans were unable to regain the White House for twenty years afterwards. The party that had won all but four of the presidential elections between 1860 and 1932 suddenly found itself in a most unusual role: it was the obstacle that unsuccessfully attempted to stand between Franklin D. Roosevelt and his vast array of domestic and international achievements. The Republicans also had some strong political divisions among themselves that made their difficult electoral prospects even more so. Ideological moderates and conservatives fought every four years over the presidential nomination only to see their hopes vanish with yet another Democratic victory. Political control of either Congress or the Presidency seemed beyond the grasp of Republicans throughout the Roosevelt years. To some extent, Republicans attributed their seemingly endless series of defeats to Roosevelt but became somewhat optimistic that their long absence from power might be coming to an end when they gained control of both chambers of Congress in the recession year election of 1946. They were particularly disappointed by the results of the 1948 election, however, when Truman won what many of them thought should have been a certain victory for Thomas Dewey. Moreover, they also lost their recently acquired control of Congress and thereby began to see their future prospects as even more fearful.

Republicans were rescued from their misfortunes in 1952 when Eisenhower won a sweeping national victory and provided them with coattails that were long enough to win control of Congress. Eisenhower was the one unifying leader in the party. He had the personal imagery of a national hero and of a statesman who was "above politics" and his popular following made victory possible. He could also accommodate the views of a variety of party factions. His importance to the party was all too readily apparent throughout the 1950s as Republicans lost control of Congress in 1954 and suffered even more losses in subsequent years. The recession of 1958 cost the party innumerable public offices at all levels of government, but Eisenhower's popularity remained strong. He was their one leading source of electoral success. Now that Eisenhower was about to retire, the Republicans feared a return to the Democratic dominance of the 1930s and 1940s. They would likely have nominated Eisenhower for a third term in 1960 had that been possible. Since it was not, they sought the next best thing—a surrogate for Ike.

Nixon began his campaign as the overwhelming front-runner in what appeared at the time to be a battle among three candidates. His support was so widespread that his two potential rivals eventually decided against opposing him. Both the moderate leader, Nelson Rockefeller, and the conservative spokesman, Barry Goldwater, decided against entering the campaign when they apparently realized they lacked any chance of defeating Nixon. Rockefeller announced in April of 1960 that he would not be a candidate and met with Nixon shortly thereafter, while Goldwater had his name placed in nomination at the national convention but withdrew at that time. After winning several uncontested primary elections and the support of virtually all party leaders, Nixon captured the nomination on the first ballot when he received the votes of all but ten of the more than 1,300 delegates who attended the late July national convention in Chicago.

Rockefeller and Goldwater quite simply had not enjoyed the same levels of favorable television exposure and the opportunities it provides for developing a strong partisan following as Nixon had for eight years. A majority of Republicans did not consider either man to be the leading surrogate and heir apparent of Eisenhower. The support that Nixon had attained among his party's activist core because of his presence in two national campaigns and because of his partisan efforts during his tenure as Vice President negated any possible advantages that Rockefeller or Goldwater might have enjoyed from their respective vantage points as the moderate governor of the nation's most populous state or as a leading conservative spokesman in Congress. Years of television news coverage had provided Nixon with opportunities for exploiting the visibility of his position so that he could convince his fellow Republicans that he—not Rockefeller, Goldwater, or anyone else—was the rightful heir of Eisenhower. He did this very effectively and thereby became one of the youngest men ever nominated for President. He eventually came within one-fifth of one percent of the popular vote from joining the very small number of men who have been elected President before the age of fifty.

I raise a point of caution. One should not conclude that the presence of television alone and the ensuing news coverage of Nixon in the role of Vice President determined the outcome of the 1960 Republican nomination. The mere possession of the vice presidential office does not by itself automatically confer a nomination. In order to acquire the nomination, a Vice President must persuade the leaders, activists, financial contributors, and primary election voters of his own party that he is indeed worthy of their support. A Vice President who lacks the requisite political skills and personal credibility for doing so will almost certainly encounter great difficulties in rallying even his own partisans to nominate him for President, despite the advantages accruing to him because of his office. Nixon did not encounter these problems. While he derived some very unique opportunities from his position, he also had some very substantial political and communicative skills and used them effectively.

The Humphrey Nomination of 1968

The acrimonious nomination victory of Hubert Humphrey in 1968 differed considerably from the virtually unanimous one of Nixon in 1960. Unlike Nixon, Humphrey did not begin the year as a presidential candidate. Instead, he planned to seek a second term as Vice President and entered the race for the top position only after Lyndon Johnson withdrew following a disappointing performance in the New Hampshire primary. Humphrey announced his candidacy in mid-April, a relatively late time for a television age campaign. Although he began after the filing deadlines had passed for every state primary, Humphrey won the nomination on the first ballot at his party's national convention.

Humphrey's strategic position was quite unlike Nixon's. The battle for the Democratic nomination began more as a campaign with a weak incumbent than as the one with a surrogate incumbent that it eventually became. At the outset, Johnson appeared to be seeking a second term. The two other candidates, antiwar Senators Robert Kennedy (New York) and Eugene McCarthy (Minnesota), certainly formulated their strategies with such an assumption. After Johnson withdrew, Humphrey sought the Presidency as the surrogate of an unpopular incumbent and had to run on the legacy of the previous four years.

Johnson's problems, which soon became Humphrey's, derived primarily from two issues: the war in Vietnam and the domestic unrest associated with the nation's racial dilemma. Johnson was particularly responsible for the war but not necessarily for the racial unrest. He had made the critical policy choices that led to the escalation of the American military effort in Southeast Asia. While one cannot place all of the blame for the nation's failed Vietnam policy on Johnson (the problem had existed since the end of the Second World War and would continue until 1975), Johnson did order the bombing raids that expanded the American military role from advisory to combat. He rejected the dissenting opinions of some of his key advisors on several occasions about the futility of attempting to win a military conflict and pursued an unworkable policy that eventually generated widespread domestic opposition.

Johnson was not the primary cause of the considerable racial unrest that occurred in many cities during the late 1960s: the racial problem has existed in this nation since the beginnings of slavery. The 1960s marked a period in which the frustration of American blacks became important politically. Johnson was a significant figure in the drive for racial equality—political, social, and economic—with his leadership in securing legislative approval of the civil rights law, the voting rights act, open housing legislation, and the broad range of social programs that became known as the War on Poverty. Despite their widespread applicability, these measures were not enough to overcome the anger that had developed among blacks because of centuries of racism. Johnson received much of the blame for the ensuing domestic unrest, partly because of the fact that he was President at the time.

The televising of these problems and their aftermaths helped bring about a sharp decline in Johnson's popularity and made him an embattled incumbent as the campaign of 1968 approached. The televised visual images of the war conveyed two simultaneous messages that ultimately proved harmful to Johnson's electoral prospects. One image was the explicit illustration of death and destruction, which many viewers found gruesome. The second, but more implicit, image depicted the nation engaging in a war that it was not winning or perhaps could not win. Johnson was also harmed by the televising of antiwar demonstrations. While many viewers appeared to dislike both demonstrations and the young people who participated in them, the scenes of the widespread domestic opposition to the war reinforced popular perspectives of the apparent failures of the Johnson policies. Televised news coverage of racial disturbances also accelerated the decline of Johnson's public standing. The emphasis upon such themes as crime and violence, breakdowns in law and order, black antipathy toward whites, and the tendency of television news media to illustrate these controversies through action and emotion-related pictures first created and then reinforced mass perceptions of an impending revolt and a threat to the tranquility of society. American society seemed to be on the verge of disintegration.

While Johnson's problems were serious and suggested that he could very well be a one-term President, they were not strong enough to cause most of the leaders, elected officials, and activists of his party to abandon him. Like the weak incumbents Ford and Carter of later years, Johnson enjoyed the support of most of the leaders and elected officials of his party and would almost certainly have defeated his challengers had he continued with his efforts. Many party chairmen, Governors, Congressmen, local and state officials, and leaders of Democratic-oriented interests were supporting Johnson and securing places on delegate slates for the national convention. While many antiwar activists supported his two opponents, most had little influence over the selection of convention delegates. Most of the party leaders who supported Johnson eventually backed Humphrey.

The Humphrey bid pitted the Vice President, who was also the candidate of the presidential component of the party, against challengers whose political support rested elsewhere. Humphrey's opponents drew much of their support from political interests that had developed in the years immediately preceding the election. They attained greater backing from suburban professionals and students rather than the Democratic core constituency of labor union members, southerners, and residents of industrial cities. Despite some important differences in their levels of divisiveness, the campaigns that led to the nominations of Nixon and Humphrey were quite similar. In each instance the Vice President mobilized the most ardent supporters of the retiring incumbent and then won the right to be his party's standard bearer.

Several significant events occurred before Humphrey announced his candidacy. McCarthy opposed Johnson in the New Hampshire primary on the second Tuesday in March. He nearly won, with 43 percent of the vote compared to Johnson's 48 percent write-in vote. The strength of the McCarthy challenge encouraged Kennedy to enter the race within one week of the primary and perhaps underscored the depth of opposition to Johnson's policies. Johnson now seemed vulnerable to defeat in the general election and decided to end his tenure in office after only one term. He announced his decision to retire before the end of March.

Johnson's decision to relinquish the Presidency dramatically altered the nomination campaign. It left McCarthy and Kennedy as the only announced candidates but did not lead to a surge in support for either of these two administration critics. Instead, the withdrawal led to considerable speculation about when, not if, Humphrey would enter the race and about how much of the Johnson support the Vice President would inherit. Humphrey began efforts on his own behalf virtually as soon as Johnson ended his own quest.

The campaign took place on two different fronts after Humphrey announced his candidacy. Since it was no longer possible to compete in any primaries, Humphrey concentrated his efforts on winning the backing of the many Johnson supporters who dominated the state conventions where most of the national convention delegates were selected that year. Kennedy and McCarthy had limited followings there. Instead, they spent the months of April through June running against each other in several primaries. Kennedy captured Indiana, Nebraska, West Virginia, and California, while McCarthy finished first in Wisconsin, Massachusetts, and Oregon. The Oregon primary was the only instance where McCarthy actually defeated Kennedy. Humphrey acquired the support of more delegates through his efforts than either of his two rivals attained through theirs. A majority backed his candidacy at the conclusion of the primary election season.

Perhaps the most significant vote at the convention indicating the relative strength of the two factions—the Johnson administration and its surrogate, Humphrey, versus its antiwar opposition—was on the minority report relating to the Vietnam War. The majority report endorsed the policies of the Johnson administration, while the minority one opposed them and asked for an earlier withdrawal from the conflict. The majority report prevailed by a margin of about 60 percent of the vote to 40 percent. Shortly afterwards, virtually all of the supporters of the majority report voted for Humphrey as the presidential nominee. Humphrey attained the votes of about two-thirds of the delegates in winning the nomination.

Humphrey's nomination, while occurring within such a cauldron of political divisiveness, is an even stronger illustration than the nominations of Nixon and Bush of the tremendous advantages that a modern Vice President enjoys when seeking a presidential nomination. Humphrey presented himself to the Democratic Party as the leading surrogate and heir apparent of Lyndon Johnson. Humphrey's tenure as Vice President provided him with advantages that were not enjoyed by any of his rivals. As Nixon had been in 1952, Humphrey was a political figure of some importance prior to becoming Johnson's running mate. After serving two terms in the Senate in which he was one of the more important liberal spokesmen, Humphrey became one of the leading contenders for the 1960 Democratic presidential nomination. He ended his unsuccessful quest after losing both the Wisconsin and West Virginia primaries to John F. Kennedy. He then won a third Senate term. As several other Presidents of the television age have done, Johnson selected a running mate in 1964 who enjoyed considerable stature of his own and who could complement his own strengths. Johnson sought to strengthen his support among northerners and liberals. The selection also provided Humphrey with even more opportunities than ever for generating a personal following and, as a surrogate of an incumbent President who was popular among Democratic leaders and activists in 1964, to become a contender for a future presidential nomination. Many Democrats soon looked upon Humphrey as the likely nominee of their party on the conclusion of a hoped-for second Johnson term in 1972.

Humphrey's acceptance speech for the Vice Presidency, in which he depicted Goldwater as a candidate far from the mainstream of American political thought, was particularly well received by Democrats, and its central idea served as a major theme in that year's campaign. As Vice President, Humphrey's public appearances on behalf of Johnson helped him develop a strong personal following among the most loyal members of the President's constituency. Humphrey used his opportunities very effectively. He also possessed the communicative and political skills necessary for manipulating the unique opportunities offered by the Vice Presidency for winning a future presidential nomination.

There is a popular argument that says Humphrey won the nomination only because of the death of Robert F. Kennedy. Otherwise, so goes the argument, Kennedy would have expanded upon his victory in the California primary and generated the delegate support needed for victory. I disagree with this argument. Kennedy was not the front-runner at the time of his death and was not gaining the support that might have placed him in that role. Like Humphrey, he had entered the campaign at a relatively late date, mid-March. While Humphrey relied upon the organizational efforts that many party leaders had been carrying out on behalf of Johnson, Kennedy attempted to rally voters to his cause by competing in the small number of state primary elections that existed in 1968. Most states had already chosen delegates who were favorable to Johnson and his policies before either Humphrey or Kennedy launched their candidacies. Many of those same delegates transferred their loyalty to Humphrey shortly after Johnson ended his candidacy. At the time of the California primary in early June, Kennedy faced the dilemma that most of the delegates who would be attending the convention had already been chosen and were not supporting him. Instead, they were supporting the Vice President and surrogate of the retiring incumbent.

The Bush Nomination of 1988

The duration and intensity of the campaign that led to the nomination of George Bush by the Republican Party in 1988 rested somewhere between those of Nixon and Humphrey. In winning his party's nomination, Bush also relied upon many of the same political advantages of the Vice Presidency that Nixon and Humphrey had done in their earlier efforts. Bush differed from the other television age Vice Presidents, however, in that he won the ensuing general election. He convinced substantial numbers of people from both his own party and from among the broader electorate that he was the leading surrogate of a popular and retiring incumbent and that he deserved their support as a potential successor.

The key to Bush's successes in 1988, particularly in light of the fact that he was defeated for a second term in 1992, rests in both the widespread popularity of Ronald Reagan and in Bush's development of the public imagery whereby many people saw his election as the equivalent of a third Reagan term. Reagan's accomplishments as President were considerable. He had led his party to electoral and policy successes that could hardly have been imaginable in earlier decades when Republicans seemed to be a permanent minority. Indeed, a number of political observers believed that the Republican Party had become the nation's majority and that it would remain so for many years to come. More people identified themselves as Republicans during the Reagan years than at any time in the history of public opinion surveying. Moreover, this growing identification was particularly noticeable among younger voters. First-time voters were more favorable to the Republican Party than were most older voters. These younger voters were attracted by Reagan's emphasis on libertarian values and his goals of limiting the size and scope of government. The possible allegiance of these voters to Reagan and the Republicans could very well confine the Democrats to minority status, a role they had not held since the 1920s. Republican hopes were so high under Reagan that some partisans even talked about an electoral lock that would virtually bar Democrats from the Presidency. Since most states in the Southeast, Great Plains, and Rocky Mountain regions could be expected to vote Republican in any given election, this partisan head start, or electoral lock as some observers called it, would force the Democratic nominee to capture nearly every one of the remaining states in order to win the election. If the Republican candidate could win just a few states from the Northeast, Great Plains, or Pacific Coast, support from the Republican strongholds would guarantee victory.

Reagan constructed a political coalition from a wide variety of contradictory interests and perpetuated it by offering a number of tangible and symbolic rewards to its component parts. He derived some of his backing from the traditional constituency of the Republican Party, those individuals associated with the business and professional worlds who usually prefer minimal governmental regulation and taxation. He retained their support by weakening the effects of federal regulatory activity and by securing tax reductions for higher income groups. Reagan also acquired the backing of the religious right, those conservative Christians who often favor a stronger governmental role in promoting their version of personal morality. He used methods that were more symbolic than tangible in retaining the support of these people. One can see an example of Reagan's attempts at balancing the competing demands of his various constituents in his policies relating to abortion. He would use the anniversary of the Roe v. Wade decision each January to tell his anti-abortion supporters, often by the use of a tape-recorded message but not through a personal appearance, that he was taking some action toward achieving their goals. At the same time, his attempts to secure passage of any constitutional bans of abortion were limited, thus reassuring another part of his constituency that they could rely on him to protect their interests.

George Bush spent much of his eight years as Vice President developing the public imagery by which he appeared to many of his own partisans as Reagan's leading surrogate and preferred successor. He abandoned many of the differences that he had with Reagan, particularly those from the early stages of the 1980 nomination, and eventually became an advocate and defender of Reagan's policies. While many of Reagan's original supporters remained skeptical of Bush and did not really consider him to be a true conservative to their liking, they nonetheless supported his nomination. He was, after all, the surrogate of their champion.

The nomination did not fall to Bush as an inheritance however; he had to compete for it. In fact, there were more candidates for the nomination of the presidential party in 1988 than there had been in either 1960 or 1968, six in all. Despite this number, the race narrowed to just two major candidates shortly after the first electoral tests of 1988: Bush and Senate minority leader Robert Dole. Bush and Dole both had long and distinguished public careers, each covering more than two decades. They were two of the nation's most well-known Republicans at the beginning of 1988, were approximately the same age, sixty-four, and were moderate conservatives. The two differed in that each had spent virtually his entire career exclusively in one institution, the competing institutions of Congress and the executive branch.

Dole was a man of Congress. He was elected to the House of Representatives from Kansas in 1960 and moved on to the Senate eight years later. He remained in the Senate continuously after that, serving during the 1988 election campaign. Altogether, Dole had spent twenty-eight years in Congress when he sought the Presidency. The most significant events of his congressional career occurred during the eight years of the Reagan Presidency. During the first four years of Reagan's tenure, Dole was chairman of the Finance Committee. This is usually one of the more important committees of the Senate and was of added significance through the taxing and spending battles of the early 1980s. As chairman, Dole was one of the leading Senate proponents of Reagan's programs. He was elected Republican floor leader in 1985 and held that position through the 1988 elections. This was made possible by the retirement of the previous Senate leader Howard Baker (Tennessee) after the 1984 elections. Dole spent the next two years, 1985 to 1987, as majority leader. He then became minority leader after the Republican Party lost eight seats in the 1986 congressional elections. Dole became the most prominent Republican congressional spokesman during Reagan's second term and was a familiar personality in television news. While his few excursions into the presidential component of his party were limited, they were extensive enough to provide important opportunities for even more television news coverage. He spent two years during the early part of the Nixon administration as the chairman of the Republican National Committee and was in the television spotlight during the 1976 election campaign as Gerald Ford's running mate. He made an unsuccessful attempt to win the Republican presidential nomination in 1980.

George Bush, by contrast, spent most of his public career as an executive branch official. He was elected to the House of Representatives from Texas in 1966 but remained in that institution for only four years. His congressional tenure ended in 1970 when he lost a bid for a Senate seat to Lloyd Bentsen. Afterwards, he held a number of executive positions under various Republican Presidents. He also spent two years during the early 1970s as chairman of the Republican National Committee and served as the director of the Central Intelligence Agency, Ambassador to the United Nations, and Special Envoy to the People's Republic of China at various times during the Nixon and Ford administrations. He held no governmental posts during the Carter Presidency but returned to the executive branch as Vice President after the Reagan victory in 1980 and spent eight years in that office. Like Dole, he had been defeated by Reagan for the 1980 nomination.

Bush and Dole each sought to convince Republican Party activists and primary election voters that he was the heir apparent of Reagan. This campaign differed from that of the Democrats in 1968 in that the opposition the Vice President encountered did not originate from ideological or factional differences about the administration's policies. Instead, this campaign revolved around the efforts of a number of aspirants who sought to convince Republicans that each of them was the best choice to succeed a popular two-term president. The contest was short-lived. Dole recorded his only significant victory of the year when he won the Iowa precinct caucuses in mid-February. Bush came back with a triumph of his own in the New Hampshire primary one week later after mobilizing that state's Republican organization and by charging that Dole might support a tax increase. The four weaker candidates—Representative Jack Kemp (New York), television evangelist Pat Robertson, former Governor Pierre DuPont (Delaware), and former Secretary of State Alexander Haig—either had already withdrawn or were effectively eliminated from contention by this time.

Helped by a new political event created by southern Democrats, Super Tuesday, Bush concluded the campaign by the end of March. Fourteen southeastern and border states had scheduled their primary elections for the second Tuesday in March in hopes that a candidate less liberal than the 1984 aspirants Walter Mondale and Gary Hart, and preferably a Southerner, would win and emerge as a contender for the Democratic nomination. In addition, Massachusetts and Rhode Island voted the same day. The first electoral test in the Southeast was the South Carolina primary, scheduled for the Saturday before Super Tuesday. Bush won and then defeated Dole three days later in all sixteen Super Tuesday primaries. He acquired about seven hundred convention delegates with these victories, about two-thirds of the total needed for the nomination. The campaign ended a week later when Bush received about 60 percent of the vote in Illinois. This outcome forced Dole to withdraw and made Bush's nomination virtually certain.

The institutional advantages of the Vice Presidency contributed to the Bush victory. Unlike Nixon and Humphrey, Bush could not count on elected officials and party leaders to deliver the votes of large blocs of supportive convention delegates. The parties had made changes in their delegate selection rules after 1968 that were so extensive that the methods Nixon and Humphrey had relied on to win delegate support were no longer available in 1988. Bush and his rivals had to campaign in more than thirty primaries in order to win the nomination.

Nonetheless, the Vice Presidency proved to be an advantageous position from which to do so. The televising of his performance as Ronald Reagan's leading surrogate through two national campaigns and eight years in office provided Bush with the same opportunities for generating the personal and emotional support from his fellow partisans that Nixon and Humphrey enjoyed in their earlier efforts. Bush raised more money and attained more support from party activists and key leaders in important primary states than any of his rivals. He was particularly helped by Governors John Sununu, Carroll Campbell, and James Thompson in New Hampshire, South Carolina, and Illinois respectively. His campaign was financially and organizationally stronger than any of his rivals in the weeks before the climactic battles of early March.

Despite his high standing in Washington political circles, Dole failed to attract the requisite support from activists, financial contributors, and party officials that would have translated into a nomination victory. Instead, those same groups were quite influential in advancing the candidacy of George Bush. A leadership position in Congress simply had not given Dole sufficient opportunities to convince Republicans that he, and not Bush, should be Reagan's heir. Once again, the Vice Presidency had proven to be a far more valuable position from which to seek the nomination of the presidential party upon the retirement of the incumbent.

This review of three campaigns supports my contention that the nomination of the presidential party will fall to a leading member of the executive branch, and usually the Vice President, when the incumbent does not seek another term. Regardless of the procedural rules that have been employed or the strengths of ideological or congressional-based challenges, incumbent Vice Presidents have occupied an invaluable strategic position and have enjoyed important advantages in seeking the nomination when Presidents have retired. Modern Vice Presidents have brought such high political status with them into office and have garnered so much televised news attention throughout their campaigns and tenure in office that they now enjoy the best opportunities of all candidates for convincing their party's presidential constituency, at both the activist and voter levels, that they are the surrogates and appropriate heirs of retiring incumbents.

Succession to a nomination by the Vice President is not, as I have argued earlier, necessarily deterministic. It is quite possible that in some future election the presidential party may not nominate the Vice President as the successor of a retiring incumbent. For that matter, the Vice President may not even be a candidate. The question is then, who would be the nominee in such a circumstance? The outcomes of the Nixon, Humphrey, and Bush campaigns allow a forecast. The nominee should be an official of the executive branch of the national government and a member of what

Thomas Cronin calls the inner cabinet. This consists of the heads of the four major departments whose policy roles place them in frequent contact with the President and with television news media: State, Defense, Treasury, and Justice. These officials are the most important political actors in an administration after the President and Vice President. A candidate who holds one of these positions would have opportunities generally unavailable to others to prove to his party's activist core that he is the surrogate and heir of the retiring incumbent. The demands that are now made of these officials and the extensive political skills that many of them attain prior to their appointments suggest that such a strategically placed candidate might very well exploit those opportunities in some future election quite effectively. Other candidates whose political strength lies elsewhere, such as in Congress or state government, would probably encounter great difficulty in competing against the candidate of the executive branch.

OPPOSITION PARTY NOMINATIONS

Overview

The campaigns that led to the nominations of John F. Kennedy (1960), Richard M. Nixon (1968), and Michael Dukakis (1988) by the opposition party were similar in a number of ways. Each campaign started without an obvious winner or even front-runner and as a result attracted a number of major candidates. All three campaigns were quite lengthy and competitive but surprisingly exhibited little of the divisiveness that one might have expected. As a consequence, none of these campaigns compromised their party's prospects in the general election. These similarities were not random but were related to the particular circumstances that the opposition party faces in an election where the incumbent does not seek another term of office. Moreover, these similarities were enhanced by television news coverage of both the Presidency and of its election campaigns.

Like virtually all human actions, a nomination campaign involves the interplay of certain events that originate from the political context of the time with other events that originate from the needs and choices of the participating actors. The context of a nomination campaign includes those influences that derive from a variety of environmental and institutional factors such as domestic or foreign conflicts and from the interests of political parties, the Presidency, and television news media. Within such contexts, individual candidates tend to pursue those actions that they believe will most enhance their chances of winning the nomination. For a divisive campaign to occur, the demands that arise from both the political context and from the needs of the individual candidates must be mutually supportive of one another. Such a combination did not exist in any of these three campaigns.

Kennedy, Nixon, Dukakis, and their many rivals began their respective campaigns in similar contexts and each had many of the same needs. In each instance, their party faced an ambiguous set of opportunities and dilemmas. From recent events, the party had some good reasons for being optimistic about its chances of winning the Presidency, but it faced the dilemma that it lacked the one standout candidate who could readily lead it to victory. As candidates, Kennedy, Nixon, Dukakis, and their rivals all faced the overriding problem that each needed either to establish or, as in Nixon's case, reestablish his credibility as a possible nominee for President. Kennedy and Dukakis were national candidates for the first time and were only beginning to emerge as possible leaders of their party. Few people looked upon either of them as the foremost national spokesman of the Democratic Party at the outset of the 1960 and 1988 election years respectively. While Nixon was an important Republican leader at the beginning of 1968, his defeats in his two most recent attempts at gaining public office had helped to create the popular image that he was a loser and that he could not lead his party to a national victory. Kennedy, Nixon, and Dukakis were not alone in their troubles however. All of the aspirants who sought the nomination of the opposition party in these elections were candidates in search of constituencies at the outset of their campaigns. Moreover, all of them had to spend virtually all of their available time competing against other candidates who, like themselves, were also in search of constituencies. Rather than attempting to serve as spokesmen for party factions, these many candidates directed their energies primarily to the more pressing demands of generating the organization and money that would enable them to compete effectively for the nomination.

The political contexts necessary for a divisive campaign to occur were missing. The opposition party had been out of power for a long enough period of time in each of these instances that the divisive issues of previous years had subsided, while more recent circumstances had made the party more optimistic about its prospects in the upcoming election. There is a certain rhythm that appears to take place in the behavior of American political parties. Historically, the parties have been broad-based coalitions of diverse and sometimes contradictory interests whose primary goal has been to seek control of government. They are not well suited to emulate European parliamentary democracy where ideologically distinct parties advance policy agendas and then exert sufficient discipline over their elected officeholders in order to implement those agendas. The constitutional doctrines of federalism and separation of powers, including state control of election laws, divide the institutions of American government among so many centers of power and create so many political subdivisions that no one party can realistically hope to take complete control of the many governments in the nation and then enact its agenda. Consequently, American parties tend to specialize in the contesting of elections and in staffing and organizing government once in power but are only one of many institutions and interests that determine the content and direction of public policy. As election-contesting organizations, the parties make appeals to a wide variety of voters from many different constituencies in hopes that they can win as many elections as possible. These appeals vary across political subdivisions and thereby contribute to the creation of diverse and contradictory voter coalitions whose members may disagree with one another about a wide variety of issues. The public officials elected by such coalitions often reflect those disagreements. While these coalition-building strategies are often very useful for contesting elections, they can create problems when a victorious party attempts to govern. The party may not have the necessary unity among its elected officeholders for enacting some parts of its program or to convince all of its constituency to support it.

The presidential and opposition parties differ from each other in that the presidential party has an identifiable leader, the incumbent, under whom it often unites, while the opposition party usually lacks such a leader. This unity is not always easy to come by, however, even for the party that holds executive power. In order to gain the support of every component of his diverse party, a President often must display some of the same contradictions in his own actions that characterize his party. Ronald Reagan, for example, manipulated the differences that exist among Republicans over the issue of abortion and united supporters of both camps behind his candidacy in each of his electoral bids. The two largest voter groups that comprised the core of the Republican coalition during the 1980s and early 1990s were the moralizers and enterprisers, as some observers have designated them. The moralizers, who often support a strong governmental role in matters relating to personal behavior, sought to ban abortion in virtually all circumstances. The enterprisers tended to resist these efforts and preferred that abortion be considered a matter of personal choice. This latter group is closely affiliated with business and commerce, and its adherents generally resist proposals that call for much governmental regulation. Reagan won the support of both groups by using contradictory messages: he emphasized his opposition to abortion to the moralizers while indicating to the enterprisers that he was not likely to do much to seek its abolition. Many contradictions within a party may be submerged during a campaign and possibly for some time afterwards, but they cannot be submerged forever. They take on greater significance and frequently prove detrimental to a political party either when the incumbent has failed to consolidate power and no longer appears to be a certain electoral winner or in the years immediately after an election in which the party loses the Presidency and is driven from power.

Intra-party factional fights tend to originate when a party controls the Presidency and erupt when that party is no longer dominated by a strong incumbent. The fights are grounded in the contradictions that exist within the diverse electoral majority that had made past victories possible. They often expand those divisions to the point where unity and victory are no longer possible, at least in the short term. The fights are of limited duration, however, since prolonged absence of a party from power helps to diminish the intensity of its conflicts or even resolve them. Since an opposition party can no longer implement the divisive policies that encouraged its factionalism, it tends to become more unified as it focuses its attention upon the more immediate goal of regaining executive power by winning an election. However, the unity that will make such a future victory possible may not occur immediately after the party ceases to occupy the Presidency. There may need to be some time for political bloodletting to occur within the party before unity is possible.

Eventually, a prolonged absence of the party from power, the needs of slightly known candidates for office to devote their time to generating personal support, and the patterns of television news coverage of the Presidency and of its related election campaigns encourage an opposition party to downplay its internal differences and unite in its quest for the Presidency. This usually occurs not later than the second election after the party loses power. A review of the factional fights that have taken place during the television age supports this contention. In each of the six elections between 1964 and 1984, one of the parties was involved in a divisive fight that compromised its electoral chances. The fights occurred in the presidential party in 1968, 1976, and 1980 and in the opposition party in 1964, 1972, and 1984. In each of these latter instances, the opposition party had been out of power for only four years. The presidential party lost each of the elections from the first group, while the opposition party failed in each of those from the second.

The opposition party in each of the elections of 1960, 1968, and 1988 had been out of power for eight years and had engaged in serious factional fighting during the preceding election. The Democrats entered the 1960 and 1988 campaigns after having been the victims of their own divisiveness and of Eisenhower's and Reagan's sweeping reelection triumphs of 1956 and 1984 respectively, while the Republican campaign of 1968 took place four years after that party had suffered its worst factionalism and presidential defeat in nearly three decades.

From early in the twentieth century until at least the 1960s, the Republican Party was divided into conservative and moderate factions. The moderates were stronger in the more industrialized states, including those of the Northeast, Great Lakes, and Pacific Coast regions, while conservatives attracted more supporters from less industrialized areas. The moderates controlled presidential nominations between 1940 and 1964 and advanced an agenda calling for acceptance of many of the legislative enactments of the New Deal period relating to social and economic welfare, while conservatives often sought the repeal of many of those same enactments. The superior influence of the moderates was evident in the victory by Eisenhower over the conservative Senate leader Robert Taft (Ohio) at the 1952 national convention. Eisenhower's subsequent victory in the general election led to a submerging of Republican factionalism, but the moderates became dominant only in the executive branch of the national government; conservatives often spoke for the party within the Democratic-controlled Congress. Although these divisions appeared to be submerged, they were still present throughout Eisenhower's tenure as President. They also existed, but were again latent, during Nixon's campaign of 1960. Despite the size of his overwhelming nomination victory, Nixon faced some faction-related problems relating to the content of the party platform. He needed to reconcile the conflicting demands of the two factions. Goldwater reflected the long-standing frustration of conservatives in 1960 when he urged them to take back their party. He reemphasized those themes in his acceptance speech for the 1964 nomination when he said that extremism in the defense of liberty was no vice and that moderation in the pursuit of justice was no virtue.

Eisenhower's retirement and Nixon's defeats led to the absence of a strong leader who could prevent factional fighting as conservatives eventually challenged moderates for control of the party. A damaging power struggle erupted and resulted in the bitter and divisive nomination campaign in 1964. This power struggle, with the help of television news media as discussed earlier, also contributed to the subsequent landslide defeat that the party suffered at the hands of the strong incumbent, Lyndon Johnson. By 1968, after having been the opposition party for eight years, the Republicans set aside their differences, but conservatives held the stronger position. As partisans rather than ideologues, they seemed far more concerned with uniting behind a ticket that could win the election.

The divisive battle among Republicans in 1976 was also a factional struggle over control. Although this election did not involve a surrogate incumbent, its events support my contention about the nature and duration of factional fights. The two factions fought each other for the right to succeed Nixon. Nixon advanced a number of policies that were somewhat more moderate in their orientation than those advocated by conservatives. Nixon chose to leave much of the Democratic legislative enactments of the Johnson years intact while at the same time seeking the improvement of relations with China and the Soviet Union. These latter goals contrasted with long-standing conservative preferences for strong and active opposition to communism. The fall of Nixon and his Vice President, Spiro Agnew, from power and their replacement by Gerald Ford and Nelson Rockefeller, both of whom were political moderates, opened the door to a new struggle for power within the party. Ford's appointment as President and his subsequent decline in popularity after the Nixon pardon left Republicans without a dominant leader who could suppress the internal divisions. Ford was the moderates' candidate, while Ronald Reagan soon became the spokesman for conservatives. The battle lasted throughout the year before the election, extended through the entire primary election season, and concluded only at the national convention after the nation's attention turned from Republicans and focused more on the general election. These struggles also contributed to Ford's subsequent defeat in that election. The differences subsided afterwards, thus enabling Reagan to unite the party under his conservative leadership in 1980.

The Democrats had power struggles within their party during the latter days of the Truman, Johnson, and Carter administrations. In all three instances, the struggles were divisive while the incumbent remained in office and became even more so after his departure. The divisions existing between the supporters of Adlai Stevenson and Estes Kefauver, which were to some extent based on support and opposition to the policies of the Truman administration, divided the Democrats through the elections of both 1952 and 1956. The two factions that developed primarily from the differences over the Vietnam War fought over the nomination in both 1968 and 1972. Finally, the factions that divided over the policies of the Carter administration and that supported the rival candidacies of Carter and Edward Kennedy in 1980 continued with their struggle four years later in the candidacies of Walter Mondale and Gary Hart. All three of these conflicts were resolved by the beginning of the campaigns of 1960, 1968, and 1988 respectively.

The Democrats' improved prospects in these elections derived from more than the mere subsiding of their recent factionalism, although these declines contributed significantly to the development of the unity that made victory possible. For one thing, the incumbent who had humbled them in the preceding election four years earlier—Eisenhower, Johnson, or Reagan—was not seeking another term of office. His likely successor as the nominee of the presidential party, the Vice President, appeared to be a far weaker candidate. Moreover, the opposition party was also encouraged about its prospects by the outcome of the most recent congressional elections where it had made substantial gains. These gains suggested that the strains of governing were reducing the magnitude of support that the incumbent had attained in the previous election.

The Democrats had gained thirteen seats in the Senate and thirty-eight in the House of Representatives during the recession year election of 1958. This ended the partisan balances that had characterized Congress during the first six years of the Eisenhower administration and gave the Democrats more than three-fifths of all congressional positions. As an indication of the nature of these earlier partisan balances, the Democrats held forty-nine Senate seats compared with forty-seven for the Republicans after the conclusion of the election of 1956. These gains, particularly when coupled with the thought of Eisenhower's upcoming retirement, encouraged the Democrats to be optimistic about their chances of winning the Presidency in 1960.

Virtually all of those new Democratic senators managed to win second terms during the Johnson electoral triumph of 1964. Moreover, the Democrats gained an additional thirty-eight seats in the House of Representatives that year and thus expanded their numbers to 295, their largest total since the 1930s. The Republicans made some important inroads in 1966 however. Helped by the growing divisions among Democrats over the Vietnam War and race relations, they gained forty-seven House seats. These gains suggested that Johnson's legislative successes were coming to an end and that the Republican Party might well win the Presidency in 1968.

Two decades later the Democrats were encouraged about their chances of winning the Presidency upon the retirement of Reagan when they gained control of the Senate in 1986. They ousted eight first-term Republicans from the upper chamber that year who had gained positions during the Reagan electoral triumph of 1980. The Democrats became even more optimistic about their chances when the Iran-Contra scandal became public during 1987. They were even more hopeful later in this same year after they successfully flexed their new senatorial muscles and denied conservative justice Robert Bork a seat on the Supreme Court. Moreover, Bush did not appear to be a particularly inspiring candidate for the Presidency at this time, and he certainly was not causing very many Democratic aspirants to reconsider their decision of seeking the nation's highest office.

The Campaigns

Despite these enhanced prospects, the opposition parties had some good reasons for being uneasy about their chances, for each faced the same political dilemma. None of them had a strong front-runner at the beginning, of these campaigns who seemed capable of overcoming and eliminating his competition before the national convention and thereby sparing the party a prolonged and potentially destructive battle over the nomination. Certainly Kennedy led his rivals in voter surveys taken in the early weeks of 1960, Nixon outdistanced his competitors during similar periods in 1968, and Dukakis was as strong as any of the Democratic aspirants at the beginning of 1988. All three eventually won nominations, but their victories were not obvious at the outset of these election years. Each eventually triumphed in a campaign that involved a fairly large number of candidates and that extended through the conclusion of his party's national convention. Kennedy and Nixon were not assured of their nominations until they actually won them on the first convention ballot. Dukakis effectively clinched his victory by winning several primary elections between March and June, but a majority of states had already selected their convention delegates before he recorded his most important victories.

Each of these three campaigns attracted large fields of candidates for essentially the same reasons discussed earlier: television age opposition parties lack effective institutional methods for selecting unifying leaders prior to the outset of a presidential campaign. The leading contenders for the nomination tend to be individual aspirants for office who are not powerful leaders of the national government and who present themselves to the voters as solitary champions of justice. With rare exceptions, such as with Nixon in 1968, the aspirants are also little-known political figures and must therefore spend a great amount of their time simply attempting to become known to most voters. These candidates also generally lack any opportunities for becoming leaders or spokesmen for ideological factions. Consequently, none of these campaigns developed into the divisive struggles between two role-playing candidates that have so often compromised the opposition party's chances in other election years.

The Democratic campaign of 1960 attracted five major candidates, each of whom began by seeking to consolidate the support of a particular constituency of his party and then expanded that support into a nomination victory. Two relatively young and liberal senators from northern states, John F. Kennedy (Massachusetts) and Hubert H. Humphrey (Minnesota), had fairly similar strategies. Both men were first-time presidential candidates lacking extensive public recognition. Each initially strived to demonstrate his ability to win votes by contesting several of the limited number of primary elections that existed at the time. The successful candidate, whomever it might be, would then use those victories and attempt to convince state and local party leaders that he could unite the party and win the general election. Another candidate, the majority leader of the Senate, Lyndon B. Johnson (Texas), opted for an alternative strategy. With the assistance of his friend and mentor, longtime House Speaker Sam Rayburn, Johnson sought to translate into delegate support the power he enjoyed in Congress and the personal associations he and Rayburn had developed over the years with many of the members of that institution. He believed that little could be gained from the primary elections and thus avoided them. As argued in earlier chapters, such a strategy rarely proves effective for winning a nomination: congressional power does not readily translate into votes either in primary elections or at national conventions. Johnson attained very little support from states outside the Southeast. The two remaining candidates, Senator Stuart Symington (Missouri) and former Governor and two-time party standard bearer Adlai Stevenson, Jr. (Illinois), relied instead upon hopes that none of the other candidates would be able to generate the support needed for winning the nomination. The resulting deadlocked convention would then be forced to turn to one of them as a unifying and acceptable alternative. Symington, who had the support of former President Harry S Truman, sought to present himself to the convention as an ideological moderate from a border state who could run well in both north and south. Stevenson wanted to rely primarily upon the prestige that he had attained as the nominee in the two preceding elections and hoped to regain the leadership of the party if and when the other candidates failed in their endeavors.

Four candidates sought the nomination of the Republican Party in 1968. Former Vice President Richard Nixon was the favorite of many elected officials and party leaders, but he had a serious and potentially fatal political problem—the public image of being a loser. He had acquired this image from his defeats for the Presidency in 1960 and for the governorship of California in 1962. He desperately needed to erase it in order to be taken seriously by the Republicans as a potential nominee. He tried to accomplish this by using television advertising and a number of public appearances to create a different image by which voters would see him as the "New Nixon." If successful, much of the voting public would look upon him as an experienced and well-qualified statesman who could lead the nation through its current foreign and domestic difficulties. Nixon also strived to convince his fellow Republicans that he was the one candidate who could unite the party and lead it to an electoral triumph. Three governors opposed him at various times during the campaign. Two of his rivals, George Romney (Michigan) and Nelson Rockefeller (New York), were moderates who sought to mobilize party leaders and elected officials from the Northeast and Midwest. If either succeeded, his next step would be to convince conservatives that he had a far greater chance of winning the electoral votes of the major industrial states than any of the other candidates, including Nixon. In contrast, Ronald Reagan (California) was telling his fellow partisans that he could advance conservative viewpoints, unify the party, and then win the election. Other conservatives, however, including Senators Everett Dirksen (Illinois), Strom Thurmond (South Carolina), and even Barry Goldwater, believed that Nixon offered the better hope.

The Democratic campaign of 1988 attracted a variety of candidates who reflected virtually all of the party's ideological and geographic constituencies. The candidates ranged from Reverend Jesse Jackson, whose support appeared strongest among racial minorities, to a number of northern liberals such as Governor Michael Dukakis (Massachusetts) and Senators Gary Hart (Colorado), Joseph Biden (Delaware), and Paul Simon (Illinois), and the more moderate southern and border state candidates Senator Albert Gore Jr. (Tennessee), Representative Richard Gephardt (Missouri), and former Governor Bruce Babbitt (Arizona). While Jackson directed much of his efforts at mobilizing support from what he called the Rainbow Coalition—racial minorities and the poor and disaffected—the other candidates set out to duplicate the successful Carter strategy of 1976. Each sought to win at least one important caucus or primary at the outset of the campaign, such as Iowa, New Hampshire, or several of those from the Southeast, and then to acquire the extensive television news exposure that Carter had attained after his early victories. Each hoped that such television exposure would increase his familiarity with voters in other states and enable him to generate the momentum, support, and monies that would lead to even more electoral successes.

Despite the fact that a front-runner emerged during the first weeks of each of these campaigns, quite some time elapsed before any one candidate demonstrated enough support that his rivals and their followers actually considered him as the certain winner of the nomination. Many observers acknowledged Kennedy as the Democratic front-runner during the early weeks of 1960 because of his standings in national surveys. Kennedy could actually claim that role after he scored a modest victory over Humphrey in the Wisconsin primary during the first week of April. He strengthened his claim by defeating Humphrey in the West Virginia primary five weeks later. These setbacks encouraged the Minnesota senator to abandon his candidacy. Despite these victories, however, Humphrey was the only rival that Kennedy had eliminated by the time the Democratic convention convened in Los Angeles in mid-July.

The Republican campaign of 1968 developed in a similar fashion. Nixon acquired the front-runner role early during the year partly because of the unwillingness of Rockefeller and Reagan to announce their intentions and partly because the Romney effort was unraveling. Nixon had raised far more money, acquired more key endorsements, and attained higher survey standings than any of his rivals. He strengthened his claim to the front-runner role after Romney withdrew from the New Hampshire primary two weeks before the voting took place. Romney decided to abandon his candidacy before the vote so that he could avoid a humiliating defeat. Nixon had opened up such a commanding lead in the nation's first primary state that Romney was left with no recourse except to withdraw. Despite this victory, Nixon nonetheless encountered some strong challenges from both Rockefeller and Reagan at the national convention, which was held in Miami during the first week of August.

The Democratic campaign of 1988 differed from these two in that Dukakis virtually clinched the nomination in late April, about six weeks before the national convention, after winning the New York primary. His victory became certain by early June after he attained the endorsements of a majority of the delegates. One can attribute Dukakis' relatively early victory to the extensive changes that have occurred since the 1970s in the methods the parties use for selecting convention delegates and to the revised scheduling of many of the primaries of 1988. These changes have helped move nomination decisions from the summer national conventions to earlier parts of the year and have expanded the influence of grass roots activists and voters over the outcomes while diminishing the influence of the party leaders and elected officials who dominated them in 1960 and 1968. The majority of states now conduct their primaries or caucuses before the end of March. While these changes certainly encouraged the opposition party to resolve its nomination much earlier than it had in 1960 or 1968, the Democratic campaign of 1988 was remarkably quite similar to those earlier ones. Even though Dukakis had emerged as the front-runner by the second Tuesday of March ("Super Tuesday"), his nomination was far from certain at that time. Five of the eight candidates remained in the race at the conclusion of that day's voting. It would take another six weeks for Dukakis to secure his victory.

A noticeable aspect of these three campaigns was the absence of the one leading adversary who could serve as the antithesis of the front-runner and as the rallying point for his opposition. This absence existed primarily because of the lack of the requisite contexts for factional fighting and from the needs of the candidates to generate their own personal support instead. In addition, the attainment of party unity in hopes of regaining the Presidency after a prolonged absence from power was a strong motivating factor within the opposition party in each of these years. Many activists and voters seemed far more willing to support the early front-runner than to engage in a divisive battle to obstruct or prevent his nomination. Kennedy, Nixon, and Dukakis were able to unite their parties, despite the fact that each needed to devote a considerable amount of time and effort to winning the nomination from a large number of rivals. The number of aspirants who choose to seek a nomination and the amount of time and money they spend as candidates are not the critical variables that make a nomination campaign divisive. The more crucial variables are the contexts in which the campaigns occur and the needs of the individual candidates to adapt to them. Divisive campaigns occur within the presidential party when a weak incumbent is challenged over some of his policies and because of differences that exist within the governing coalition. Moreover, the challenge comes from a rival whose political support rests outside the executive branch of government. The opposition party may undergo a divisive campaign during the first election after it falls from power over differences that originated while it last held office. As demonstrated in earlier chapters, television news media, while not creating the contexts of these fights, report them in ways that enhance the electoral prospects of strong incumbents while damaging those of weak ones. In the three campaigns that are the subject of this chapter, many members of the opposition party could find no particularly compelling reasons for attempting to deny the nomination to the early front-runner. One of the candidates for each nomination was thereby able to convince many of his fellow partisans that he was a promising leader who could bring about unity and victory. He emerged as the front-runner fairly early during the campaign and then defeated a variety of individual opponents to win the nomination. At no time did the rivals of the front-runner ever unite into a coalition behind one candidate. Instead, each attempted to build political support only for himself and each eventually withdrew as his inability to do so became more and more obvious.

Kennedy was the front-runner for several weeks before the beginning of the national convention, but he lacked the support of enough delegates to claim victory. The remaining candidates—Johnson, Stevenson, and Symington—shared the goal that each one of them had to prevent Kennedy from winning so that he could continue with his own efforts. Despite this commonality of purpose, each was also prepared to do battle with the others if Kennedy failed. All three worked from the assumption that they might stop the growing Kennedy bandwagon if they could collectively garner enough votes to deny the Massachusetts Senator a first-ballot nomination victory. There was a widespread belief at the time that Kennedy would achieve his strongest support on the first ballot and would then lose support on subsequent ones. Kennedy's rivals were hoping for a repeat of his fate as an unsuccessful candidate for the Vice Presidency in 1956. During that previous campaign, Stevenson did not designate a running mate but left the choice to the convention instead. Kennedy finished in first place on the initial ballot but lost the support of several hundred delegates on the second one and was eventually defeated.

Johnson was Kennedy's strongest remaining rival. He allegedly had some assurances from the leaders of several delegations who planned on voting for Kennedy on the first ballot that they would switch their support to him if the convention reached a second ballot. Johnson believed that he could replace Kennedy as the strongest candidate after the initial ballot and that he could then translate his congressional power into a nomination triumph. Stevenson and Symington supported Johnson's efforts to block Kennedy's nomination, but they also planned to oppose Johnson if that effort succeeded. Their hope was to force a deadlocked convention which would turn to one of them as an acceptable compromise after several additional ballots. They were more optimistic about stopping Johnson since they believed that he would gain little support outside the Southeast.

The divisions that existed among the Democrats in this campaign were not so much ideological as they were based instead upon the needs of the candidates to generate enough personal support to win the nomination. The attainment of party unity after such a campaign is relatively easy, as the aftermath of the voting shows. Kennedy gained the support of several of the undecided delegations and won on the first ballot with slightly more than eight hundred of the approximately fifteen hundred convention votes. Johnson finished second with about four hundred votes, while Symington and Stevenson together gained about 150. The Democratic Party was unified when Kennedy selected Johnson as his running mate.

The divisions among Republicans at their 1968 national convention were similar to those of the 1960 Democrats, related more to the needs of particular candidates than to the animosity of ideological factions. Like Kennedy, Nixon entered the convention with more delegates than any of his rivals but did not have enough to claim the nomination. He needed the support of several uncommitted delegations. His two remaining opponents, Rockefeller and Reagan, tried to prevent his victory on the first ballot in order to keep their own hopes alive. There was a widespread assumption that Nixon would achieve his greatest strength on the first ballot and would lose some of his support on subsequent ones. Nixon had campaigned on the theme that he was not the predominant spokesman for any one faction of the party but was a unifying leader who could bring Republicans of all viewpoints together and win the election. Some of his more conservative supporters would likely have shifted their allegiance to Reagan if Nixon had ceased to be a viable contender for the nomination, while some of the more moderate ones would have backed Rockefeller in such a likelihood. Any possible alliance that might have existed between Nixon's two rivals was temporary and designed mainly to prevent him from winning on the first ballot. Reagan and Rockefeller would then have opposed each other if they had succeeded in stopping Nixon.

Nixon's rivals threw a strong challenge at the former Vice President but failed to stop him. At the conclusion of the many nominating speeches that were made on behalf of the three major candidates and several favorite sons, Reagan led one final effort to stop Nixon when he moved to adjourn the convention for the evening and delay the first ballot until the following morning. He hoped that some delegations might drop their support of Nixon overnight and back him instead. His motion failed on a close roll call vote. Shortly thereafter, about seven hundred of the thirteen hundred delegates voted to make Nixon the nominee.

The 1988 Democratic campaign was similar to these two earlier ones in that it too lacked the bitter ideological divisions that often lead to electoral defeat and also in the sense that it was mostly a battle among candidates. For the first few months, as in 1960 and 1968, the campaign was essentially a Hobbesian world of "a war of every man against every other man": each of the eight candidates sought to gain strategic advantages over his rivals. After Dukakis emerged as the front-runner, each of his rivals in turn fell by the wayside. At no time did any of them occupy the role as the one leading adversary of the front-runner who could pose a serious threat to the inevitable Dukakis nomination. The number of candidates had narrowed from eight to six by January of 1988 with the withdrawals of Hart and Biden for personal reasons. Hart had abandoned the race after extensive media coverage of his alleged extramarital affairs contributed to a large drop in his popularity, while Biden quit following media discovery (with some help from the Dukakis campaign) that he had plagiarized a speech given by British Labor Party leader Neil Kinnoch. Babbitt was the next to depart after losing both the Iowa caucuses and the New Hampshire primary in February. Gephardt followed Babbitt and withdrew in late March after losing in all but one state on Super Tuesday and after losing again in the Michigan caucuses two weeks later. Simon pulled out of the race in early April after his fourth place finish in the Wisconsin primary where he garnered only 7 percent of the vote. Gore quit in late April after running out of money and suffering an overwhelming setback in New York where he attained only 10 percent of the vote. These departures reduced the number of active candidates to only two: Jackson, with his constituency of racial minorities and some white liberals, and Dukakis, who by now had the support of virtually everyone else in the party. While Jackson chose to perpetuate his efforts until the national convention in mid-July, he lacked the following to constitute a serious threat to Dukakis. One can hardly describe him as the leading adversary of the front-runner in the sense that he had a realistic chance of denying the nomination to Dukakis. The Democratic campaign essentially ended with the New York primary. In a period of about two and a half months, ranging from the mid-February Iowa caucuses to the aftermath of the New York primary in late April, Dukakis went from being only one of the pack, to the front-runner, to the virtually certain nominee.

One cannot attribute the Dukakis victory to successful ideological or factional appeals. Dukakis, in fact, even denied this in his acceptance speech when he said that the election was about competence, not ideology. His appeals were general enough to attract a wide variety of Democrats. This approach also characterized the campaigns of all the Democratic aspirants except Jackson.

Television news media played an important role in this campaign. They implicitly helped Dukakis generate consent among his own partisans by directing much of their attention to the "horse race" and to the efforts of the candidates to seek advantages over the others, in much the same way they had done in the two earlier campaigns involving Kennedy and Nixon. The coverage downplayed whatever differences might still have existed among Democrats and enhanced the rapid departure of the other candidates from the campaign. Two of them, Gephardt and Simon, spent much of their time and money in Iowa in the hopes that victory in the state's caucuses would help them generate the exposure via television that would set them on a course for the nomination. Neither man attained very much from Iowa that actually helped him in contesting the nomination. The final Iowa vote was very close among the top three contenders with Gephardt finishing first, Simon second, and Dukakis third. The identity of the winner was not obvious from the initial returns and did not become apparent until the very early hours of the following morning. The closeness served to help Dukakis because it denied Gephardt the opportunity to gain any immediate publicity from his eventual first place finish and because it also encouraged television news media to direct even more of their attention to the outcome of the Republican vote. The major news stories that finally came out of Iowa were about Republicans: the third place finish by the front-runner George Bush, the victory of Bush's leading adversary Robert Dole, and the surprising second place finish of Pat Robertson. Gephardt and Simon received their fifteen minutes of fame and each soon faded away. One week later both candidates lost the New Hampshire primary to Dukakis and essentially disappeared from the airwaves. By this time, they were also out of money.

The same fate awaited Gore. He had decided to center his strategy on achieving great successes in the southern primaries on Super Tuesday. Like Gephardt and Simon, he divided the Democratic vote and subsequent publicity with two others—in this instance Dukakis and Jackson—and, like Gephardt and Simon, became a victim of the fact that the major news of the day was also about Republicans, the sweeping victories of George Bush in all sixteen states. Gore attained his fifteen minutes of fame and then he too disappeared from the airwaves without registering very strongly in the public's consciousness.

The genre of books that began with Theodore White's *The Making of the President 1960* and that continued in the many imitations that have appeared after every presidential election since then have placed great emphasis upon the individual competition for the office. The writers of these books often convey implicitly, as White did with Kennedy, that the eventual winner of a prolonged and highly contested election battle has proven to the nation that he is the most qualified of all candidates to be President. The campaign is an ennobling experience for would-be Presidents and is the truest test of their political virility. Similarly, in a televised campaign in which media depict individual efforts and victory as the ultimate political virtues, the winner of a nomination campaign for a party that has been out of power for at least two terms will very likely appear as a unifying individual who possesses the personal skills that people expect of a President. Television news media followed this script of White in all three of these campaigns and treated the successes that the individual candidates had at raising funds, acquiring high survey standings, and winning primary elections as political virtues while depicting the failures of the other candidates to accomplish these same tasks as vices and as signs of personal limitations. This manner of reporting was particularly adaptable to the contexts of these three years and appears to have helped Kennedy, Nixon, and Dukakis generate even greater support among the activists and voters of their own parties and to appear to those partisans as unifying leaders. These three nominees had passed the televised test of leadership by vanquishing the many rivals they had encountered in their quest for office and each was now ready to take on the Vice President.

GENERAL ELECTIONS

Surrogate's and Challenger's Dilemmas

Each political party encountered a recurring dilemma in these three elections that appears to be unique to its own particular vantage point. The presidential party had the dilemma that its nominee was an executive branch surrogate of the retiring incumbent, in each instance the Vice President, who had inherited only some of that incumbent's popularity. Each Vice President had successfully manipulated the advantages of his office that derived from television and had convinced many of his fellow partisans that he, as the one leading surrogate of the incumbent, deserved the nomination. These Vice Presidents were less successful at winning the support of many independents and opposing partisans who had voted for the incumbent in one or both of the preceding elections however. A great number of Eisenhower Democrats, Johnson Republicans, and Reagan Democrats declined to support Nixon, Humphrey, or Bush. They did not necessarily see these Vice Presidents as statesmanlike leaders. As a result, the presidential party began these elections with reduced prospects of retaining the White House.

The limitations of surrogate incumbency and the strength of the challenge that the Vice President will eventually face from the unified opposition party often become apparent during the weeks between the end of the primary election season in mid-June and the onset of the national conventions in July or August. By this time, the eventual winners of the nominations of both parties are usually obvious. Consequently, the two likely nominees tend to change the focuses of their campaigns by directing their attention toward the general election instead of the primaries and begin concentrating more upon their future rival and less upon their previous ones. Television news media tend to change their patterns of reporting during this time as well and direct more of their attention to the eventual nominees while virtually ignoring other aspirants. The events of these weeks are often crucial. Many voters make their final electoral choices during this time, and a particularly large number of them decide in favor of the challenger. The growth in support for the challenger is often large enough that the Vice President falls permanently behind his rival by Labor Day. Vice Presidents Nixon, Humphrey, and Bush led challengers Kennedy, Nixon, and Dukakis in the variety of public opinion surveys that were taken during the primary election seasons of their respective campaigns but each lost his lead during the weeks that followed the conclusion of the primaries. Only Bush regained his lead and went on to win.

One factor that encourages the growth of support for the challenger during these weeks is the implicitly supportive news coverage that he often receives from television media. They help him appear to be a new political leader of presidential quality. With the conclusion of the primary election season, the challenger begins to dominate the televised news coverage of his party at a time when he is attempting to change both his political status and his public image. He no longer is simply one of the many aspirants in quest of the nomination but instead is emerging as the new and unifying leader of a previously leaderless opposition party. The rise of such a new leader to prominence tends to affect the political perceptions of many of that party's activists and voters. They begin to imagine the real prospect of a change from the immediate past and the defeats that characterized it to a more promising future that can be made possible only with an electoral victory. While some of them may have voted for other candidates earlier in the year, they now begin shifting their support to the challenger as he closes in on the nomination. This growing support enables the challenger to unify his party even more.

Television news media illustrate the growth of this support and unity and the emergence of the challenger in much the same manner that they illustrate the consolidation of power by a strong incumbent President. They direct more of their attention to the aftermath of the challenger's achievements than to the achievements themselves. Earlier in the year, they had depicted the challenger as only one of many candidates in the nomination horse race. Now that he has vanquished his rivals and unified his party, they begin depicting him more favorably. This, in turn, helps the challenger appear to be a leader of presidential quality. Through these patterns of coverage, television news media are both sanctifying the processes of the nomination and implicitly telling their audiences that the candidate who triumphs is qualified to be President. By depicting the challenger in this manner and only at this time, television news media are providing a favorable and supportive context in which he can expand his voter support.

The corresponding expansion of the challenger's support is not necessarily limited to his own partisans however. A number of other voters also begin to sense that the upcoming change in national leadership may involve more than just the mere replacement of a retiring incumbent with a surrogate. Partly because of the aforementioned patterns of television news coverage, these other voters also begin to see the challenger as a leader of presidential quality and decide that they too will support him. The Vice President now faces a dilemma because of these circumstances. He has developed a public image whereby many voters see him primarily or only in the role of surrogate. Because of this, the Vice President often cannot convince many voters other than his own partisans that he is or can be a leader of presidential quality. His lack of a political identity other than that of surrogate now becomes an obstacle to his electoral prospects. Consequently the challenger begins to seize the lead from the Vice President in national surveys.

For example, a Gallup survey taken during the first week of July 1960, shortly before the convening of the first national convention of the year, indicated that Kennedy led Nixon by 4 percentage points, 50 to 46. In contrast, Nixon had led Kennedy by 6 points in a January poll. A Gallup survey taken at a comparable time in 1988, in early July before the convening of the first convention of that year, showed Bush trailing Dukakis by 6 points, 47 percent to 41. This reversed a 12-point lead of Bush over Dukakis in March. Finally, a Gallup survey compiled in late July, shortly before the first of the 1968 conventions, showed Humphrey trailing Nixon by 40 percent to 38 with Wallace at 16. One month earlier, Humphrey had been ahead of Nixon by 6 percentage points.

Two of these three Vice Presidents fell even further behind their challengers as the convention periods unfolded. Humphrey, in particular, lost support as a result of the divisions over the Vietnam War that polarized his party's national convention. Humphrey's 2-point gap of July expanded into a 16-point deficit by late August. He garnered support from only 29 percent of the respondents compared to Nixon's 45 percent and Wallace's 18. While Bush headed toward a unified Republican convention in mid-August 1988, Dukakis expanded his 6-point preconvention lead to 17 percentage points, 54 to 37, by the end of July. Granted, some of this additional support was illusory and can be attributed to the post-convention "bump" where a candidate appears to gain support after a week of extensive publicity, but Dukakis still maintained a lead of 7 percentage points, 49 to 42, two weeks after the Democratic convention.

In contrast to the extensive shifts of support in 1968 and 1988, the electorate of 1960 showed relatively little volatility. Neither of the two candidates gained or lost much support during the conventions. Kennedy maintained his lead into mid-September as he led Nixon by a margin of 47 percent to 45 at that time. He expanded his lead to five points, 50 percent to 45, by early October.

While the opposition party avoided the divisiveness in these three campaigns that might have undermined its general election prospects, it had a unique and recurring dilemma of its own. Far too much of the summertime support for its nominee was illusory and could well disappear by the time of the general election. The illusion of support derived from the political contexts of the nomination campaigns and from television news coverage of the actions of the various candidates. Kennedy, Nixon, and Dukakis were victors in the campaigns of an opposition party that had been out of power for at least eight years and which very much wanted to set aside past differences and win the election. Without the divisive context of the preceding election and with the consensus-building role provided by television news media, the challengers eventually defeated their rivals and united their parties. They did so by advancing broad but vague appeals that were interchangeably linked with their own personalities and that held out the promise of victory. Kennedy, as a young and dynamic member of a new generation, promised to "get this country moving again." Nixon, as the heir to the popular Eisenhower, had a "secret plan to end the Vietnam War." Dukakis, who had used the imagery of his role in a so-called Massachusetts economic miracle to gain support throughout the primaries, offered voters a campaign that was "about competence, not ideology." Each candidate became the early front-runner for his party's nomination and developed into a consensus leader through the use of these personal images and policy appeals and through his corresponding successes at raising money and organizing voters. Since these nomination campaigns had effectively been reduced to a number of personal quests for office, candidates who failed in the early electoral tests were soon unable to rally enough support to perpetuate their efforts. Television news media, as discussed earlier, helped front-runners Kennedy, Nixon, and Dukakis secure their victories and generate consensus by depicting the other aspirants as losers and thereby enhancing their rapid departure from the campaigns.

Favorable public images grounded in the euphoria of primary election successes, such as the ones of these challengers, can change for the worse during the intensity of a general election campaign. These changes occur as the challengers are subjected to attacks from the Vice President and his supporters and to increasing doubts of skeptical voters about their abilities. As these general election campaigns developed, the vague images of the challengers proved troublesome. Once again, Kennedy seemed to be far too young and inexperienced for the Presidency, Nixon was the "Tricky Dick" of recent memory, while Dukakis appeared to offer little more than a return to the bad old days of the Johnson and Carter administrations. Each of the three needed to respond to those attacks and doubts or his summertime lead could disappear. The effectiveness of the responses varied considerably. Kennedy and Nixon were successful and won their elections, while Dukakis failed to grasp the extent of his difficulties and lost.

Candidates' Strategies

Dukakis emerged from the pack of aspirants and became the front-runner for the Democratic nomination during April after winning the Wisconsin and New York primaries. By mid-May, with his nomination virtually certain, Dukakis changed the focus of his campaign toward the upcoming battle with George Bush. He soon gained the backing of most of the supporters of his rivals who had already withdrawn from the campaign, which by now included every candidate other than Jackson. He combined the votes of these new supporters with those of his earlier ones and garnered even stronger victories in the final primaries. He eventually gained the backing of Jackson's supporters after the national convention and then became the undisputed leader of his party. Since he had not been associated with the unpopular Carter administration, Dukakis seemed to offer the prospects of both change and victory. Dukakis was no longer simply one of many aspirants for the nomination; he was the one remaining alternative to a possible Bush administration. It was during these weeks that Dukakis gained the lead from Bush in national surveys.

Dukakis' lead was as illusory as his image was vague. The generality of the appeals that had enabled him to unite his own partisans had also left many gaps in the minds of other voters as to the nature of his qualifications for the Presidency and of what he might do if elected. Rather than attempting to close those gaps, however, Dukakis sought to perpetuate them. He continued to emphasize his competence to hold the Presidency but failed to demonstrate for what uses that competence might prove important. He even spent some time after the convention attending to Massachusetts governmental matters rather than seeking to alleviate the public doubts about his image. While Dukakis apparently had no intention of addressing his problems, the Bush campaign certainly did.

George Bush had an unusual dilemma that derived from his role as Vice President and surrogate. He had begun the year as the front-runner for the Republican nomination and had driven each of his rivals from the campaign by the end of March. By this time he had convinced most of his fellow partisans that he should succeed Reagan as President. The Republicans were as united behind Bush in April as the Democrats would be behind Dukakis in July. Bush had several more weeks available than Dukakis to orient his efforts toward the general election. With the benefit of such a long head start, Bush might have used the time to open up an insurmountable lead over his Democratic rival by the onset of the conventions. Unfortunately for Bush, there were other factors at work. With the Republican nomination resolved, television news media directed most of their coverage of electoral politics to the campaign among the Democrats. In doing so, they provided Dukakis with the opportunities for gaining widespread exposure and a corresponding increase in political support. Bush suffered from the limitations of his role of surrogate. Unlike the President, a Vice President cannot use the Rose Garden strategy in a general election campaign. A strong incumbent who clinches his nomination early during an election year, as Reagan did in 1984, will continue to receive substantial television news coverage thereafter simply because of the fact that he is President. This fact does not apply to the Vice President since his activities are not always newsworthy.

Bush was trapped by the surrogate's role. He had used it effectively to win the Republican nomination but was now encountering some difficulty in using it to win the support of many of the independent voters and Democrats who had supported Reagan. Reagan remained popular in 1988 and quite likely could have won a third term had such an undertaking been constitutionally possible. To win the election, Bush had to extend his surrogate's appeal beyond Republicans to those same voters who had supported Reagan but who were now looking favorably upon Dukakis. He had to convince them that a Bush victory would result in the equivalent of a third Reagan term. Dukakis faced quite the opposite task. He needed to convince those same voters that change from the status quo was preferable to a Bush Presidency and that he was the man to lead that change.

The problems that Kennedy and Nixon encountered in 1960 were similar to those of Dukakis and Bush. Kennedy, like Dukakis, had been one of many aspirants for the Democratic nomination. His party had lost the two preceding elections but was optimistic about its prospects this time because of the retirement of Eisenhower. The Democrats faced the institutional problem of a modern opposition party in that it did not have a unifying leader before the beginning of the campaign. Kennedy emerged from the pack of candidates, defeated his rivals, united the party, and offered the nation the prospect of a change from the status quo. As it was eventually to do with Dukakis, television media focused extensive news coverage upon the personal imagery and vague appeals of Kennedy while these events were unfolding. They enhanced Kennedy's efforts to generate consensus among his own partisans and to develop and project a favorable public image to many voters who had supported Eisenhower in the previous election. Kennedy gained his lead over Nixon in the polls during this time and never relinquished it.

Nixon, like Bush, used his position as Vice President to clinch his party's nomination long before Kennedy had clinched his. Nixon was also the surrogate of a popular incumbent who could have won a third term if that option had been possible. As with Bush, Nixon was unable to use his early victory to dominate television news throughout the summer months because he too was the Vice President and the Vice President's actions are not always newsworthy. Nixon fell behind Kennedy in the surveys of early to mid-summer when the Massachusetts Senator changed his status from aspirant for the nomination to one of the two final contenders for the Presidency. The tasks for Nixon and Kennedy were the same as they were to be for Bush and Dukakis: Nixon had to convince voters that his election would translate into the equivalent of a third Eisenhower term, while Kennedy had to alleviate the doubts about his abilities that still existed among many voters because of the vagueness of his image and convince them that he was the man who could bring about the necessary change that the nation supposedly wanted.

The major difference between these two elections was that the challenger of 1960, Kennedy, successfully addressed his image problems and eventually convinced voters to view him as the preferred agent of change, while the challenger of 1988, Dukakis, failed on both counts. The surrogate of 1988, Bush, finally persuaded voters that a third term for the retiring incumbent was preferable to the change proposed by the challenger, while the surrogate of 1960, Nixon, failed to make such a case. Kennedy effectively countered the strongest doubts about his image, that of his youth and inexperience and that his Roman Catholic religion might affect his actions as President. In the televised debates he assured a number of voters who were skeptical about his lack of qualifications for the Presidency when he appeared to be at least the equal of Nixon. He successfully addressed the religious problem during his address to the Greater Houston Ministerial Association in which he spoke of the need for the separation of church and state. Finally, his themes that an upcoming generational change could lead the effort to "get the country moving again" helped convince enough voters that the election of a surrogate of the popular Eisenhower was not the preferable response to the beginning of a new decade.

Dukakis failed to provide a convincing rationale for his candidacy and left voters to choose between himself and four more years of Reagan through a Bush Presidency. The Bush strategists dominated the rhetoric of the campaign from this point and helped fill the gaps in the vaguely defined Dukakis image. They attacked Dukakis about several issues that they believed would help retain the support of many of the independents and Democrats who had voted for Reagan. Dukakis did not respond effectively to most of the attacks. By the time the campaign ended, Bush had depicted Dukakis as unwilling and incapable of addressing problems relating to crime, patriotism, national defense, or the environment. When given a choice of continuing with the proven record of the Reagan years versus the poorly defined and uninspiring promises and personality of Dukakis, many of the voters who were targeted by the Bush campaign voted for him.

As the challenger in 1968, Nixon faced problems that were similar to those of Kennedy and Dukakis. After he emerged as the Republican frontrunner during the early months of the campaign year, Nixon sought to define himself as an experienced statesman who could lead the nation out of its current difficulties. His reemergence as the leader of his party and the promise that he held out for victory were reassuring to many of his fellow partisans, particularly in light of the divisiveness that had existed among Republicans during the Goldwater campaign. The juxtaposition of the consensus-building coverage of Republicans and the dissensus-oriented reporting about Democrats by television news media during the summer months of 1968 aided Nixon in seizing the lead from Humphrey in national surveys. The combination of the choice of a surrogate as the standard bearer of the presidential party and the emergence of a unifying leader from an extensive field of individual candidates in the opposition party had once again helped create a campaign in which the challenger appeared headed toward certain victory.

Humphrey faced problems that were far different and much more difficult to overcome than those of the other two Vice Presidents. Unlike Nixon and Bush who were surrogates of strong and popular incumbents, Humphrey was the surrogate of a weak incumbent who probably would have been defeated had he sought another term. Humphrey could not have won the election if his main strategy had been to convince voters of his intentions to extend the Johnson administration for another four years. Nixon sought to convince voters of that possibility. Instead, Humphrey tried to run as a partial surrogate of Johnson. In late September he said he would stop the bombing of North Vietnam if elected. This was the first clear indication of Humphrey's intentions to pursue an alternative approach to the war. While he attempted to make a major departure from Johnson in this one important policy area, Humphrey campaigned to extend the far more popular social welfare components of Johnson's legacy. Johnson had enjoyed his greatest popularity and subsequent electoral triumph as a strong incumbent in 1964 when voters identified him as the heir of John F. Kennedy and as the architect of the Great Society programs. Humphrey wanted to recreate this aspect of the two previous Democratic administrations and extend it into a third one. He sought to create a public image whereby he appeared to voters as the surrogate of the Lyndon Johnson of 1964 and 1965. He nearly succeeded in his endeavor.

The combination of voter uncertainties about Nixon and the increase in support for the partial surrogate Humphrey almost reversed the Nixon lead. Far too many voters were beginning to see the "Old Nixon" during the concluding days of the campaign. Humphrey gained steadily throughout October and eventually came within one percentage point of overtaking Nixon. Nixon managed to retain his lead and win the election by successfully exploiting several of the divisive social issues that had risen to prominence in the late 1960s. These issues included the insecurities that had developed among a great number of white voters about increases in crime, changing race relations, and the emergence of a so-called counterculture among middle class college students. Nixon attained and held the support of enough working class, suburban, and southern voters to win the election by appealing to this "great silent majority" for support against the trends of the decade.

Despite their efforts to address the doubts of skeptical voters and to maintain their promising summertime leads, all three challengers lost support during the final days or weeks of their campaigns. The sharpest decline, of course, was that of Dukakis. After a month of complacency following his nomination, Dukakis found that his lead over Bush had been replaced by a 4-point deficit. A Gallup survey of August 21, taken shortly after the Republican national convention, showed that Bush had regained his lead of the primary election season and now led Dukakis by 48 percent to 44. Dukakis fell even further behind throughout the remainder of the campaign. By mid-September he trailed Bush by 8 points, 49 percent to 41, and eventually lost the election by that same margin, 54 percent to 46.

Challengers Kennedy and Nixon avoided the eventual fate of Dukakis and maintained their diminishing leads long enough to win their elections. The last Gallup survey taken before the 1960 election showed Kennedy's lead had narrowed to only one point, 49 percent to 48, while the final Gallup survey in 1968 indicated that Nixon's lead over Humphrey had declined to only 2 points, 42 percent to 40, with Wallace at 14 percent. The final results of both elections were even closer than these polls suggested. Kennedy attained 49.7 percent of the final popular vote compared to Nixon's 49.5, while Nixon defeated Humphrey by a margin almost as small, 43.4 percent to 42.7.

State and Regional Partisanship

The combination of the short-term electoral effects that derived from the interplay of incumbency and television with the long-term effects of partisan alignments produced one final victory for the Roosevelt coalition in 1960, albeit by a reduced margin. Kennedy won most of the states and electoral votes in two of the nation's four major regions, the Northeast and Southeast, while Nixon dominated the Midwest and West. Kennedy's strongest region was his native Northeast where he carried nine states. In doing so, he virtually restored the same state-level coalition that had supported Roosevelt in 1940 and 1944. He carried every state in the region other than Maine, New Hampshire, and Vermont. Roosevelt had lost only Maine and Vermont in each of his two final victories. Kennedy's success also reversed the misfortunes that the Democrats had been suffering in the Northeast since Roosevelt's time. In 1948 Truman won only Massachusetts, Rhode Island, and West Virginia. Stevenson fared even worse; he carried only West Virginia in 1952 and lost every state in 1956.

With the help of Lyndon Johnson, Kennedy retained the support of the Democratic coalition that existed within the Southeast during the 1950s. He carried seven states: Alabama, Arkansas, Georgia, Louisiana, North Carolina, South Carolina, and Texas. This corresponded with Stevenson's performance in the two preceding elections. Stevenson won eight states in 1952: Kentucky, Mississippi, and every one that Kennedy carried other than Texas. He retained six of them in 1956, failing in Kentucky and Louisiana. With the exception of Mississippi, which voted for an unpledged slate of segregationist electors in 1960, Kennedy carried every southeastern state that had voted for Stevenson in both 1952 and 1956. In contrast, most of the states that abandoned the Democrats in 1952 remained Republican in 1960. Virginia, Florida, Tennessee, and Oklahoma, which were also Roosevelt's weakest states in the region, voted Republican for the third consecutive time in 1960.

Kennedy won only four midwestern states but restored the Roosevelt coalition in the region, once again by reduced margins in the popular vote. He carried Illinois, Michigan, Minnesota, and Missouri, the same four midwestern states that voted for Roosevelt in 1944. Kennedy could not restore the Democratic coalition in the West however. The western realignment toward the Republicans in 1952 remained intact. Kennedy won only three states—Hawaii, Nevada, and New Mexico—and Hawaii was voting in a presidential election for the first time.

The effects of televised incumbency interacted with more volatile patterns of state-level partisanship in 1968 and helped bring about the end of the series of Democratic victories that had marked presidential elections since the 1930s. The addition of the 1964 southeastern regional realignment to the western one of 1952 provided a foundation for this Republican victory. The electoral weaknesses of Humphrey, as the surrogate of an unpopular incumbent, combined with these more long-term changes and provided the context for the Nixon triumph. In addition to winning the election, Nixon also fashioned a Republican presidential majority in 1968 that has resurfaced in several elections since that time. Despite the closeness of the popular vote, Nixon recorded a lopsided victory in the electoral college. He carried thirty-two states while losing to Humphrey in only thirteen states and the District of Columbia and to Wallace in five states. Once again, Nixon's weakest region was the Northeast. This time he carried two of the states that he won in 1960—New Hampshire and Vermont—while adding two others, Delaware and New Jersey. Nixon's two strongest regions were the Midwest and West, just as in his previous effort. He restored the same state-level coalition that supported him in 1960 as he carried every state in these two regions except for Michigan and Minnesota in the Midwest and Hawaii and Washington in the West.

The Southeast was the only region that had a competitive outcome involving all three candidates. Nixon was the strongest and garnered the electoral votes of seven states. He built his coalition on much the same base that initially emerged for Eisenhower in 1952 while making some important additions. He carried the same five states that he won in 1960: Florida, Kentucky, Oklahoma, Tennessee, and Virginia. He then became the first Republican since Herbert Hoover in 1928 to carry North Carolina. Nixon also kept South Carolina, which voted for Goldwater in 1964, in the Republican column. He could not win the remaining Goldwater states, however, and lost Alabama, Georgia, Louisiana, and Mississippi to Wallace. Wallace also won in Arkansas. Finally, Humphrey was the weakest candidate in the region as he managed to carry but one state, Lyndon Johnson's Texas. This was the poorest performance in the Southeast by a Democrat during the twentieth century thus far and clearly demonstrated that the Roosevelt coalition no longer existed in the region.

The size of George Bush's victory in 1988 was greater than those of either Kennedy or Nixon. Bush garnered 53.4 percent of the popular vote, while Dukakis attained only 45.6 percent. Bush also carried forty states and a majority of the electoral vote in each of the four regions. His greatest support came from the Southeast where he won each state by a popular vote tally that exceeded his national showing. While his victories in several northeastern states were close, Bush won every state there except Massachusetts, Rhode Island, New York, West Virginia, and the District of Columbia. He lost three midwestern states—Iowa, Minnesota, and Wisconsin—and three western ones—Washington, Oregon, and Hawaii.

These outcomes reflected recent electoral patterns but also suggested that some important changes might be under way in state partisanship. The modern Republican tendencies of the Southeast resurfaced once again and helped make Bush the third nominee of his party to carry every state since 1972. The northeastern vote was also fairly consistent with recent trends. Dukakis ran stronger in six states then he did nationally: Maryland, Pennsylvania, and the four mentioned above. These six states consistently vote more Democratic than the nation. The votes of most midwestern and western states were also consistent with past trends, but several states departed from these trends and gave some indications that the Reagan coalition might be losing its appeal. The Republican strongholds of Indiana, the Great Plains states of Kansas, Nebraska, North Dakota, and South Dakota, and the eight states of the Rocky Mountains provided Bush with some of his greatest margins of victory. However, four states in these two regions that rarely vote Democratic supported Dukakis. The midwestern states of Iowa and Wisconsin and the Pacific Northwest states of Oregon and Washington usually vote Republican and tend to depart from that practice only when Democrats win the Presidency or lose it narrowly. The fact that each of these states voted Democratic in a year in which the Republican ticket was winning a national election by nearly 8 percentage points was indeed unusual. This behavior suggested the possibility that some realignment toward the Democrats might be taking place in these two regions. Indeed, several other Republican-leaning states from these regions voted for Bush but did so by margins that were below national trends. Included here are California, Colorado, Illinois, Montana, and New Mexico. This trend toward the Democrats accelerated in 1992 when Clinton carried a majority of the states from both the Midwest and West.

Conclusions

Several patterns appear to be common to elections in which the incumbent retires, and they will probably resurface in future years. By far the most important is the succession of the Vice President to the nomination of the presidential party. As an officeholder and candidate, the modern Vice President has an invaluable opportunity to present himself to his fellow partisans as the one leading surrogate of the retiring incumbent who is most deserving of their support. While his selection as successor of the incumbent is not deterministic, a Vice President will most likely possess the political skills required for manipulating the advantages of his position and winning the nomination. The Vice President does not need to be more skilled at campaigning than any or all of his rivals. Instead, the advantages of his position will likely enable him to defeat a candidate of equal or perhaps of even greater personal ability. It is now a monumental accomplishment for any candidate whose political base rests outside the executive branch of the national government to defeat the Vice President for the nomination of the presidential party.

Surrogate incumbency appears to be a mixed blessing for Vice Presidents however. It has proven to be a powerful asset when one seeks a nomination, but it is often of limited value in general elections. Many of the independent voters and opposing partisans who supported the retiring incumbent in one or more of the preceding elections are less willing to support the Vice President in the current one. They do not necessarily see him as either the equal of the retiring incumbent or as a candidate who necessarily has presidential abilities.

The Vice President will quite likely face the dilemma that the opposition party will nominate a candidate who is a relative newcomer to national politics and who appears to have excellent prospects of winning the general election. In all likelihood, this newcomer will vanquish many unknown or slightly known rivals during the nomination campaign, will unite his party, will project a favorable public image through the televised reporting of his accomplishments, and will be offering an undefined but appealing change from the status quo. Moreover, the issues that divided his party during its recent defeats will probably have subsided by the current campaign. This development will likely contribute to the creation of a political context that helps make the rise of such a unifying new leader possible. The challenger should benefit from the theme of consensus building that is often implicit in televised news reporting of the actions of front-running candidates in the closing stages of modern nomination campaigns. The tendency of television news media to personalize their reporting will provide invaluable opportunities for this challenger to appear as a competent and popular champion from outside of government who has overcome the personal obstacles that stand between himself and the nomination. This implicitly supportive coverage should provide this challenger with invaluable opportunities for developing support from voters other than his own partisans. He will accomplish much of this during the summer months of the election year after he first begins to appear as the last remaining alternative to the Vice President.

The nomination of such a candidate is not necessarily a political disaster for the Vice President however. It creates a unique opportunity that he can exploit and thereby attain an electoral triumph that might not have otherwise been possible. The challenger may appear to have widespread support at the beginning of the general election campaign, but some of that support is likely to be illusory and might very well decline by the end of the campaign. The Vice President may be able to provide the necessary assistance for facilitating that decline. The vaguenesses of image and promise that helped make the nomination of the challenger possible may also provide the circumstances that help the challenger fail in the general election. Voters may become far more skeptical about the challenger as doubts that were submerged during the televised showing of partisan unity and personal triumph that marked the national convention period resurface during the final weeks of the campaign. George Bush exposed the illusory nature of the appeal of Michael Dukakis through his attacks on the undefined imagery of his rival. Dukakis failed to counter the attacks effectively, saw his public image redefined, and watched his efforts end in defeat.

There does not seem to be any particular advantage that is inherent for either the Vice President or his challenger in an election with a surrogate incumbent. The outcomes of all three elections were decided by an interplay between a short-term factor—the responses by the candidates to the unique dilemmas and opportunities that derived from their respective vantage points of surrogate and challenger—and a long-term factor, the existing alignments of partisanship. Future elections in this category will likely be decided in the same manner. The limitations of the Vice Presidency as a strategic position from which to win a general election are apparent from the fact that Nixon and Humphrey both lost, while Bush looked very much like a loser during the summer months. In contrast to this, there were sufficient opportunities for the Vice Presidents to win, as many voters remained skeptical about the qualities of the challengers.

Challengers Kennedy and Nixon (1968) reassured voters about their strengths, while Dukakis failed to make such reassurances. Of the surrogates, Bush convinced voters that he would continue Reaganism, while Nixon (1960) could not make a convincing argument that his administration would perpetuate the popular aspects of the Eisenhower years. In contrast, Humphrey nearly disassociated himself from the unpopular foreign policies and political unrest associated with Johnson and almost won after promising to return the nation to the more favorable domestic policies of the earlier Johnson years. Finally, all three elections were influenced by the existing patterns of partisanship. The Democratic party remained the majority party in presidential elections in 1960, which contributed to the Kennedy victory. The Democratic majority no longer existed by 1968, however, and Nixon led a developing Republican presidential majority into national office. George Bush led that same partisan majority in 1988 to what may prove to be one of its final electoral victories.

4

Elections with Weak Incumbents

Despite the opportunities for electoral success that it often provides, presidential incumbency is not a virtual guarantee of reelection. Three incumbents have failed to win second terms since 1960, while a fourth, Lyndon Johnson (1968), withdrew from a campaign in late March that appears, in retrospect, to have been developing very much like the unsuccessful efforts of the other three. Gerald Ford (1976), Jimmy Carter (1980), and George Bush (1992) joined William Howard Taft (1912) and Herbert Hoover (1932) as the only incumbents defeated for reelection during the twentieth century. Each of the unsuccessful incumbents of modern times, Johnson included, was in political trouble at the outset of his reelection bid. None of them had effectively consolidated power within his own party. As a consequence, all were unable to manipulate televised news coverage of the Presidency and project images whereby voters could see them performing in the statesman role. Their troubles were reflected in the fact that each was opposed for renomination by at least one prominent member of his own party: Ford by former Governor Ronald Reagan (California), Carter by Senator Edward Kennedy (Massachusetts), Bush by conservative commentator Patrick Buchanan, and Johnson by Senators Eugene McCarthy (Minnesota) and Robert Kennedy (New York). Both Ford and Carter repulsed their challengers but paid very high prices while doing so. Each won the nomination but only after engaging in many months of intense competition and only after defeating his challenger at a divisive and televised national convention. Ford and Carter soon found, as they lost their respective general elections, that their renomination triumphs had been Pyrrhic victories. While Bush defeated Buchanan relatively early during the primary season and ended this challenge to his renomination, the divisions that Buchanan exposed among Republicans eventually opened the door to the independent candidacy of Ross Perot. Perot attracted the support of many Republicans and other conservatives who had supported Bush in 1988 and thereby helped bring about the end of Bush's Presidency.

This chapter discusses elections with weak incumbents. While the campaign of 1968 had no incumbent after the withdrawal of Johnson, it began very much like those of 1976, 1980, and 1992. Therefore it is considered part of the campaign in which Johnson was a candidate.

Television news media responded to the challenges of these incumbents by directing most of their attention during the nomination season to three candidates: the incumbent, his leading adversary, and the one aspirant who emerged, or whom they helped to emerge, as the front-runner for the nomination of the opposition party. Their reporting helped weaken the reelection prospects of the incumbents while enhancing those of the opposition party. They directed more attention to the campaign events of the presidential party than to those of the opposition and used the incumbents as the anchors by which they reported and interpreted most of those events. This practice derives from the importance that television news media give to the Presidency as a news source. Their treatment of the reelection efforts of these weak incumbents differed from their treatment of the efforts of the strong incumbents however. They depicted these incumbents as politicians fighting for power rather than as statesmen leading the nation. Their reporting affected how many viewers of televised politics perceived and interpreted events, evaluated the personal abilities and promises of the candidates, and eventually cast votes.

In contrast, their reporting of the campaigns within the opposition party enhanced that party's electoral prospects. They directed much of their attention to the front-runner, downplayed or ignored the other candidates, and used that front-runner as the anchor by which they defined these campaigns. Shortly after the votes were cast in the earliest primaries and caucuses, television news media began treating the actual or alleged front-runners—Carter (1976), Reagan (1980), and Clinton (1992)—as if they had already won their respective nominations. They also illustrated these front-runners as presidential-appearing alternatives to the beleaguered incumbents.

A caveat is in order here. I assume that the individuals who challenged the nominations of the incumbents were rational politicians motivated by the goal of electoral victory: they would not have run unless they believed that their chances of success were realistic. That they did run indicates they had fairly strong reasons for believing that the incumbents could be or would be defeated for renomination or reelection. It is important to raise this argument because of some recurring features in elections with weak incumbents. Each incumbent faced a challenge for the support of his own partisans that eventually left that constituency divided while denying him the invaluable opportunities of appearing presidential and statesmanlike before television audiences. The prolonged and divisive campaigns that followed were also the leading political news stories of the first months of these election years. Such campaigns cannot occur within the presidential party unless political figures of the stature of Reagan, Kennedy, and Buchanan are willing to oppose the incumbent. This is because television news media face some difficulty in finding other means of describing the political troubles of an incumbent. The candidacies of prominent intra-party rivals of the incumbents provide them with these means.

Prolonged and divisive nomination campaigns contribute to the defeat of incumbent Presidents by enhancing already existing mass perceptions of their personal and political limitations. Another word of caution however: one should view such campaigns more as symptoms of the initial weaknesses of incumbents than as primal causes of election outcomes. If an incumbent's own partisans perceive him to be strong and effective, they will not challenge his renomination. The candidacies of Reagan, Kennedy, and Buchanan were not the leading causes of the eventual defeats of Ford, Carter, and Bush. The incumbents were already weak at the beginning of their campaigns for reelection.

The three challengers who eventually defeated these weak incumbents relied upon the combination of two political factors in winning the Presidency. The first was the apparent willingness of many of their own partisans to set aside past differences and unite behind a candidate who held out the promise of victory. The second was that televised news coverage of the campaigns enhanced the generation of consensus within the opposition party and behind the candidacies of these initial front-runners. The combination of these two factors enabled the challengers to clinch their nominations very early during the primary election season, even though they each faced a number of major rivals. Each had become virtually unbeatable for the nomination by the end of April. Their emergence as the new leaders of their respective parties by such an early date allowed them sufficient time to generate an even broader following from among voters other than their own partisans. Carter, Reagan, and Clinton thereby opened up substantial leads over the weak incumbents by the conclusions of the national conventions, and they never relinquished them during the remainder of their campaigns.

PRESIDENTIAL PARTY NOMINATIONS

Overview

Each weak incumbent began his reelection effort while enjoying relatively limited public approval. Moreover, each failed to reverse this shortcoming during his campaign. Gerald Ford, the first chief executive not elected as either President or Vice President, entered office without a strong personal following and was not particularly successful at building one. Jimmy Carter won office in a close election in 1976 but expanded his popularity during his first year in office. His support declined by the late summer of 1979, however, at times becoming about as low as that of any President since public opinion polling developed in the 1930s. George Bush carried forty states in his successful attempt for the Presidency in 1988 and eventually saw his approval rating reach an all-time high for modern chief executives during the early months of 1991 shortly after the conclusion of the Persian Gulf War. His support declined substantially during that same year, however, as he seemed unable or unwilling to confront a growing recession.

All three were responsible for some of their own difficulties but in other instances were unlucky victims of unusual circumstances. Gerald Ford came into office by a most unusual method, the forced resignation of a President and Vice President, but this alone did not damage his popularity. His support was initially high, perhaps partly because many people were grateful that Nixon had finally left office. Ford lost much of his support in September 1974 after pardoning Nixon. The pardon was a choice by Ford, much as the escalation of the Vietnam War was a choice by Lyndon Johnson. Ford was responsible for the political problems he faced because of the Nixon pardon, but, as with Johnson, he was also the victim of problems not of his own making. The nation underwent both high inflation and high unemployment during his administration, although the causes for these problems rested more with the policies of Johnson and Nixon and with various foreign events that were somewhat beyond Ford's control. Much of the inflation derived from Johnson's decision to finance an expanded war without an offsetting tax increase. The larger federal deficits that resulted eventually contributed to higher inflation. The Arab-led oil embargo of 1973 that developed as a consequence of the Yom Kippur War between Israel and its neighbors contributed to even more inflationary increases and helped to expand the already high rate of unemployment. Ford may not have been directly responsible for these economic difficulties, but he was the recipient of much of the public's wrath.

Ford also had the problem that he was an unelected President who had attained office without the benefit of a national campaign. In all other elections of the television age, the incumbent was either running for a second term or was attempting to win on his own after a previous campaign as a vice presidential candidate. Without such experiences, Ford lacked the opportunities usually enjoyed by incumbents for developing the political and personal ties with state party leaders and activists that often enhance the consolidation of partisan power. Consequently he began his effort in 1976 with a relatively weak political position for an incumbent. In fact, public opinion surveys of early 1973 indicated that few Republicans considered that Ford, at the time a member of Congress, would even be a candidate in 1976. Far more preferred Ronald Reagan.

Jimmy Carter faced many of the same economic problems of Ford when he sought reelection in 1980. Inflation by now had reached such unpopularly high levels that many voters began venting their anger upon the most available political candidates and ballot issues. There was, for example, an unusually large amount of turnover in the Senate during the late 1970s and early 1980s. Twenty new members were elected in 1978 alone. Taxpayer revolts were at their zenith in 1978 as well. A number of ballot measures that sought to place lower limits on state and local taxes succeeded, with Proposition 13 in California being the most famous and far-reaching. Voters there slashed local property taxes by more than one-half and placed major limits on the size of future increases.

The economic troubles derived from Carter's policies to some extent, but also to events for which Carter had not been primarily responsible. Carter's fiscal policies encouraged even more inflationary increases. His intent was to reduce unemployment, but instead he acquired even more inflation and higher interest rates by 1979. This inflation was enhanced by yet another oil embargo by Middle Eastern nations, particularly Iran, where in 1979 the pro-American government of Shah Reza Pahlavi was overthrown and replaced by an anti-American Islamic fundamentalist regime led by Ayatollah Khomeini. The new Iranian leaders began an oil embargo that eventually contributed to a rapid acceleration of fuel prices in the United States and to a subsequent decline in Carter's popularity. Carter also suffered the public consequences of other Iranian-related events, including the hostage crisis. His inability to attain the release of fifty hostages taken from the embassy in Teheran and held captive for 444 days helped to undermine his prospects for reelection by making him appear incapable of protecting American interests and personnel abroad.

The hostage crisis resulted both from Carter's choices and from circumstances over which he had little control. Carter precipitated the crisis by allowing the Shah to receive medical treatment in the United States. This decision prompted angry Iranian mobs to attack the embassy and seize its personnel. However, Carter may have been a victim of the general hostility of the new Iranian regime to the United States, a problem that owed its origins to several decades of American governmental support for the Pahlavi dynasty. Carter was also a victim of television news coverage of the hostage problem. Televised reports such as ABC's nightly program, "America Held Hostage," and Walter Cronkite's evening litany where he concluded his telecast by saying, "and that's the way it is on day 'xyz' of the hostage crisis," drew continuing attention to the unending and apparently insoluble hostage story. This coverage helped undermine public support for Carter and contributed to his eventual downfall by making him appear incapable of resolving the crisis.

George Bush faced the same pattern of contradictory circumstances in 1992. He enjoyed mixed success during his Presidency as his far-reaching accomplishments in foreign policy were offset by some noticeable disappointments in domestic and economic matters. Perhaps *Time* magazine accurately captured this dilemma when it chose Bush as its Man of the Year for 1990. The authors depicted Bush as a man with two faces—one smiling, one frowning. The smiling Bush was the President successful in foreign policy; the frowning one was the man of limited domestic achievements.

George Bush held office during the most abrupt period of change in American relationships with foreign powers since the conclusion of the Second World War. The bloc of Eastern European communist nations that had been this nation's adversary for more than four decades ceased to exist between 1989 and 1991, thus ending the Cold War and ushering in a new and somewhat uncertain era. The period of uncertainty and threat that marked American foreign policy for more than four decades finally came to an end. Bush supplemented the enhanced public esteem that he enjoyed because of the end of the superpower rivalry with a military victory over Iraq. This one-sided victory boosted American self-esteem, a need that developed from the failures of Vietnam.

While these foreign successes may have bolstered Bush's popular standing, growing economic difficulties eventually led to his defeat. The recession that began in late 1991 and lasted through most of 1992 was particularly severe in California, New England, and the Midwest. California was also affected by declines in defense spending and soon incurred a state governmental budget crisis of monumental proportions. The economic difficulties translated into major political problems for Bush as many voters began to believe that he had few available solutions.

Bush's economic problems, as those of previous weak incumbents, resulted partly from his own efforts and partly from circumstances over which he had limited control. The costs of many of the policy initiatives of the twelve years of the Reagan and Bush administrations were becoming due. The taxing and spending changes of the first years of the Reagan administration stimulated the national economy and induced significant growth and low inflation by the time of the 1984 presidential election. Reagan and Bush gained accordingly, as their reelection theme of "It's Morning in America" demonstrated. The prosperity of the 1980s was purchased at a tremendous price however. The effects of the soaring federal deficits created when taxes were lowered while defense spending was increased and that of entitlement programs left untouched began to be felt. High interest rates, low investment, and a general stagnation in wages and purchasing power left the economy anemic. Economic growth was the lowest in decades, while bankruptcies and foreclosures soared. The new outlays made necessary by the scandal in the savings and loan industry and the increasing proportion of the national budget spent for interest on the accumulated debt reduced the discretionary spending that might have helped reduce the effects of the recession.

The recurring deadlock between the Democratic Congress and the Republican Presidency presented Bush with additional political problems that eventually helped to undermine his support even among his own partisans. Bush had to reach an accommodation with his partisan adversaries in late 1990 in order to gain congressional approval of his budget. He accepted some tax increases and in doing so broke a major campaign promise of 1988: "Read my lips—no new taxes!" This angered many conservatives who were already skeptical about what they perceived as Bush's lack of interest in their social agenda. Conservative anger over Bush's preoccupation with foreign issues and his breaking of the tax pledge encouraged Pat Buchanan to enter the campaign.

The television news media practice of linking major social problems with the Presidency eventually helped to undermine the political strength and public support of these incumbents. One should realize, of course, that television news media did not create the aforementioned problems. They illustrated their effects and implicitly suggested that the incumbents were unwilling or unable to alleviate them. The televising of the apparent failures of an incumbent to resolve the problems of his time indicates to viewers that he lacks the personal and political skills required for the Presidency. Moreover, the coverage also reflects an underlying fact about the incumbent: he has not consolidated power within his own party.

The decline in Gerald Ford's public support, as with that of Lyndon Johnson, was also enhanced by televised news reporting of controversial events. Television news media often depicted Ford as though he was not in charge of events and, with help from some comedians, as an awkward and stumbling fool who could not lead. They reported about a number of economic difficulties, such as the sharp price increases for gasoline and home heating oil, and attempted to link them to Ford's policies. Ford was one of the first public victims of the new problem of "stagflation," the combination of high inflation and low growth. The rather abrupt change from the more optimistic economic conditions of the preceding decade caused much uncertainty and anxiety among voters after 1973. The oil embargo of that year served as a symbolic turning point for popular viewpoints about the condition of the American economy. Not only were energy prices greater than before, but public perceptions were developing in which a long-term decline in the American standard of living seemed to be unfolding. Inflation was high, unemployment was growing, energy was scarce, and real wages were no longer increasing. There was growing talk about an era of limits to growth and prosperity. There was increasing apprehension that American influence might be diminishing throughout the world. The hostility of Arab nations to the United States and the unsuccessful conclusion of the Vietnam War, where the nation's policy had finally failed, led to uncertainty and pessimism among large numbers of people.

Ford became President after the two greatest failures of modern American government, Vietnam and Watergate. The damaging effects of these two failures did not fall merely on the actors involved however: government itself was damaged. Public faith in the ability of government to deal honestly and effectively with matters of foreign policy and political ethics suffered accordingly. Ford seemed increasingly incapable of dealing with problems that derived from pessimism and lack of faith. The controversy relating to his pardon of Nixon compounded this difficulty, helped undermine his personal standing with voters, and contributed to his eventual demise. The weakness of his leadership and the apparent depth of the troubles in the Republican Party because of the fall of Nixon and the worsening recession became all too obvious to Ford's potential rivals when the party suffered unusually large setbacks in the elections of 1974. The Republicans lost fifty-two seats in the House of Representatives and several governorships, including those of California and New York. Shortly afterwards, Reagan announced that he would seek the presidential nomination.

While Jimmy Carter began his administration amidst considerable optimism, he was unable to accomplish two necessary political and communicative tasks: alleviating the nation's economic problems and manipulating the symbolic dimensions of the Presidency in ways that might have created a strong personal following. After an initial period of relatively high public support, Carter underwent a gradual decline in his popular standing. This decline began after he announced his energy program, which he called the "moral equivalent of war," in the first half year of his Presidency. Carter then faced a variety of dilemmas, some of which were not unlike those encountered by Ford. The economic problems that troubled Ford increased in magnitude during the Carter years.

Carter was an outsider in Washington. He was elected in 1976 partly because of his appeal that he was not part of the Washington establishment in which the public had lost faith. While this appeal was helpful in Carter's initial election efforts, it later appeared to be more of an obstacle in his efforts at governing. Carter did not enjoy the broad-based personal relationships with many power holders in Washington that his predecessors had often used for advancing their own agendas. He seemed to lack the skills for constructing the coalitions necessary for attaining congressional approval and public support for new policies. This was unfortunate for him in that his Democratic Party controlled both houses of Congress during his administration. Carter's political and public relations failures soon enhanced highly publicized divisions among Democrats. Liberals were angered over what they considered as failures to focus on many of the problems they wanted addressed. Television news media all too readily transmitted this anger to their audiences. The divisions had become fairly extensive by 1978, as seen in the enthusiastic reception in Memphis for Edward Kennedy at the Democratic Party's second national convention held during an off-year election.

Carter was also relatively ineffective at manipulating the symbolic dimensions of the Presidency. Initially he had developed a fairly strong following from Southerners and had the necessary emotional bonds with them for maintaining a following. Unfortunately his inability to persuade voters that he had answers to the nation's more intractable problems undercut his support even in his native region. His problems became even more evident during the late summer of 1979 when he delivered a nationally televised speech about the problems of the American spirit, his so-called "malaise" speech. This speech did not produce the intended effect; instead it made Carter appear even more ineffective and uninspiring as a President. His popularity declined even further afterwards. Perhaps the final blow to his popular standing was the series of events resulting from the turmoil in Iran.

Television news media illustrated many aspects of the loss of power and public esteem by George Bush. While Bush attained many far-reaching successes in foreign policy and acquired substantial news coverage of his accomplishments, television news media also reported about some of the apparent limitations of those same accomplishments. For example, while Bush's most significant accomplishment was the military victory over Iraq, television news media responded to the aftermath of the war by illustrating what had not happened—the elimination of Saddam Hussein from power. They depicted the plight of the Kurds and the devastation that Hussein was inflicting upon them as if advancement of the political autonomy of that people was a problem Bush had neglected. Moreover, continuing news coverage of Hussein's resistance to the efforts of United Nations inspectors to begin dismantling his capacity to create weapons of mass destruction and of the environmental and political problems of Kuwait underscored the theme that the United States and the Bush administration had not completed its mission.

The conclusion of the Cold War would appear to be a time for rejoicing, but the tendency of television news media to focus attention on controversies and conflicts encouraged reporting about the many difficulties arising from the successor regimes of the defunct communist political systems of Eastern Europe. Ethnic strife in the former Soviet Union and Yugoslavia, and the uncertainty and potential instability that existed in those disintegrating nations, reduced some of the euphoria that had become widespread in the immediate aftermath of the end of the Cold War. Eastern Europe no longer seemed peaceful and unthreatening now that communism had fallen. The potential for war and continued strife seemed very real. Finally, the continuing emphasis by television news media upon the still unresolved Iran-Contra scandal and the possible role that Bush might have played in it as Vice President suggested that Bush had not been honest about his involvement. This variety of themes in television news reporting suggested that Bush was not a political mastermind who could manage foreign affairs in ways that would prove valuable for the best interests of the nation.

Television news media also focused attention on the effects of the recession and on other domestic problems during the later Bush years. They broadcasted many reports about unfavorable economic statistics and trends and about the various job losses that affected well-known corporations and entire industries and regions. Some of these reports emphasized the personal suffering of people in such key primary and general election states as New Hampshire and California. Bush was also damaged by the televising of the events and violence associated with the Los Angeles riots of 1992. This coverage had much the same effect, albeit by reduced margins of voter insecurity, that coverage of the riots of the late 1960s had upon the popularity of Lyndon Johnson. Bush appeared uninterested in or incapable of alleviating the underlying social and economic problems that contributed to these particular riots or to the personal and economic difficulties of so many other people in different parts of the nation.

The Campaigns

The candidates who eventually opposed these incumbents had problems of their own that derived from their unique vantage point of intraparty challengers of incumbent Presidents. Even weak incumbents have extensive support among their fellow partisans. If a challenge to the renomination of an incumbent is to have any chance of succeeding, it must by necessity be united behind one strong candidate who enjoys widespread appeal within the party or behind one powerful and far-reaching issue. A broad array of challengers and causes will very likely enhance an incumbent's renomination prospects by dividing the available political support and television news coverage among many aspirants. The incumbent will almost certainly defeat each of his many challengers in turn and quite likely will do so very early during the primary election season. A unified challenge can direct television news coverage and public attention to one candidate, however, and can eventually help personify that candidate as the challenge itself. The old adage "united we stand, divided we fall" applies to candidates who challenge the renomination of an incumbent. This requisite unity of candidates and causes occurred in all four of these elections and thereby made significant challenges possible.

Ronald Reagan and Edward Kennedy enjoyed enough respect among their fellow partisans at the beginning of the 1976 and 1980 election years respectively that their candidacies soon eclipsed the possible plans of others and consequently provided this unity. Both Reagan and Kennedy were major national spokesmen for the leading ideological components of their parties. Their candidacies virtually assured that the incumbents would face significant challenges.

Reagan, as Governor of California (1967–75), emerged as the nation's most prominent conservative spokesman among Republican officeholders after Barry Goldwater lost the 1964 presidential election. Reagan was an unsuccessful candidate for the 1968 nomination but left little doubt at the time that he eventually planned to seek the Presidency again at a later date. He remained popular within his party and was particularly well received by his fellow partisans as the keynote speaker at the 1972 national convention. In fact, many Republicans at the time looked upon Reagan as the probable successor of Richard Nixon in 1976, long before the Watergate scandal forced Nixon from office. Some people have even speculated that Ford's ascension to the Presidency in 1974 initially deterred Reagan's probable candidacy. Shortly after Ford's selection of Governor Nelson Rockefeller (New York) as Vice President, Reagan became the most prominent Republican leader outside the executive branch of the national government.

Kennedy enjoyed substantial respect among Democrats in 1980. As the last of the Kennedy brothers, he became the subject of considerable speculation as a future presidential nominee after Robert Kennedy's assassination. Surveys in the years immediately after 1968 indicated that Democrats preferred Kennedy more than anyone as their nominee in 1972 and 1976. While Kennedy inherited substantial popularity because of the careers of his brothers, he also established a national reputation of his own as a leading spokesman in the Senate for liberal causes. He was the most well-known Democratic officeholder during the late 1970s who did not have a post in the Carter administration. His popularity among Democrats remained strong throughout the years after his brothers' assassinations, despite the fact that he did not seek the Presidency before 1980.

Unlike Reagan or Kennedy, Patrick Buchanan and Ross Perot had never held public office. The two were such prominent political figures, however, that their decisions to oppose George Bush virtually guaranteed that the incumbent would face a significant challenge to his prospects for a second term. Buchanan had been a leading spokesman for Republican conservatives for many years and had once served as a speechwriter for Richard Nixon. Prior to his efforts in 1992, he worked both as a nationally syndicated columnist with editorials appearing in a number of newspapers and as a commentator for Cable News Network (CNN) where he regularly argued the conservative perspective on "Crossfire." In both forums, Buchanan emphasized a growing theme of opposition to the direction of the foreign and domestic policies of the Bush administration. Conservatives had been among the most vigorous opponents of communism throughout the Cold War years, but Buchanan urged them to take a more isolationist stance now that the Eastern bloc powers no longer offered a credible threat to American interests. His positions were similar to those of pre-Cold War conservatives who had often resisted the attempts of Wilson and Roosevelt for a more internationalist American role in world affairs. Moreover, his writings also reflected the disappointments that conservatives had with Bush over the issues that comprised their social agenda.

While Perot had a number of associations with past and present Republican administrations, his readiness to use his vast financial fortune in a presidential bid posed a threat to Bush. Many independent candidates of past campaigns lacked the requisite funds for placing their names on the ballots in all fifty states and for conducting effective nationwide campaigns via television. Perot's wealth helped make him substantially more threatening to the two-party dominance of elections than previous independent candidates, including George Wallace and John Anderson. Those earlier candidates lacked the financial resources to compete effectively against the partisan candidates as the general elections developed. Their support, as measured in national surveys, declined during the final weeks of their respective campaigns. This decline was not to be the fate of Perot.

One issue that needs addressing is why these challengers opposed the incumbents when they did. It would seem that a far more promising approach would have been to wait until the next election when the current incumbent would no longer be a candidate. In fact, Robert Kennedy initially made such a decision in late 1967 before Lyndon Johnson announced that he would not seek another term. Nonetheless, the challengers apparently believed that their aspirations might very well incur critical and perhaps fatal setbacks if they chose to forego the current campaign. The incumbents seemed to be vulnerable Presidents whose tenure in office could very likely conclude during the upcoming election. If any of the challengers decided against opposing the incumbent and waited until the next election instead, he could very well sacrifice his best opportunity of winning the Presidency.

The experiences of Reagan illustrate two recurring dilemmas that potential challengers of weak incumbents tend to encounter. First, it was quite possible that Ford would lose the election to a Democrat, as eventually happened. The potential Democratic President might then become a strong and popular incumbent and be virtually unstoppable in his quest for a second term. Reagan would then find that a campaign against a strong Democratic incumbent in 1980 would be considerably more difficult than challenging the weak Republican incumbent of 1976. The possible replacement of the vulnerable Ford by a powerful Democrat would then create the additional problem for Reagan that his next serious chance of winning the Presidency would be delayed for at least eight years. During this interim, new rivals within both the Republican and Democratic parties might rise to national prominence with the likely consequence that support for a future Reagan Presidency would decline. It might well have been too much of a gamble for Reagan to wait for eight years as the Republican presidential nominee-in-waiting until a strong Democratic incumbent retired.

Reagan's second dilemma was that another Republican might enter the campaign and defeat Ford for the nomination and then win the general election. This result could also delay Reagan's chances for at least eight years while allowing enough time for new rivals to gain prominence in both parties. One can see the seriousness of this dilemma in the lesson of Robert Kennedy. After Kennedy initially decided against opposing Johnson, the little-known McCarthy announced his candidacy and soon developed a personal and political following from much of the same constituency that Kennedy had been courting. McCarthy nearly eclipsed Kennedy by the time the New York Senator finally entered the campaign. If Kennedy had not announced his candidacy within days after the New Hampshire primary, as he eventually did, his chances for the Presidency might very well have been compromised for several years. From Kennedy's perspective, Johnson might fail to win another term, but someone else, such as McCarthy or Humphrey, or even Nixon, would become President. Johnson's successor, Democrat or Republican, might then prove far less vulnerable to defeat in 1972 than Johnson did in 1968. Certainly, Nixon demonstrated in 1972 that a new incumbent can expand his support considerably within four years.

Edward Kennedy encountered many of these same dilemmas. While his effort helped demonstrate that important personal obstacles could deny him the Presidency in any election, his response to the context of 1980 appears correct. By losing the election, Carter helped provide Reagan with the unique opportunities offered by the televised Presidency for developing a strong personal following. Reagan used those opportunities and won a sweeping reelection triumph. New Democratic leaders such as Gary Hart, Jesse Jackson, Walter Mondale, and Michael Dukakis gained national prominence after 1980. Kennedy would have needed to oppose them, in addition to Reagan or George Bush, if he had delayed his candidacy until 1984 or 1988. He must have realized that 1980 was his best opportunity of winning the Presidency since he chose to oppose the relatively weak Carter.

While his chances of winning the Republican nomination were quite limited, Buchanan appeared to find 1992 relatively promising. Since no other party leader was willing to oppose Bush, Buchanan had a unique opportunity to emerge as the leading spokesman for conservative resentment of the administration and its policies. By this time, there was already an extensive list of possible contenders for the 1996 nomination. If Buchanan had decided to postpone his candidacy until that time, he would have to face one or more of the leading members of the Bush administration including Vice President Dan Quayle, and the Secretaries of State, Defense, and Housing and Urban Development—James Baker, Dick Cheney, and Jack Kemp. Other candidates might also emerge from Congress and state government. Even if he could defeat all these potential rivals, Buchanan might then have to face an incumbent Democrat in the general election. For Buchanan, it was either 1992 or not at all.

Perot would eventually run as an independent, but his background and ideology suggested that he would attract more votes from Republicans and other conservatives than from liberal Democrats. He would likely garner more votes from people who supported Bush in 1988 than from those who backed Dukakis. His best chance of winning as an independent would be in a year with a weak contender from each of the major parties. Not only did Bush appear vulnerable, but the Democrats seemed to be offering little or no prospects of nominating a strong candidate and of making an effective challenge. While the Democrats eventually chose Clinton and won, such an outcome was not apparent at the beginning of the year. It was also quite possible that new contenders could emerge in both parties by 1996 and thereby make an independent candidacy by Perot even more difficult. As with Buchanan, Perot seemed to find his best chance in 1992.

The campaigns within the presidential party were the kinds of struggles that television news media often enjoy reporting. Each was a two-candidate affair from the outset with a beleaguered incumbent matched against a prominent spokesman from one of the party's ideological factions. Television news media encountered no difficulty in finding both an available front-runner to serve as the anchor for their coverage and a leading adversary whom they could depict as the antithesis of that front-runner and as the personification of his political obstacles. The incumbent and his one challenger filled these roles quite early and quite effectively.

It is a monumental, and thus far unaccomplished, task for anyone to defeat an incumbent President for renomination during the television age. Except perhaps for a most unusual period, such as during the days that preceded the resignation of Richard Nixon from the Presidency in August 1974, the majority of a President's own partisans do not abandon him. This is particularly true during renomination campaigns. The public relations opportunities that derive from televised incumbency are so overwhelming that Presidents almost always enjoy powerful advantages over their rivals. A President's most intensive detractors are not his own partisans but members of the opposition party. A President's own partisans, who quite likely supported him in the preceding election, are the most supportive of all voters of his renomination effort. While it is true that several incumbents encountered strong resistance from within their own party, that resistance was limited. Nomination challengers of incumbent Presidents generally cannot convince a majority of their own partisans that they can better represent the party than the incumbent. Consequently all have failed to win. A majority of a President's partisans will support him for renomination either because they agree with him on the critical issues of the day or because they believe that he will be a stronger candidate in the general election or both.

The difficulty of denying renomination to an incumbent is reflected in the results of the New Hampshire primary. Despite the fact that the state's leading newspaper, the *Manchester Union-Leader*, endorsed Ronald Reagan, Gerald Ford turned back the efforts of his challenger by about 3 percentage points. Jimmy Carter, buoyed by his earlier and substantial victory over Edward Kennedy in the Iowa precinct caucuses, defeated Kennedy by more than 10 points. After a slow start because of his failure to realize the strength posed by the challenge of Pat Buchanan and the depth of resistance to his renomination, George Bush defeated his conservative rival by a margin of 53 percent to 37. This proved to be the high point of the campaign for Buchanan as he failed to attain 37 percent of the vote in any other primary.

The incumbents never relinquished their leads. Both Ford and Carter added to their New Hampshire successes by winning enough support in the primaries and caucuses that followed that they secured first ballot victories at their respective national conventions. Neither had an easy time however. While both won frequently after New Hampshire, each encountered some major setbacks that indicated the difficulties they would eventually face in their general election campaigns. The existence of strong opposition to their nominations reflected the extent of the widespread voter dissatisfaction that would finally drive them from office. Despite the fact that they repulsed their rivals, Ford and Carter could not force Reagan and Kennedy to end their candidacies before the national conventions. Reagan and Kennedy generated enough support to sustain their efforts until that time.

Ford defeated Reagan in three consecutive primaries during the weeks immediately after New Hampshire. He won in Massachusetts on the first Tuesday in March, Florida on the second Tuesday, and Illinois on the third. Each victory was by a margin greater than that of New Hampshire. The Reagan effort began to look as if its days were numbered, but it was not over yet. Despite his victories, Ford had to face Reagan in North Carolina, and this turned out to be Ford's greatest loss of the campaign. With the assistance of conservative Senator Jesse Helms, Reagan defeated Ford and won his first victory of the year. The defeat did not pose any great danger to Ford's nomination—he would have many future triumphs—but it hurt him because it helped prolong the Reagan challenge until the national convention. If Ford had won North Carolina, it is quite possible that he could have forced Reagan to abandon his candidacy.

Ford and Reagan divided the remaining primaries, with Ford winning the ones in the Northeast and Midwest and Reagan capturing most of those in the Southeast and West. While Reagan could rely on his victory in North

Carolina as an opportunity to sustain his candidacy until the convention, there was never any chance that he could actually defeat Ford. Ford won the nomination by slightly more than one hundred delegate votes, 1187–1070.

The aftermath of the New Hampshire primary of 1980 bore many similarities to the Ford-Reagan struggle. Carter defeated Kennedy in several additional primaries and was never in any great danger of losing the nomination. Like Ford, however, he could never generate enough support to defeat Kennedy in every state and drive him out of the race. After New Hampshire, Carter and Kennedy engaged in a battle in Illinois that would decide the nomination. Illinois is the largest midwestern state and in 1980 was the key to that region. Jane Byrne, the mayor of Chicago, chaired Kennedy's efforts, while Richard M. Daley, her leading rival, headed those for Carter. Carter recorded a sweeping triumph with nearly two-thirds of the Illinois vote. His victory was large enough virtually to eliminate any chance that Kennedy might win the nomination. Unfortunately for Carter, it did not end Kennedy's efforts. Kennedy continued his campaign and won enough primaries (New York, New Jersey, Pennsylvania, and California) to perpetuate his challenge until the national convention.

While both Ford and Carter won the support of enough delegates to assure their nominations, each spent far too much time at his party's convention fighting in yet another battle with his rival. These battles were the most televised political events of the initial days of the conventions. Ford and Carter won, but in doing so lost any opportunities of manipulating television and appearing presidential. Instead, each seemed more like an unstatesmanlike candidate who was involved in some unsavory political manipulations of party rules in order to defeat his rival.

In what turned out to be a major surprise, Reagan named his running mate before losing the roll call vote when he selected Senator Richard Schweiker (Pennsylvania) for that honor. He then sought to overturn party rules and require all candidates (i.e., Ford) to name their running mate prior to the balloting for President. Reagan hoped that Ford would lose support once he announced the identity of his running mate. This questionable logic and Reagan's limited delegate strength were insufficient to overturn the rules and derail Ford's candidacy. Ford turned back the challenge and went on to win the nomination two days later.

In a similar late challenge, Kennedy entered the Democratic convention with only about half the number of delegates as Carter but sought to alter the likely outcome. He hoped that his victory in the California primary would encourage hundreds of delegates previously supportive of Carter to abandon the President and support him for the nomination instead. In order to gain this new support, Kennedy proposed a change in the convention rules that would allow all delegates to be freed from the commitments they had made at the time of their selection. Thus freed, they supposedly would vote for Kennedy. Kennedy failed to understand that most of the delegates who supported Carter did so freely. His efforts failed badly, but he succeeded in making Carter look very unpresidential. Carter's victory in this procedural vote indicated that he enjoyed the support of a majority of the delegates. Like Ford in 1976, Carter won the nomination two days later.

Unlike Reagan and Kennedy, Buchanan could not generate enough support to sustain his efforts through the entire primary season. Nonetheless, he was a challenger of some political strength. His first challenge of Bush, and what turned out to be his strongest, came in the New Hampshire primary. Throughout his campaign in that economically depressed state, Buchanan charged that Bush had failed to advance conservative goals. Bush survived the challenge, but the size of the Buchanan vote reflected the depth of Republican and conservative disenchantment with his administration.

Although Buchanan lost, he continued his efforts. The outcomes of the four primaries that occurred within the two weeks immediately after New Hampshire indicate the importance that television and other media play in transmitting the events of one state throughout the nation. Although he did not commit comparable amounts of time and money to any of these later elections, Buchanan virtually duplicated his New Hampshire support in each state. He acquired between 30 and 36 percent of the vote in Maryland, Georgia, South Dakota, and Colorado. Regardless of the magnitude of his efforts or of the geographic location of any primary, Buchanan was capable of garnering about one-third of the vote in any given state. He had exposed a significant political fact: a large minority of Republicans were dissatisfied with George Bush and were willing to vote for another candidate.

Buchanan's challenge weakened after this initial round of primaries however. He had not actually won in any state. Moreover, he did not appear to have a remote chance of ever winning a primary. All available surveys indicated that Buchanan would likely attain at most only about one-third of the vote in any state. In addition, Republican rules did not require states to distribute their delegates proportionately among the candidates. Instead, the winner of the Republican primary in many states receives all or most of that state's delegates. Buchanan had won only a small number of delegates thus far. There was even a strong chance that he would fail to win enough delegates to have his name placed before the convention. A candidate needed the support of a majority of the delegates from five individual states in order to have his name placed in nomination.

Buchanan's support soon weakened. His percentage of the vote declined to only about 20 to 25 percent of the vote from any state in the next group of primaries. He soon withdrew, although his name remained on the ballot in a number of states. His withdrawal posed a dilemma for television news media as it left them without a nomination campaign to report. By this time, the campaign among the Democrats was over, with Clinton the certain winner. Three months remained before the onset of the conventions. This was much too long a period of time for television news media to lack action, pictures, competition, and controversies about which to report, particularly considering the extent of their financial investment in this campaign. They needed a new rival for Bush. The time had come for them to begin directing their attention to Ross Perot.

Television news media reported about the Perot campaign in a most unusual manner. Perot indicated in February that he was considering an independent effort. By early April, he was actively encouraging the efforts of "volunteers" to circulate petitions in order to place his name on the ballot in each state. As discussed earlier, television news media prefer for the complete campaign picture to be reduced to only three major contenders by this time, the obvious winner of the nomination of one party and a front-runner and his leading adversary in pursuit of the other. Clinton was the obvious nominee of the opposition, but the embattled incumbent, Bush, suddenly lacked a leading adversary. Ross Perot did not fit into any of these three predefined roles. If Buchanan had been a stronger candidate, television news media could have reported about his efforts in a prolonged struggle for the Republican nomination with Bush and then could have illustrated the futile attempts of the eventual winner, Bush, in a battle with Clinton.

In most election years, the three major candidates of late spring reduce to only two nominees by the conclusion of the national conventions, but Perot was apparently planning on being a major player in the general election. Television news media faced an unusual dilemma in reporting about his efforts at this stage of the campaign. The nominations were resolved, but the general election campaign, regardless of whether it would involve two candidates or three, was not yet ready to begin. Television news media responded by treating Perot at this time as if he were a candidate for the Republican nomination and then began depicting him as the equivalent of the leading adversary of George Bush. They placed him in essentially the same role they had placed Reagan and Kennedy in 1976 and 1980, as the antithesis of the embattled incumbent and as the personification of his political obstacles.

For several weeks during the latter stages of the primary election season and in the weeks that preceded the conventions, television news media directed much of their political reporting to a campaign that apparently existed between only two candidates, Bush and Perot. They either ignored or downplayed Clinton throughout much of this time. There was a similar theme in much of their reporting. They would begin many of their politically related narratives by illustrating the effects of some economic problem and of how Bush had not resolved it. Afterwards, they would direct attention to Perot and focus on the promises for improvements that he seemed to be making. The contrast was vivid. While Bush appeared incapable of alleviating the problem of the day, Perot seemed ready and able to solve it. If Bush was unable to break the partisan deadlock of Washington, Perot, the champion of non-partisan justice from outside the Beltway, would "just do it." For all intents and purposes, the campaign for the Republican nomination was still under way. Perot actually gained survey leads over both Bush and Clinton during this time.

The Democratic convention was a significant turning point. Within days of its convening, television news media began directing more attention toward Clinton. He was now starting to appear more as the leader of the opposition party than as a candidate in quest of the nomination. Perot attained much less coverage and soon lost his survey lead. Within two weeks, Perot declined by about 15 percentage points in the national surveys and dropped into third place.

The Perot effort had provided television news media with what they prefer at this time in an election year—the appearance of a contested battle for the nomination of one party. While the outcome of the Republican nomination was not at stake, the two protagonists seemed to be fighting each other for much of the same constituency, the support of Republicans and other conservatives. Perot did not win this battle or the general election, but he and Buchanan together accomplished what Reagan and Kennedy had done individually in their earlier campaigns. They exposed the political weaknesses of the incumbent and denied him invaluable opportunities for manipulating television news coverage and appearing presidential. The main difference between the two previous elections and that of 1992 was that two candidates were needed in the latter to accomplish what one candidate did in each of the others. The effects were the same however: the incumbent was damaged enough so that a presidential-appearing challenger from the opposition party would defeat him in the general election.

These divisive and prolonged nomination battles, when combined with the personal and institutional strengths and weaknesses of the various incumbents, helped make the presidential party the focal point of much of the televised news coverage during the first half of these years. Due to the centrality of the Presidency in government and politics, the incumbents were the anchors that television news media used for reporting and interpreting events. They described the events of these campaigns from the vantage point of an incumbent fighting for renomination against a formidable challenger who could not defeat him but whom he could not drive from the race. They also depicted the challenger as the antithesis of the incumbent rather than as a candidate in his own right. The challengers attained meaning mostly in relation to the incumbent they were opposing.

In an earlier chapter, I argued that television news media depicted the strong incumbents as performing more in the role as President leading the nation than in the role of candidate seeking renomination and reelection. This pattern of reporting implicitly encouraged viewers of televised politics to perceive the incumbents as more qualified and statesmanlike than their general election opponents. Those opponents often appeared to those same viewers as little more than political combatants who were unqualified to hold the nation's highest office. These mass perceptions were reversed in the weak incumbent elections. Television news media treated the actions, utterances, policy proposals, and travels of the weak incumbents more as campaign devices for gaining advantages over rivals than as actions related to governing. The effect of this reporting was to deny weak incumbents the opportunities enjoyed by strong incumbents for appearing presidential and as statesmen whose behavior is "above politics."

While the strong incumbents successfully manipulated the presidentially centered coverage of television news into an invaluable reelection asset, the weak incumbents found this coverage to be an immense political liability. The weak incumbents were, of course, able to create imagery on a number of occasions whereby they appeared in the governing role, but television news media also illustrated them far too frequently for their own political good as troubled politicians unable to vanquish their rivals for the nomination. Television news media reported about these incumbents' unpresidential-appearing actions because such actions placed the incumbents' efforts at consolidating power into the realm of actions, pictures, competition, and controversy during an election year, which is the domain of television news. The weak incumbents had not consolidated power within their parties prior to their reelection efforts in the more subtle ways that the strong incumbents had done. Instead, their highly publicized power-seeking efforts created the unfortunate side effects of making them appear more as politicians than as statesmen and eventually cost them the immeasurable opportunities that derive from televised incumbency of appearing more qualified than their opponents. They were reduced to the status of ordinary candidates and to very controversial ones at that. These embattled incumbents spent so much time in divisive nomination campaigns that by the time they finally defeated their challengers, they appeared to lack the qualities that Americans have come to expect of their chief executive.

OPPOSITION PARTY NOMINATIONS

Overview

The beginnings of the campaigns for the nomination of the opposition party in the nine elections that comprise the television age have generally been quite similar. Many aspirants were seeking the nomination, but the winner was not readily apparent. This occurred regardless of whether the incumbent was challenged (1976, 1980, 1992) or unchallenged for renomination (1964, 1972, 1984) or of whether he was constitutionally ineligible for another term (1960, 1968, 1988). Despite this multiplicity of candidates and uncertain outcomes, the campaigns in those six elections where the incumbent sought reelection conformed to two very consistent but highly divergent scenarios. Television news media encouraged these scenarios through their reporting and interpreting of campaign events.

In those elections where the incumbent was unchallenged for renomination, television news media discouraged the early resolution of the opposition party's nomination behind the candidacy of the initial front-runner. As discussed earlier, they helped perpetuate a two-candidate campaign until the national convention and even continued directing additional news attention to many controversies within the party in the weeks initially after the convention. Their reporting appears to have damaged the opposition's chances in the general election. However, in those elections where the incumbent faced important competition for renomination, television news media engaged in vastly different patterns of coverage and in so doing encouraged quite the opposite results. Their reporting enhanced the early resolution of the nomination behind the candidacy of the initial front-runner. This had the effect of strengthening the party's electoral prospects.

Regardless of whether the incumbent was challenged for renomination or not, television news media identified a front-runner for the nomination of the opposition party early in each campaign and then used that front-runner as the anchor for future news emphasis. They placed different emphasis upon the campaigns of the front-runner's rivals, however, depending upon the existence of a challenge to the renomination of the incumbent. When the incumbent was strong and unchallenged, television news media directed much of their political coverage to the events within the opposition party. They placed considerable attention upon one of the front-runner's rivals and virtually ignored the others. Moreover, they often depicted that rival as the antithesis of the front-runner. In contrast, television news media either disregarded the front-runner's opponents almost entirely in the elections with weak incumbents or reported about several of them but without distinguishing any one in particular as the leading adversary. Certainly, they did not depict any of the front-runner's rivals as his antithesis. Such a reporting pattern of inclusion and omission of the front-runner and his rivals respectively helped expand the front-runner's familiarity and eventual support among primary election voters and simultaneously prevented similar opportunities from developing for his rivals. This, in turn, enhanced the front-runner's electoral prospects by facilitating the relatively rapid elimination of his rivals from contention, by enabling him to unify his party quite early during the election year, and by encouraging viewers of televised politics to see him as a qualified alternative to the embattled incumbent.

The amount of broadcast attention that television news media devote to the opposition party's campaign in any given year is inversely related to the amount of attention they devote to the campaign of the presidential party. In fact, the opposition party receives less news attention than the presidential party in those years when the incumbent is opposed for renomination. Television news media appear to prefer that one divisive and prolonged nomination campaign occurs between two role-playing candidates, a front-runner whom they use as their anchor for reporting and interpreting of campaign-related events and his one leading adversary. When such a campaign exists within the presidential party, they find few incentives for attempting to perpetuate one within the opposition party. Television news media do not necessarily need two such campaigns. The existence of one allows them sufficient opportunities for directing attention to the action, personalities, competition, and controversy that they believe will help satisfy their goal of attracting and retaining audiences with marginal viewers of politics.

The opposition party in the three elections with weak incumbents attracted numerous candidates for its nomination who represented virtually all of that party's regions, factions, and institutional bases. Jimmy Carter was one of twelve aspirants for the 1976 Democratic nomination, while Ronald Reagan faced six Republican rivals in 1980. Bill Clinton was one of six Democrats who sought the Presidency in 1992. The Democratic field of 1976 contained six liberal contenders, including Senators Birch Bayh (Indiana) and Frank Church (Idaho), former Senator Fred Harris (Oklahoma), Congressman Morris Udall (Arizona), former Peace Corps director Sargent Shriver (Maryland), and Governor Edmund Brown Jr. (California). Five moderates, including Carter, Senators Henry Jackson (Washington) and Lloyd Bentsen (Texas), Governor Milton Shapp (Pennsylvania), and former Governor Terry Sanford (North Carolina), were among the contestants. The one conservative in the field was Governor George Wallace (Alabama). In addition to their ideological preferences and regional backgrounds, these candidates differed in their political experiences. Some were members of Congress, others were Governors, while yet others had served as executives in previous Democratic administrations.

The Republican contenders of 1980 were nearly as diverse with respect to institutional background, ideology, and geography. In addition to Reagan, the field included two Senators, Howard Baker (Tennessee) and Robert Dole (Kansas); two House members from Illinois, John Anderson and Philip Crane; and two Texans, George Bush and John Connally. Bush and Connally had held major executive offices under previous Republican Presidents, Reagan and Connally were former Governors, while both Bush and Dole had served as national chairmen of their party. Reagan, Crane, and Connally were conservatives, while Bush, Baker, Dole, and Anderson were more centrist in their views.

The group of candidates who sought the Democratic nomination in 1992 were also quite diverse with respect to ideology, geographic bases, and institutional backgrounds. This field included two southeastern Governors, Bill Clinton (Arkansas) and Douglas Wilder (Virginia); two midwestern Senators, Tom Harkin (Iowa) and Robert Kerrey (Nebraska); and two former officeholders, Paul Tsongas (Massachusetts) and Jerry Brown (California). Harkin hoped to mobilize organized labor and liberal interest groups, Brown attempted to generate a following through anti-establishment appeals, Wilder sought to build his political base from blacks and conservatives, Tsongas promised a more pro-business climate than those of previous Democratic administrations, while Clinton and Kerrey emphasized their political moderation and personal experiences as progressive leaders from relatively conservative states.

The size and composition of these fields affected the actions of the individual candidates. With the possible exception of Reagan in 1980, none was the acknowledged front-runner at the beginning of any of these election years and most were nearly unknown to a majority of voters. Each needed to devote considerable time and effort simply to becoming better known. Essentially they were candidates without constituencies. They spent much of their time and effort engaging in those very activities that television news media like to report about in depicting election campaigns as races: raising money, building organizations, generating name familiarity through personal appearances and media advertising, and attacking their opponents in many places and upon a wide variety of issues. Successes or failures in these activities often serve as guideposts that television news media use in reporting about the developments of races and candidates. The content of television news in all three years was dominated by reports of how effectively the candidates pursued those activities.

Television news media may have aided the opposition party by these patterns of reporting. They helped define political reality for their viewing audiences by depicting the abilities of the candidates to raise money, draw large crowds, and win primary elections as the important tests of leadership. They treated the candidates who excelled much more favorably than they treated those who failed. They also used the successes of early front-runners as yardsticks for judging the performances of the other candidates. This reporting encouraged the creation of a political context in which the front-runner acquired a fairly rapid and unified nomination victory over a field of generally unknown and uninspiring candidates who lacked their own constituencies. Primary election voters found few compelling reasons to continue supporting losers who seemed to be engaging only in futile bids against a presidential-appearing front-runner and eventually abandoned them.

The Carter Nomination of 1976

The campaign for the Democratic nomination of 1976 opened without an obvious front-runner. This was not to be the case for long however. With the help of television and other news media, the first electoral test of the year soon provided one. Party activists in Iowa attended over 2,500 precinct caucuses on January 19 for the purpose of electing delegates to attend county conventions scheduled for several weeks later. Television news media began their coverage of the nomination campaigns in earnest at this time by reporting extensively about the Iowa-related activities of the candidates but encountered some difficulties in doing so. First, there was no battle among Republicans. While the campaign between Ford and Reagan would eventually garner far more television news coverage than that among the Democrats, that campaign would not begin until the New Hampshire primary a month later because Reagan had decided to bypass Iowa. The absence of Reagan not only eliminated the possibility of a battle among Iowa Republicans over delegates but also diminished the chance that either of the Republican candidates would gain any substantial news coverage from the state. This gave the Democrats a virtual monopoly of the available news coverage.

In addition, none of the Democratic aspirants appeared stronger than the others. All were relatively unknown candidates without constituencies. This lack of a readily identifiable front-runner for the caucus vote created a problem for television news media in that it did not provide them with a readily available anchor on which to focus their political coverage. Instead, this absence encouraged them temporarily to disperse coverage among several candidates rather than to focus on one. In a sense, the race for the nomination had not yet begun.

The Iowa caucuses marked a major turning point in the campaign. While no candidate actually won, Carter did run better than any of the others by acquiring 27 percent of the total vote. Uncommitted finished in first place with 39 percent. Three additional rounds of voting remained in the selection of the state's national convention delegation. The aforementioned county conventions were to be followed several weeks later by conventions in each of Iowa's six congressional districts with a state convention to occur shortly afterwards. Many activists quite simply wanted more opportunities for exercising flexibility in these later rounds than would be possible from their commitment to a candidate in January.

While a number of activists were reluctant to endorse a candidate during the caucuses, television news media wanted a winner and decided that a victory by uncommitted was unacceptable. Consequently they declared Carter, despite his second place finish and limited support, to be that winner. This media-engendered declaration of success soon provided Carter with invaluable opportunities for attaining a bonanza in public relations payoffs. Television news media not only declared him the Iowa winner, but also named him as the national front-runner and provided him with such extensive coverage afterwards that he soon expanded his name familiarity with voters and then became the actual front-runner. After Iowa, Carter received more television news coverage than all of his nomination rivals combined, over 70 percent according to Doris Graber. This near monopoly soon distinguished him from the rest of the field. With a front-runner and anchor for future news reporting now available, television news media ceased depicting the campaign as a struggle among twelve little-known aspirants and redefined it as a battle between Carter on the one hand and his eleven rivals on the other. They did not identify any of the remaining eleven candidates as the one leading adversary of Carter but focused attention on virtually all those that still remained in the campaign. This lack of a single adversary upon whom voters could focus their attention aided Carter. He soon led his rivals in national surveys and shortly thereafter began a string of primary election victories that eventually made him the nominee.

Carter benefited from both the themes and images of television news coverage. This coverage illustrated him quite favorably as a Georgia peanut farmer, a former naval officer, a devout born-again Christian, and a successful modern governor of a southern state. This biographical attention had the effect of strengthening Carter's personal identification among voters and of thereby enhancing his chances of winning the nomination. Television news media did not direct comparable biographical attention to any of Carter's rivals during this time. The visual images of televised news showed Carter campaigning. These action-related pictures, particularly since they were not juxtaposed with pictures of a rival who would have appeared as his antithesis, helped Carter by indicating to viewers that he was overcoming the electoral obstacles that stood between himself and the Presidency and that he was both a winner and a leader.

Television news media personalized the campaign and made it into the story of Carter running for President, much like Theodore White had personalized the 1960 campaign as the story of Kennedy running for President. Carter became the central personality in the unfolding drama and was presented implicitly by television news media as a new leader who held the answers to the nation's difficulties that had apparently eluded Gerald Ford. A campaign thus defined became one that necessarily concluded very quickly. There were not enough well-known candidates other than Carter able to sustain a prolonged race for the nomination. Television news media had placed such little emphasis upon the other candidates that many voters knew little about them. Many viewers of televised politics saw these other candidates mostly as uninspiring aspirants for power who were unable to win primaries, raise money, or attain high survey standings. Consequently, Carter became virtually unstoppable in his quest for the nomination. He did suffer a few setbacks, however, but nonetheless continued receiving the highly favorable televised new coverage that helped him project the image that he indeed was a qualified alternative to the embattled incumbent, Gerald Ford.

One should not assume that Carter received all the news attention; some of his rivals received extensive coverage before the Iowa vote. In fact, some actually received more news coverage than Carter. One should realize, however, that much of this coverage occurred long before the people who are most susceptible to the influences of television gave much attention to the campaign and the candidates. Many of these people began paying attention after the casting of the first votes. At this formative time, television news media made Carter the anchor for their reporting and interpreting of campaign events, while they began downplaying or excluding his rivals from coverage.

The New Hampshire primary occurred five weeks after the Iowa caucuses. Television news media could now report about an intense Republican battle that was taking place between Ford and Reagan. This change of circumstances eliminated the Democrats' virtual monopoly of televised political news which they had enjoyed shortly before and after the Iowa vote and thereby reduced the amount of air time available for them. This loss of time had the ironic effect of helping Carter. By now, television news media were interpreting events related to the Democratic campaign from the perspective of how they might affect Carter. It was the other candidates, not Carter, who suffered from the loss of air time to the expanding Ford-Reagan campaign.

Carter soon made his media-proclaimed front-runner role a reality in New Hampshire as he won that primary with about 30 percent of the vote and defeated four rivals: Udall, Bayh, Harris, and Shriver. He suffered his first setback one week later after finishing fourth behind Jackson in Massachusetts while acquiring about 14 percent of the vote. Jackson had about 30 percent, approximately equal to Carter's support in New Hampshire. Television news media did not treat Jackson's victory with the same reporting intensity as they had treated Carter's earlier performances however. Jackson did not acquire anything comparable to the personalized coverage that Carter had already received, nor did he become the anchor for televised reporting of the campaign or even occupy the highly valuable role as Carter's leading adversary. In fact, televised coverage of Jackson faded within days. Jackson soon reverted to his post-Iowa role as one of Carter's many rivals for the nomination who in this instance had inflicted a temporary setback on the front-runner.

Shortly afterwards and throughout the remainder of March, television news media continued directing more of their attention to events within the Republican Party but focused their coverage of the Democratic race mostly upon Carter. Carter was now running in two southern primaries, Florida and North Carolina, where his main opponent was Wallace. These primaries pitted two candidates against each other who stood for contrasting views of the role that the South should play in national politics. Carter constructed a biracial coalition and carried both states and, for all intents and purposes, ended Wallace's candidacy. Carter had overcome yet another obstacle on his way to the White House.

Throughout both April and May, television news media divided their electoral coverage between the intense two-candidate battle within the Republican Party and the story of Carter running for and winning the Democratic nomination. With Wallace out of the way, the Democratic front-runner had to confront two additional obstacles in April and two more in May, and he successfully overcame both of them. The first was the liberal Udall in the Wisconsin primary in early April, while the second was Jackson, the favorite candidate of organized labor. He faced Jackson in the Pennsylvania primary during the latter part of the month. Carter won both primaries, thus causing Jackson to withdraw and Udall to reduce his future efforts. Once again, the front-runner was beating the obstacles.

May brought out two additional challengers for Carter. Church won the Oregon primary, while Brown captured the one in Rhode Island. Carter was not deterred by either of these defeats, however, nor did television news media change the focus of their coverage. Neither of Carter's new rivals attained anything like the extensive and favorable coverage that Carter acquired earlier during the year. The news coverage of the victories by Church and Brown was more akin to that of Jackson after the Massachusetts vote, intense but fleeting. Within days after these primaries, television news media continued to direct attention to the Ford-Reagan battle in one party and to the continuing story of Carter running for President in the other.

The campaign ended shortly afterwards. Carter defeated Udall and Church in the Ohio primary during the first week of June. After receiving some key endorsements from Edward Kennedy and Chicago Mayor Richard J. Daley within days of his Ohio victory, Carter had enough delegate support to claim the nomination. While he faced many obstacles and overcame most of them, at no time did he need to confront the political and media problem of having one leading adversary who could expose his limitations and undermine his candidacy; instead he had a multiplicity of adversaries. One week he was competing with Bayh, Shriver, Harris, and Udall, the next week with Jackson, followed by Wallace, Udall, Jackson again, then Church, Brown, Udall, Church, and so on. Viewers of televised politics could not direct their attention to any one leading adversary of Carter as they could with Ford's rival, Reagan, in the Republican campaign. Without such an adversary who could unite the opposition, the television-enhanced momentum of the front-running Carter was virtually unstoppable.

Media professionals place great importance upon the value of objectivity. They consider themselves to be observers of events, not participants in them, and believe that their reporting and interpreting of events is detached and impartial. One can, from this perspective, defend the extensive news coverage about Carter's performance in Iowa and in the primary elections that followed because he had, after all, beaten his rivals and news reporting involves the coverage of events. While one may argue that this coverage was objective, the actual reporting of political events often influences their outcome. For television news media to focus attention on Carter, even if only to report that he received more votes than anyone else, was to distinguish him from the other candidates and to redefine the reality of the campaign to those persons whose knowledge of it derived primarily from television news. When they went beyond this and proclaimed Carter as the front-runner, and then made him the anchor for future news reporting and interpretation, they helped create the self-fulfilling prophecy discussed earlier. The media-proclaimed front-runner eventually became the actual front-runner and then went on to win the nomination.

The Reagan Nomination of 1980

The campaign for the Republican nomination in 1980 was, in many ways, quite similar to the Democratic one of 1976 but was shorter in duration because of the initial existence of a front-runner. Ronald Reagan was the acknowledged front-runner at the beginning of the year because of his candidacy four years earlier and because of his continued actions as a national spokesman for conservative political goals. The fact that Reagan had already acquired the front-runner designation at the outset meant that television news media did not need to wait until after the first votes were cast before they could direct their coverage toward one candidate and use him as the anchor for reporting and interpreting the events of the campaign. Reagan became the leading contender for the 1980 nomination shortly after Gerald Ford suffered his general election defeat in 1976, and he assumed the role of front-runner in early 1977.

Much as they had done in 1976, television news media began their daily coverage of the 1980 nomination campaigns in January and directed most of their initial attention to the first electoral test of the year, the Iowa caucuses. Their coverage of the campaign within the opposition party differed from that of 1976, however, because of the prior existence of a front-runner. They did not have to help create one. Reagan began the year leading his rivals in a variety of indicators that television and other news media generally use for estimating the political strength and likely fate of individual candidates. He led his rivals in public opinion surveys, in the number and importance of endorsements from elected officials and prominent party leaders, and in funds raised. Consequently, television news media made Reagan the anchor for their coverage from the beginning of the year and interpreted events from the perspective of how they might affect his chances. The predominant theme in their coverage of the campaign was the continuing story of Reagan running for President against a disparate field of six other candidates.

An important similarity between the campaigns of 1976 and 1980 was the existence of an intense battle within the presidential party between two role-playing candidates, the weak incumbent and his one leading adversary. The race between Carter and Kennedy attracted a considerable portion of the broadcast time available for election-related news. This reduced the portion of air time available for Republicans. Reagan, like Carter four years earlier, gained from this as he continued receiving substantial coverage because of his front-runner role. The other candidates, as with Carter's earlier rivals, were the political victims of this reduced time and suffered accordingly. None of them ever received the intense and long-term coverage that would have given them the opportunities to expand their support and advance to the roles of either front-runner or leading adversary.

With the exception of a temporary setback suffered in Iowa, Reagan led his rivals throughout the campaign and drove all of them from the field by mid-May. Bush managed to pull an upset of sorts when he finished first in Iowa by scoring a narrow victory over Reagan. Both Bush and Reagan garnered about one-third of the vote. Bush hoped to expand the momentum he gained from this victory with a public relations bonanza of news coverage comparable to Carter's. Unfortunately for him, this was not possible in the context of the 1980 campaign. With the Democratic battle limiting the broadcast time available for Republican candidates and with Reagan virtually monopolizing much of that, Bush gained only a few days of fleeting publicity and then reverted to the role of one of front-runner Reagan's many rivals. He did not achieve anything comparable to the extensive biographical and personalized coverage that Carter acquired after his Iowa success. Television news media treated the results of Iowa more as a setback for Reagan than as a success for Bush and speculated often about how that might affect Reagan's chances. They actually devoted very little of their air time to introducing Bush to the American public as they had done with Carter. While not particularly useful to Bush at this time, this pattern of media coverage paid important political dividends for him in 1988 when, as front-runner, he lost the Iowa caucuses to Dole. Television news media, true to form, were far more concerned with discussing the implications of Bush's setback than in evaluating Dole's victory.

One can see an example of the central role that television news media continued giving Reagan as the anchor for their political coverage in the reporting that followed a candidate debate in New Hampshire. The most important segment that they selected for national coverage was when Reagan said, "I paid for this debate," after some of the debate promoters attempted to turn off the microphones when Reagan brought all of the other candidates except Bush into the debate. The promoters had wanted the debate limited to just Reagan and Bush.

Reagan soon ended any chance that Bush might actually win the nomination when he countered with a sweeping victory in the New Hampshire primary. Reagan attained about one-half of the popular vote, virtually doubling Bush's total. The campaign concluded within weeks. Two of Reagan's six rivals, Baker and Dole, withdrew shortly after their New Hampshire defeats, while Connally ceased his efforts in mid-March after suffering an overwhelming loss to Reagan in the South Carolina primary. Crane was the next to leave the field, doing so in late March after losing his home state of Illinois to Reagan. The next to depart was Anderson, but he did so in order to pursue an independent candidacy. He had attracted some fairly strong support in several primaries in the Northeast, particularly Massachusetts, although much of that support came from independents rather than Republicans. This encouraged Anderson to seek the Presidency as an independent. His refocused candidacy left Bush as Reagan's final nomination rival. Bush concluded his campaign shortly afterwards because of his poor showings in several states, including Texas. With Bush's departure, Reagan was assured of the nomination.

The television news coverage of this campaign bore a striking similarity to that of the Democrats in 1976 in that Reagan appeared to face a multiplicity of candidates rather than one leading adversary as he progressed through the primaries. While Bush became his main opponent in Iowa, several candidates in addition to Bush were his adversaries in New Hampshire. These included Anderson, who began gaining national prominence at this time, and both Baker and Dole, who already enjoyed it. Connally, meanwhile, staked his hopes on a strong performance in South Carolina which he thought might open the door to his possible sweep of the southern states. He declined to accept federal matching funds and the spending limitations that accompanied them in order to concentrate his money in South Carolina in hopes that he could beat Reagan there and generate enough momentum to carry the rest of the South. While his efforts on his own behalf were in vain, he helped Reagan in the sense that he eclipsed Bush and prevented him from becoming Reagan's one leading adversary.

After disposing of Connally, Reagan took his campaign to Illinois where Anderson and Crane were his major opponents. With those candidates gone, he faced Bush once again in a campaign that had finally narrowed to only two candidates. By now, it was too late for Bush. Reagan had already developed such widespread support that he easily drove Bush out of the campaign in Texas.

Throughout the campaign, Reagan's major opponent, like Carter's in 1976, changed constantly. Bush was the initial rival, but later Baker and Dole had their chances. Soon it was Connally, then Anderson and Crane, and then Bush again. As they had done in 1976, television news media did not focus attention on any one of the other candidates for a long enough period of time to allow that candidate any real opportunities to emerge as Reagan's one leading adversary. Instead, each of these candidates ended up playing the role of one of the many political obstacles that the front-runner needed to overcome on his way to the White House. With the existence of such a campaign context, it was only a matter of time before Reagan overcame each of his rivals and won the nomination.

Shortly after the New Hampshire primary in both 1976 and 1980, television news media defined the composition of the complete campaign picture, that is, the small number of candidates who remained as viable contenders for either of the party nominations, as limited to three role-playing candidates. These roles were that of embattled incumbent, his one leading adversary for the nomination, and the front-runner for the nomination of the opposition party. For all intents and purposes, television news media considered the nomination campaign within the opposition party to be resolved with the earliest caucus and primary voting. Meanwhile, they considered the campaign for the nomination of the presidential party as just beginning. Shortly after the first votes of 1980 were cast in Iowa and New Hampshire, television news media depicted the complete campaign picture as a battle with Jimmy Carter, Edward Kennedy, and Ronald Reagan fulfilling those respective roles.

George Bush came very close to becoming the one leading adversary of Reagan and perhaps could have attained that role if Carter had been a strong incumbent and thereby unchallenged for the Democratic nomination. The lack of a strong challenge to Carter would have made more broadcast time available for the Republican campaign. Television news media would almost certainly have shown a greater interest in encouraging a battle between two role-playing Republican candidates, if there had not already been a parallel campaign among the Democrats. The amount of television news coverage that non-front-runner candidates for the nomination of the opposition party receive after a first or second place finish in the Iowa caucuses or New Hampshire primary appears to be related far more to the context of their election year and the needs of television news media for encouraging or discouraging a contested nomination battle than to the total percentage of the vote they receive. While there are two different party nomination campaigns in any election year, television news media tend to focus more attention on the one they consider to be more newsworthy. In years when strong incumbents are candidates, the more newsworthy campaign occurs within the opposition party. Television news media seek to perpetuate these campaigns, for without them no races would exist for either nomination. This partly explains why McGovern and Hart received so much televised news coverage after their second place finishes behind front-runners Muskie and Mondale in their respective election years.

The more newsworthy of the nomination campaigns in 1976 and 1980 were in the presidential party however. There was little need for television news media to attempt to extend the campaign until the national convention, and they did not do so in either year. This partly explains why they found that a Bush victory in Iowa with 33 percent of the vote over front-runner Reagan was less newsworthy than a victory with 27 percent by front-runner Carter in 1976. Television news media needed Carter as the front-runner in order to help complete the cast of three role-playing contenders for the party nominations but had little need for a successful Bush candidacy against Reagan in 1980.

The Clinton Nomination of 1992

The campaign among the opposition Democrats of 1992 unfolded in a fashion similar to these other two election campaigns. The Democrats began without an obvious front-runner and began their efforts relatively late. One reason for the late start was that the Persian Gulf War and the ensuing popularity of George Bush discouraged a number of potential candidates from seeking the Presidency and encouraged others to reconsider their plans. This delay was no small matter. The recent rule changes concerning fund raising and delegate selection have forced candidates to start their efforts at increasingly earlier dates. Most now begin during the first half of the year that precedes the election. Since most candidates are also little-known aspirants in search of constituencies, the campaigns tend to be quite lengthy. The candidates must spend a considerable amount of time raising money and generating support and name recognition so they can compete in the initial primaries and caucuses of the election year. The Iowa caucuses and the New Hampshire primary are now held in February. Opposition party nominees McGovern (1972), Carter (1976), Reagan (1980), Mondale (1984), and Dukakis (1988) had started their efforts by July of the year before their nominations.

Despite the delay, the six candidates who sought the 1992 Democratic nomination were campaigning earnestly by early autumn, but their success at generating support and resources lagged behind those of many candidates of recent campaigns. None had raised much money by the end of 1991 and, with the exception of Brown, were still relatively unknown. Harkin's candidacy encouraged the others to avoid the Iowa caucuses, thus making the New Hampshire primary the first test of the year. Television news media expanded their coverage of the developing campaign during the first part of January at approximately the time that Wilder, who had failed to generate much enthusiasm, withdrew from the race.

For the reasons discussed earlier, it is imperative for television news media to have a front-runner who can serve as their anchor when they report and interpret campaign events. Since there was no initial front-runner in this race, television news media set out to create one. They began structuring their reporting, virtually from the outset, with Clinton filling that role. The designation of Clinton in January as the front-runner was problematic. There had as yet been no votes cast, so reliance upon the outcome of the initial electoral test did not justify the designation of Clinton. Funds raised or survey standings might have been better indicators, but none of the candidates enjoyed much of an advantage there either. In fact, Clinton was in second place behind Harkin in fund raising, and none of the candidates held a lead in the surveys. Nonetheless, some news organizations began treating Clinton as the front-runner. While the above-mentioned indicators of support were not definitive in identifying a front-runner, several more subtle indicators of potential electoral success suggested that Clinton might win the nomination. At this stage of the campaign, Clinton appeared to be gaining the support of more party leaders than any of his rivals, particularly from the ranks of both his fellow Governors and Southerners. He also seemed to be the most electable candidate. Liberal nominees from the Northeast and Midwest had not fared well in recent elections, while more moderate candidates from the Southeast, such as Johnson and Carter, had led the party to victory. Clinton had been fairly skillful at both winning office and governing in a conservative southern state. Since Clinton appeared to be the "most likely to succeed," television and other news media proclaimed him to be the front-runner when in fact no votes had been cast and when he had not assumed an actual lead in such objective indicators of support as fund raising or survey standings.

Assigning Clinton to the role of front-runner led to a reorientation of campaign news reporting. This, in turn, redefined the campaign and helped transform it into the story of Clinton running for President. After such a change, the other candidates appeared more as obstacles between Clinton and the nomination than as political figures in their own right. The front-runner role had its pitfalls for Clinton however. He barely moved into the center stage of campaign coverage when some potentially damaging stories began appearing about his personal behavior. The initial ones, which were also the most threatening, directed attention to charges, printed in a supermarket tabloid, of a nightclub singer who claimed that she had a twelve-year sexual affair with the Arkansas governor. The substantial and expanding news coverage of these charges led to a most extraordinary introduction of the new front-runner to most voters. Clinton and his wife, Hillary, were interviewed on a special edition of the CBS newsmagazine "60 Minutes" immediately after the Super Bowl football game in late January. Clinton defended himself against the charges, stated that he had done nothing wrong, and demonstrated to his audience that he had the strong personal backing of his wife. He also convinced a fairly large number of people in the audience that his actions had been quite proper. For all intents and purposes, this was Clinton's equivalent of the Checkers speech. Like Nixon in 1952, Clinton used this unusual opportunity to increase his familiarity with voters and to begin eliminating a potentially destructive issue that posed the danger of bringing his aspirations to an abrupt halt.

There is an irony that exists in both the reporting of Clinton's problems and in his need for eventually defending himself before a national television audience. One might suspect that such coverage would destroy whatever chances he had of winning the nomination. Quite the contrary occurred however. Clinton's appearance on one of the nation's most popular television programs, and particularly the edition that occurred immediately after the most-watched sporting event of the year, provided him with an audience that he could not hope to generate by any other means. The telecast introduced the Clintons to millions of Americans. Many people were just beginning to think about the campaign and the candidates, but they could now see and listen to the new front-runner and his wife. Many of them liked what they saw and heard. Bill Clinton soon became the most well known of all Democratic aspirants, and Hillary Clinton became the most familiar of all potential first ladies. The effects of this controversy and related news coverage were comparable to the aftermath of the second place finish by Jimmy Carter in the 1976 Iowa caucuses. By directing so much attention to Clinton this early in the campaign, television news media distinguished him from the others and provided him with a unique and invaluable opportunity to become the front-runner in fact. Clinton then attained more news coverage during the early weeks of the campaign than all of his rivals combined. He followed by consolidating political power within the leaderless Democratic Party in only a few short weeks after the telecast and, with the implicit help of television news media, began projecting the image that he was a qualified alternative to the weak incumbent.

Television and other news media carried out a self-fulfilling prophecy. First, they decided that Clinton was the most likely winner of the nomination. Therefore, they proclaimed him the front-runner and used him as the anchor for reporting the campaign. As front-runner, Clinton soon attained news coverage that was potentially scandalous and therefore had to defend himself. The defense in itself was newsworthy, thus resulting in even more news coverage of the alleged front-runner. Television news media, and CBS in particular, provided Clinton with an opportunity for a public defense. Clinton accepted the opportunity, projected a favorable image to viewers of televised politics, set aside the scandal, became the actual front-runner, and then won the nomination.

Once again I would raise a point of caution. Clinton was beginning to emerge as the most likely winner of the nomination by late 1991. Television and other news media did not generate the initial support that he seemed to be attaining from Governors, Southerners, or other party leaders. Clinton accomplished this without their help. Nonetheless, when television news media began directing more attention to Clinton by depicting him as the front-runner and using him as the anchor for their reporting, they were illustrating the aftermath of his initial rise, not its actual occurrence. The limitations of the popular horse race metaphor discussed earlier are applicable here. When Clinton started to emerge from the field in December 1991, television news media started directing more attention to him. The ensuing attention then made Clinton the actual front-runner and led to the rapid elimination of his little-known rivals from the campaign.

Despite this success in attaining television coverage, Clinton's problems were not over. Many news organizations continued directing attention to personal factors and reported that Clinton had supposedly used some deceptive tactics to avoid military service during the Vietnam War. The ensuing controversy, which became one of the leading news stories in the weeks leading up to the New Hampshire primary, initially appeared to weaken Clinton's prospects in that state. The media-originated daily tracking polls compiled in the final days before the primary suggested that Clinton was losing support. This abrupt decline ended shortly, however, as several surveys had the Arkansas governor regaining some of his earlier standing. Clinton finished in second place with about 25 percent of the vote. Tsongas won with 33 percent.

The campaign did not last much longer. Despite his first place finish, Tsongas did not replace Clinton as the media-identified front-runner. Instead, reporters continued looking upon Tsongas as merely an obstacle that Clinton had to overcome on his way to the nomination. Tsongas was from Massachusetts, after all, and supposedly had won because many Democratic voters were more familiar with him than the other candidates. The next round of primaries occurred two weeks later, on the first Tuesday in March, in three different states from widely divergent regions. No definitive winner emerged from them, although Kerrey lost so badly in all three that he withdrew. Clinton won Georgia, Tsongas captured Maryland, while Brown gained his first victory of the year in Colorado. One week later Clinton garnered the lead in delegates as he won primaries in six southeastern states (Florida, Louisiana, Mississippi, Oklahoma, Tennessee, and Texas). Tsongas won Rhode Island and Massachusetts that same day. Harkin failed in all eight states and left the campaign.

The Michigan and Illinois primaries followed these by one week and marked a major turning point in the campaign. Clinton attained a majority of the vote in both states and expanded his already growing delegate lead. Tsongas ended his efforts two days later, thus narrowing the field to only Clinton and Brown. Clinton effectively ended the campaign two weeks later when he defeated Brown in New York. While Brown refused to withdraw after this defeat, he no longer posed any danger to Clinton. Clinton won every remaining primary, including the one in California. There were only nine weeks between the "60 Minutes" telecast and the New York primary. During this time, Clinton went from being a little-known candidate who needed to defend himself before a national television audience to the undisputed leader and eventual nominee of his party.

Finally, Clinton's campaign was similar to the earlier efforts of Carter and Reagan in the sense that television news media did not attempt to create a two-candidate battle within the opposition party. They did not attempt to cast one of Clinton's rivals in the role of leading adversary and then depict him as the antithesis of Clinton. As with the two earlier campaigns, they found no particular need to encourage prolonged and divisive campaigns in both parties. The Buchanan challenge to the renomination of Bush and its equivalent replacement by the potential candidacy of Ross Perot provided television news media with the one contested political battle that they wanted during the first half of that election year. Without a leading adversary for the nomination, Clinton found little trouble in demonstrating his ability to garner television news coverage, win primaries, and unite the party, while his rivals looked like losers and abandoned their failing efforts. Like Carter and Reagan in the other elections with weak incumbents, Clinton gained the lead over the incumbent during the summer months and never relinquished it.

GENERAL ELECTIONS

Candidates' Dilemmas

In an earlier chapter, I demonstrated that the three surrogate incumbents of the television age lost their leads in public opinion surveys during the latter stages of the primary election seasons or in the summer months after the conclusion of those seasons. The three weak incumbents discussed in this chapter lost their leads at approximately this same time in their respective campaigns but, unlike the surrogates, could not reverse these patterns and make their races more competitive. Ford trailed Carter by 16 percentage points, 53 to 37, in an early July Gallup survey compiled shortly before the 1976 Democratic convention. He fell even farther behind in the weeks before the August Republican convention, as much as 33 points at one time. Ford ended the summer with an 11-point gap, 51 percent to 40. The poll standings of incumbent Carter during the summer of 1980 were not much more promising than Ford's. He led Reagan in every Gallup survey taken before June but dropped behind his rival in the latter part of that month. Reagan garnered the support of 37 percent of the respondents in a survey of late June compared to only 32 for Carter and 22 for Anderson. Reagan increased his newly acquired lead to 16 points by late August when he led Carter by 45 percent to 29 with Anderson at 14. Finally, Bush led Clinton in every Gallup survey taken during the first half of 1992 but fell permanently behind his Democratic rival in July. A Gallup survey in late May showed Bush with an 11-point lead over Clinton, 50 percent to 39. An early July survey involving the three candidates who would eventually contest the general election had Bush in first place with 35 percent, Perot with 30, and Clinton with 28. Clinton gained the lead in July during the Democratic convention and retained it thereafter. He led Bush by 15 percentage points, 54 to 39, in early September after the conclusion of both conventions. Ford, Carter, and Bush eventually reduced these post-convention deficits, but they could not overtake their rivals. Ford lost the general election to Carter by 2 percentage points, 50 to 48; Carter lost to Reagan by 10 points, 51 to 41 with Anderson at 7; while Bush garnered 37 percent of the vote compared to Clinton's 43 and Perot's 19.

In their bids for reelection, the three incumbents encountered some similar dilemmas that became apparent after they secured their nominations. They had begun their quests for second terms while facing some fairly significant political divisions among their own partisans which they had not alleviated either during the primary election season or at their national conventions. The divisiveness of their campaigns in fact led to even further deterioration of their public esteem. Ford and Carter had to spend months engaging in a series of difficult battles with a formidable rival for the support of their own partisans. This denied them invaluable opportunities to appear as unifying and statesmanlike leaders. While Bush initially seemed to escape this fate when he forced his first rival, Buchanan, to depart from the race after several primaries, he eventually fell victim to it through the growing emphasis that television news media placed upon the potential candidacy of the conservative Perot. The demise of Buchanan had provided Bush with an opportunity to consolidate the support of the Reagan constituency. The rise of Perot denied Bush this opportunity and instead forced him to spend the crucial months of April through July engaging in a public battle with the Texas billionaire for the allegiance of many of the same people who had supported him in 1988.

These incumbents faced prolonged and divisive campaigns for renomination, or the equivalent of such a campaign as in Bush's opposition by Perot, both because of their initial political weaknesses and because of their failure to consolidate the support of their own partisans before the election year. As a consequence, they had to fight for power throughout the primary election seasons and national convention periods and thereby lost whatever chances that the televising of the Presidency and its related election campaigns might have provided for them to appear unifying and statesmanlike. Television news media depicted them instead as mainly aspirants for power who were preoccupied with the strategic needs of contesting their nominations. The televising of intra-party power struggles tends to undermine the public's esteem for the participants. The continuing efforts of these three incumbents to consolidate the support of their own partisans, while television news media recorded virtually their every move, left them with substantial shortcomings in public esteem at the conclusion of their nomination campaigns.

The general election opponents of these incumbents had some dilemmas of their own however. These dilemmas appear to derive from the recurring experiences that opposition party nominees tend to encounter in election years in which an incumbent has trouble uniting his own partisans. They seem comparable to the dilemmas often faced by the challengers of surrogate incumbents, as discussed earlier. Carter, Reagan, and Clinton, the challengers of the three weak incumbents, attained their nominations through similar means that eventually affected their prospects for the general election. Each began his campaign as one of many candidates seeking the nomination of the opposition party in a year when the most important political news story of the primary campaign and convention period concerned the troubled efforts of an embattled incumbent to consolidate power within his own party. All three challengers emerged as the front-runner for his party's nomination very early in the year and then served as the anchor by which television news media illustrated and reported the story of that party's choice of a standard bearer. Carter, Reagan, and Clinton dominated the televised news coverage of their respective parties from that time on, and all three soon appeared to be passing the requisite tests for political leadership that television news media tend to employ. The three were projecting vague but positive personal images in which they appeared to possess the skills expected of a President. They seemed to encounter little difficulty in vanquishing in the primaries their many slightly known rivals and in attracting larger and more enthusiastic crowds of supporters as their campaigns developed. These successes helped them attain even more televised news coverage and support which they then exploited in order to unite their own partisans around the prospect of victory. Television news media enhanced the efforts of each of these three challengers to generate a widespread consensus among his own partisans in support of his candidacy. All three challengers led united parties when they began their general election campaigns.

As with the challengers of the surrogate incumbents, Carter, Reagan, and Clinton also won their nominations in years when recent divisions within their parties had subsided and unity behind new leaders seemed increasingly possible. The Democrats underwent divisive nomination campaigns in 1968 and 1972 over issues that originated during the Johnson administration but which were resolved before 1976. The fall of Nixon led to a succession battle among Republicans that compromised that party's electoral chances in 1976, but most Republicans were far more conciliatory toward their fellow partisans by 1980. After three consecutive defeats, the Democrats of 1992 were finally ready to set aside their past differences and unite behind a candidate who held out the promise of victory and who could lead their new generation of activists to power. In each of the three elections with weak incumbents, the opposition party found a candidate that could provide the requisite unity and hope that might make victory possible.

The challengers faced a dilemma in that the positive but vague public images that helped them attain their nominations could very well deterioriate as the campaigns intensified and thus deprive them of victory. The growing uncertainty that skeptical voters tend to have about the personal limitations of challengers during the latter stages of campaigns often forces those challengers to alleviate their doubts or face defeat. Dukakis failed to address the doubts that surfaced about his abilities and lost in 1988, while Kennedy and Nixon (1968) successfully addressed theirs and were elected. However, the threats of declining support that faced the challengers of weak incumbents in 1976, 1980, and 1992 were not as pressing as those that faced the challengers of surrogate incumbents in 1960, 1968, and 1988. The incumbents in the former elections were relatively unpopular, and many voters wanted new leadership. There were no incumbents in the latter years except for retiring Presidents who either were quite popular at the time of the election or who had been popular at one time. If the challengers of the weak incumbents failed to alleviate the doubts of skeptical voters, they still might have been able to win these elections since so many voters wanted change. Carter and Clinton actually failed to set aside much of the voter skepticism about their abilities but nevertheless won, although their margins of victory were smaller than some of their earlier leads suggested. In contrast, Reagan answered many of the doubts raised by cautious voters and was expanding his support in the days immediately before the election.

Candidates' Strategies

The major party candidates in these elections faced some strategic needs that also derived from their particular vantage points of incumbent or challenger. The challengers faced circumstances not unlike those encountered by the challengers of the surrogate incumbents. All three emerged as new and unifying leaders of their parties during the nomination campaigns by holding out the promise of victory that derived from their triumphs over a number of little-known rivals who lacked constituencies. The party unity and optimism that followed these triumphs were somewhat illusory, however, in that they were based mostly upon the vague but positive images projected by the challengers and the euphoria that came from the successful conclusion of their nomination campaigns. Comparable to the challengers of surrogate incumbents, these challengers had the problem that much of their promising support could disappear during the final weeks of the campaign as increasingly skeptical voters abandoned them. They had to address the potentially damaging charges raised by the incumbent and his supporters that they lacked the personal abilities demanded of the Presidency and that they would embark upon some potentially dangerous policy changes if elected. At the very least, they had to reassure voters that they were the political equals of the embattled incumbents they sought to replace.

Perhaps the most significant political fact facing the three weak incumbents at the conclusion of their nominating campaigns was that the majority of the voters did not want to see them reelected. Indeed, a wide variety of surveys in 1992 demonstrated that a maximum of only about 40 percent of respondents preferred George Bush for a second term. The support for Ford and Carter at comparable times in 1976 and 1980 was not much better than that for Bush. Moreover, the leading events of these campaigns enhanced the crystalizing of unfavorable attitudes by many voters about the incumbents. A majority of voters disapproved of the incumbents and seemed unlikely to alter their views. This fact left the incumbents with only one remaining option that could lead to possible victory. They had to convince many of the hostile voters that the challengers would make even poorer Presidents. This strategy would supposedly induce those voters to oppose the challengers and thereby reelect the incumbents. The challengers, of course, had to convince voters that they were not less capable than the incumbents and that the changes they proposed were worthwhile. The desire by the electorate to remove the incumbents appeared to be strong enough that the challengers would probably win if they could simply demonstrate that they were equal to the incumbent they sought to replace. If voters are satisfied with a President, a challenger cannot win the election unless he convinces those same voters that he will be a better chief executive than the incumbent he seeks to replace, a task that is often quite difficult. This is not true when the incumbent is unpopular: the challenger can win if he appears to be at least equal to the incumbent.

Since 1976, presidential election campaigns have been characterized by a series of nationally televised debates among the leading candidates. The date when this pattern began is relevant to the present discussion because it means that debates occurred in all three of the weak incumbent elections, a fact not true about all of the elections that comprise each of the other categories. The debates affected the strategies of the candidates and the behavior of voters in that they created a formalized means for generating the largest audiences that would observe and evaluate those candidates during the final two months of the campaigns. They did this by providing the best available opportunities for the incumbents to raise the necessary doubts about the abilities and promises of the challengers, for the challengers to alleviate those doubts and attempt to reinforce their summertime survey leads, and for independents Anderson and Perot to demonstrate that they were indeed serious contenders for the Presidency. If the incumbents could not make effective use of these debates to reverse the direction that public opinion seemed to be taking against them, they would face almost certain defeat. All three failed to make these reversals.

There were three debates in 1976, two involving Ford and Carter and one between vice presidential candidates Dole and Mondale. The Republicans suffered setbacks in the first two that may have put an end to their hopes of raising serious questions about Carter. They may have succeeded in raising more questions about themselves instead. Ford virtually destroyed any chance that he had of appearing as the winner of the initial debate when he said that Poland was a free nation. News reporters were widely critical of this remark in the days that followed, with many of them referring to it as the one leading indicator of Ford's poor showing. Subsequent polls indicated that many viewers concurred: most said Ford lost the debate. The Republicans were unable to reverse their misfortunes in the second debate and compounded their difficulties with another unfortunate remark. This debate among the vice presidential candidates is best remembered by a statement by which Dole appeared to hold Democrats responsible for the major wars of the twentieth century, including the two world wars. News reporters and opposing partisans soon denounced his reference to "Democrat wars" with the same intensity that they had criticized Ford for his earlier remarks about Poland. Television viewers told pollsters they considered Mondale as the debate winner. These two performances denied the Republican ticket the opportunities it needed for raising the questions that would encourage an erosion of support for Carter and Mondale. Carter did not appear less qualified than Ford, nor did he seem likely to pursue any dangerous policies that Ford could use to raise further doubts. Ford could not generate the doubts that would lead skeptical voters to abandon Carter. Carter retained his lead during the final weeks of the campaign and won the election.

In light of the troubled performances by Ford and Dole, one may wonder why the Republicans would ever agree to any debates. After all, the last time the presidential party agreed to debates was in 1960, and those allowed Kennedy an opportunity to alleviate the questions that many voters had about his youth and inexperience. Nixon provided Kennedy with an audience that his challenger could not provide for himself, and Kennedy took full advantage of it. If Ford had refused to take part, Carter would have been unable to generate a comparable audience in any other setting. Since Carter also needed to alleviate some important questions that existed about his lack of experience, why should Ford provide him with one? Without such an opportunity to explain himself, Carter might eventually be undermined by voters' doubts and Ford would win the election by default. Despite the possible appeal of such an argument, Ford had little choice but to participate in the debates. His situation was not comparable to Nixon's, and Carter's was not comparable to Kennedy's. Polls revealed that many people were disillusioned with Ford, did not want to see him remain in office, and seemed to be accepting the prospects of change that Carter offered. While some of Carter's lead was illusory because of the patterns that exist in televised news coverage of the Presidency and of its related election campaigns, Ford could not afford to take the chance that skeptical voters would eventually abandon Carter and vote Republican. The favorable attitude that many voters held toward Carter could intensify and leave little room for the Republicans to persuade them to act otherwise. The Republicans had suffered a significant political defeat in the congressional elections of 1974 and were on the verge of losing once again. Ford could not allow such a defeat to happen. He needed to take part in the debates as much as Carter did.

The vantage points of the two major candidates in 1980 were similar to those of 1976, with Carter now playing a reversed role. This time he was the embattled incumbent and trailed his challenger. His strategic needs were similar to those of Ford: he had to convince a significant number of voters that his challenger, Reagan, posed a serious threat to their interests and that they should reject his bid. Since a majority of voters did not support his reelection, Carter also had only one viable option available. If he could discredit his rival, he would win as voters rejected Reagan. With this in mind, he began raising doubts about the possible consequences of a Reagan victory. Conversely, Reagan needed to alleviate those doubts and demonstrate that he offered a positive change from the status quo. Since most voters seemed to want some kind of change, Reagan could win the election if he could avoid appearing as a dangerous ideologue who was less capable of leading the nation than Carter. Once again, the televised debates had the potential for generating the largest audiences of the year and for providing each candidate with the necessary opportunities for accomplishing his leading objectives. Carter almost prevented the debates from taking place, however, since their existence posed some danger for him. As the incumbent, he did not wish to generate an audience that his rivals could not generate for themselves. Anderson needed the debates to establish his credibility as a serious candidate and to dispel some growing perceptions that he was merely serving as a vehicle for political protest. If successful, Anderson could very well compromise Carter's hopes of regaining the lead. He was attracting more support from Democrats and liberal independents than from Republicans and conservatives. Many of Anderson's supporters were unlikely to vote for Reagan under almost any circumstances. With Anderson garnering as much as one-fifth of the popular vote in some surveys, Carter did not want to provide an audience that could help Anderson gain even more votes at his expense. Carter also did not want to provide Reagan with any opportunities to alleviate the doubts that he was raising about the potential dangers of a Reagan victory. When the debate sponsors, the League of Women Voters, invited Anderson, Carter refused to take part. With no incumbent, the debates should fail.

Reagan was unwilling to let Carter deny him the opportunities that the debates offered for reassuring voters, and he therefore agreed to oppose Anderson. The ensuing debate between the two major opponents of the incumbent provided the chance that Reagan needed to make the case for a change from an unsuccessful status quo and to convince voters that he had the personal and political skills to effect that change. Carter's attempts to discredit Reagan failed as the campaign continued. With support for Reagan remaining strong, Carter was eventually forced to revise his strategy. He agreed to one debate with Reagan to be held during the last week of the campaign. Anderson's support had now fallen below 10 percent in the national surveys, thus prompting the League of Women Voters to exclude him. Carter agreed to participate for essentially the same reasons that Ford did in 1976: it offered him a final opportunity to stop his rival. The debate proved to be the final act in Carter's undoing however. Reagan appeared more competent than Carter and made two widely quoted remarks that helped propel Carter toward his ultimate defeat one week later. When Carter began with yet another attack upon his rival's agenda, Reagan retorted by saying, "there you go again." This remark belittled Carter and reinforced the growing perception that he was acting in an unstatesmanlike manner. Finally, Reagan concluded his final summation by asking, "Are you better off than you were four years ago?" With this question, Reagan emphasized once again that change was necessary and that he was the candidate who could lead the way. For all intents and purposes, the campaign ended with Reagan's concluding remarks.

The problems that George Bush encountered in 1992 were comparable to those of Ford and Carter. He had also lost the survey lead to his rival during the final weeks of the primary election season and the convention period, and there were strong suggestions that a majority of the voters did not wish to see him reelected. He had seen many potential opportunities of appearing presidential disappear during his battles with Buchanan and Perot and, like Carter and Ford, now seemed to find that his best remaining option of winning required him to attack and discredit his opponent. Bush therefore spent much of his time attacking the real or imagined shortcomings of Clinton in an attempt to persuade voters to abandon the Arkansas governor. He achieved about as little success as the two earlier incumbents. Although Bush appeared to be reducing the size of Clinton's lead in the surveys, he was unable to make the kinds of reductions that would lead to an election victory. Moreover, some of his attacks contributed to a damaging public backlash.

One such backlash developed from the efforts of the Bush campaign to use the Republican convention as a forum for attacking the social agenda of the Democratic Party. Two of the more important of the prime time speakers in this endeavor were Pat Buchanan and Marilyn Quayle, the wife of the Vice President. Each attempted to link many of the supposedly unpopular social problems of the 1960s with the Democrats. Buchanan proclaimed that the nation was involved in a cultural war, and the Republicans, of course, were on the correct side. Quayle spoke of how she was one member of her baby boom generation who had not partaken of the drug counterculture of the 1960s and that she had also chosen to forsake a career in order to raise her children. This was a veiled attack at Hillary Clinton. The remarks of Buchanan and Quayle angered more people than they converted, and the Bush campaign backed off from this cultural attack in the weeks that followed.

This campaign also featured debates that once again aided the challenger by providing him with an opportunity, which he used effectively, to demonstrate that he was at least the equal of the incumbent he sought to replace. As occurred in the other two elections, the incumbent could not afford to avoid these debates since he was trailing in the polls and could not hope to find an audience of a comparable size at any other time in the campaign. There were four debates in 1992, one more than usual since debates became a regular feature of campaigns in 1976. Three involved the presidential candidates and each included Ross Perot. The threat that Perot posed to the aspirations of Bush was similar to that posed by Anderson toward Carter. Perot had more appeal to Republicans and other conservatives than to Democrats and liberals. A credible effort by Perot could very well undermine Bush. If Bush could actually persuade skeptical voters to abandon Clinton, many of them might then decide to cast their lot with Perot. While this would help Bush by depriving Clinton of some votes and thus narrowing the difference between the two candidates, it could also induce some voters who were only reluctantly planning to vote for Bush to abandon the incumbent in favor of Perot.

The debates did not help Bush; surveys indicated that viewers believed he had not performed as well as either of his opponents. Moreover, the fact that Perot was in the debate left Bush with only one-third of the available time in which he could defend himself and attack his opponents. The presence of Perot allowed two-thirds of the debate time to be used by candidates who advocated change from the status quo. Public support for change seemed to be the main winner of the debates. Within the context of 1992, change meant voting George Bush out of office. The debates were symptomatic of the problems that Bush faced throughout the campaign. He could not avoid them but could not use them to convince voters that he deserved a second term or that his opponents could not be trusted with the Presidency.

In all three of these campaigns, the incumbents reduced the gaps that existed in their poll standings after the conclusion of their nominating conventions, but none could reverse those gaps and win. Once the opposition party completed its nomination campaign and united under new leadership that held out the promise of change from the unpopular status quo, each of the three weak incumbents was headed for the end of his public career.

State and Regional Partisanship

The patterns of state and regional partisanship in 1976 reflected those of 1960 but also hinted at the emergence of a new Democratic majority coalition. They reflected 1960 in the sense that many of the states carried by Carter had also voted for Kennedy. As with Kennedy, Carter won most of the states in the Northeast and Southeast while losing most of those from the Midwest and West. He attained 50.1 percent of the popular vote compared to 48.0 percent for Ford and carried twenty-three states and the District of Columbia. Only five of his victories were in states outside the Northeast and Southeast (Hawaii, Minnesota, Missouri, Ohio, Wisconsin). He ran strongly in the Northeast and defeated Ford in seven states (Delaware, Maryland, Massachusetts, New York, Pennsylvania, Rhode Island, West Virginia). He drew much of his support in this region from traditional areas of Democratic strength. Six of the states he carried, Delaware excepted, generally vote more Democratic than the nation.

Carter ran particularly well in his native Southeast: he carried eleven states, losing only Virginia and Oklahoma. Moreover, he ran stronger in most of them than he did nationally. His margin of victory in each state other than Mississippi exceeded his national showing. This was the strongest performance in the Southeast by a Democrat since Roosevelt won all thirteen states in 1944. While Carter appeared to restore the older Democratic coalition to majority status, at least at the state level, the underlying patterns of his support differed substantially from those of Roosevelt however. Roosevelt won his victories long before the civil rights movement induced some significant and far-reaching changes in southeastern voting patterns. Few blacks could vote during his time, but many did so in 1976. Carter failed to win a majority of the votes cast by whites in most states that he carried. He won in most states by supplementing the minority of white votes that he received with the nearly unanimous support of blacks. A victory throughout the Southeast with a biracial coalition was unprecedented in national elections, although similar coalitions had elected some state officials in the years immediately before 1976. Indeed, Carter was elected as Governor of Georgia in 1970 with the support of a biracial coalition.

Whatever possibilities the Carter victory may have offered for permanent realignment disappeared with the Reagan triumph in 1980. Not only did Carter suffer a defeat of nearly 10 percentage points in the popular vote, 50.7 to 41.0, but he encountered an even more overwhelming defeat in the electoral college. He won only six states and the District of Columbia and encountered sweeping defeats in each of the four regions. Nonetheless, the state and regional voting patterns of this election bore some similarities to those of 1976, at least in the sense that Carter's best regions were once again the Northeast and Southeast. His best showing, at least in terms of state-wide victories, occurred in the Northeast where he won Maryland, Rhode Island, West Virginia, and the District of Columbia. While Carter lost to Reagan in most of the northeastern states, he ran better in virtually all of them than he did nationally. His margin of defeat was less than 10 percentage points in all but Connecticut, New Hampshire, New Jersey, and Vermont. The region was also Anderson's strongest and Reagan's weakest. While Anderson was not competitive anywhere in the nation, as seen in his attaining only 6.6 percent of the popular vote, he garnered more than 10 percent of the vote in each of the six New England states. His greatest support came from Massachusetts where he received 15 percent of the vote. This performance may have affected the outcome in that state as both Reagan and Carter acquired 42 percent each.

Despite the fact that he lost every southeastern state except Georgia, Carter remained competitive in his native region. He exceeded his national total of 41 percent of the popular vote in ten states and actually finished within 2 points of Reagan in seven (Alabama, Arkansas, Kentucky, Mississippi, North Carolina, South Carolina, Tennessee). The only southeastern states where he actually fell behind his national vote totals were Florida, Oklahoma, and Virginia. These states had also voted Republican in every election between 1952 and 1972 other than for the Johnson landslide year of 1964. Once again, Carter's two weakest regions were the Midwest and West. This time he lost every state other than Hawaii and Minnesota. Moreover, he attained 41 percent of the vote in only four states other than the two he carried: Illinois, Michigan, Missouri, and Wisconsin.

The electoral patterns of 1992 were unusual in the sense that Clinton won states that rarely vote Democratic. While he managed to defeat Bush by less than 6 percentage points in the national popular vote, 43.0 to 37.4, with Perot at 18.9, Clinton recorded an electoral college landslide. He won thirty-two states and the District of Columbia and acquired 370 electoral votes. This was the highest total attained by a Democrat since Johnson and was the second highest total since Roosevelt. Nonetheless, the state and regional patterns bear a remarkable similarity to those of most television age elections and appear to have resulted more from short-term deviations in recent voting behavior than from any partisan realignment. The election of 1992 does not appear as yet to signal the beginning of a new and long-term Democratic presidential majority.

The outcome in the Southeast differed from those of 1976 and 1980. With the exception of those two elections, the Southeast has been one of the nation's least Democratic regions over the past three decades. Even the presence of native sons Clinton and Gore on the Democratic ticket could not reverse the recent Republican tendencies of this region. The Southeast cast a majority of its electoral votes for Bush and was the only region to do so. Bush won eight states and included the two giants of Texas and Florida in his tally. Only Arkansas, Georgia, Kentucky, Louisiana, and Tennessee voted Democratic, and Arkansas alone provided Clinton with a popular vote total that exceeded his national margin of 6 percentage points. Bush won 116 electoral votes in the Southeast but garnered only 52 from the rest of the nation.

Clinton won the Presidency by sweeping all but ten small states from the three remaining regions and by taking some states that his party had not captured since the days of Lyndon Johnson. He ran strongest in the Northeast where he carried every state. With the exception of New Hampshire and New Jersey, he also carried each state by a vote margin that exceeded his national tally of 6 percentage points. These same two states had also been Reagan's strongest in the region in 1980. Clinton carried seven midwestern states (Illinois, Iowa, Minnesota, Michigan, Missouri, Ohio, Wisconsin), while losing the same five that had been the most Republican during and since the time of Roosevelt (Indiana, North Dakota, South Dakota, Nebraska, Kansas). He ran unusually well in the West, but the patterns of his support corresponded with those of other Democratic candidates over the past four decades. Clinton's strongest support was in the Pacific states of California, Hawaii, Oregon, and Washington, as he carried each by at least 10 percentage points. These four have been the least Republican western states since 1964. Clinton became the first Democrat since Johnson to win in Colorado, Montana, Nevada, and New Mexico, but he won the first three of these states by less than 6 percentage points and may have been helped throughout the entire West by Perot. Perot ran stronger in the West than elsewhere.

Conclusions

As with the two categories of televison age elections discussed in earlier chapters, one can draw a number of conclusions about elections in which the incumbent is defeated in his quest for a second term. First, the primal causes of an incumbent's defeat will not originate exclusively during the campaign but will instead be symptomatic of the problems that already exist at the beginning of the election year. The incumbent quite likely will have generated substantial opposition from both the general population and his own partisans that is reflected in his low approval ratings and in a widespread lack of support for his reelection. This disenchantment will reflect the more significant political fact that this incumbent has not consolidated the support of his own partisans behind his bid for reelection. Many of the incumbent's own partisans would like to support another candidate for the nomination.

The incumbent will encounter substantial difficulty in uniting his partisans behind his reelection effort, and he may never actually accomplish it. There is also a strong chance that he will face a challenge to his nomination that will come from a political figure of some prominence within his own party. The challenger could very well be one of the most important leaders of the party who does not hold an office in the executive branch of the national government. This challenger may garner the support of a significant block of partisans who are disenchanted with the incumbent. The challenge can be of such magnitude that the incumbent will not be able to dispense with it early in the year. Two embattled incumbents of recent times could not destroy the challenges to their renominations until their parties' mid-summer national conventions. The intra-party opposition to another incumbent was strong enough that it encouraged an independent candidate to seek office who eventually gained the backing of many of the same partisans who had supported the incumbent in the previous election.

The efforts by a weak incumbent to consolidate power within his own party during the election year will not only be prolonged and highly divisive, they will be televised and will help make the incumbent appear less than statesmanlike. The incumbent will thereby lose whatever opportunities the symbolic dimensions of the Presidency might provide for projecting a favorable public image whereby he appears as a statesman competently governing the nation. After several months of these televised political struggles, the incumbent will instead project an alternative image in which he appears as simply another politician in search of power, an image that much of the American voting public find distasteful. The effect of televised news coverage of such a prolonged struggle will be to enhance the dissensus that already exists within the constituency of the presidential party.

A second recurring feature of these elections is that the opposition party will generally encounter little trouble in uniting behind a candidate and will probably do so fairly early during the primary election season. Indeed, Carter, Reagan, and Clinton effectively captured their nominations in April of their respective years when each recorded a series of victories over his remaining rivals. There are two reasons why the opposition party unites so readily. First, it will likely have been out of power for a long enough period of time that many of the conflicts that divided it in earlier years, and which originated when the party was last in power, will have receded. In addition, the party will likely attract a wide variety of little-known candidates who will seek to avoid those controversial issues in their individual quests for the nomination. Television news media will implicitly aid the party in its efforts to unite behind a new set of leaders as they will illustrate the nomination campaign as a race among several individual candidates who are primarily engaged in the pursuit of winning primaries. They will depict the ability of a candidate to win primaries as political virtues and the

WEAK INCUMBENTS

inability to win as vices. When the reality of a campaign develops in this manner, the constituency of this party will find few reasons for supporting the losing candidates and will unite readily behind the front-runner. The new front-runner will then monopolize television news coverage of the campaign and will soon emerge as the inspiring new leader who promises to lead the party into the White House. This challenger will take the lead over the incumbent in the election surveys compiled during the weeks between the end of the primaries and the beginning of the general election campaign. The challenger's lead will be somewhat illusory, however, because some of the voters who support him will become increasingly skeptical as the campaign heats up. Nonetheless, most of these summertime supporters will remain with this candidate throughout the campaign and will vote for him as the next President. Despite all the efforts of the embattled incumbent to convince voters that he deserves a second chance, or that they should reject his dangerous opponent and give him a second term because he is the lesser of two evils, the incumbent will fail. The challenger will begin his campaign by emphasizing that voters want change from the status quo. While voters may indeed be skeptical about the challenger, they will be sufficiently supportive of change that they will vote for him if he can convince them that he is at least the equal of the incumbent he seeks to replace. When one considers the monumental task that an aspirant for the Presidency faces in simply emerging from the pack of candidates who seek the nomination of the opposition party, any successful aspirant will most likely possess the political skills for making those reassurances. Certainly Jimmy Carter, Ronald Reagan, and Bill Clinton possessed them.

5

Conclusions and Epilogue

The discussion in the preceding chapters demonstrates that television news media do exert some fairly significant influences over the outcomes of presidential elections, but it also suggests that those influences may be limited and perhaps reflective of the strength of incumbency. While television news media played important roles in all nine elections since 1960, they were not the primary reasons that Johnson, Nixon, and Reagan consolidated power before their successful bids for reelection, nor were they the causes of the electoral failures of Ford, Carter, and Bush. They did provide these six incumbents with unique opportunities for enhancing their own political followings however. Three of the aforementioned incumbents used those opportunities quite effectively and won second terms, while three others did not. Despite these results, one can advance far stronger reasons to explain the successes of the incumbents from the first of these groups and the failures of those from the second than simply their successes at manipulating the style and content of television news. The presence of television can enhance the strengths of some incumbents while enhancing the weaknesses of others.

In a way, television news media affect the outcomes of elections in a manner somewhat akin to the modern effects of the electoral college. Through its winner-take-all allocation, the electoral vote magnifies the outcome of the popular vote and thereby provides a definitive victory for the first place finisher in a way that is not possible with the popular vote. Several Presidents who attained relatively weak popular vote totals actually won sweeping mandates in the electoral college. In 1992, for example, Bill Clinton won only 43 percent of the popular vote but also carried thirty-two states and thereby garnered nearly 69 percent of the electoral vote. This latter outcome helped transform a fairly weak popular vote triumph into a sweeping and undisputed election victory. The same can be said about the relatively close or multicandidate elections that chose Kennedy, Nixon (1968), Carter, and Reagan (1980), and such pretelevision age Presidents as Abraham Lincoln, Woodrow Wilson, and Harry Truman.

As with the electoral college, the reporting patterns of television news media discussed throughout this book can magnify the nature of other outcomes. A strong incumbent who has enjoyed a wide variety of political and personal successes, and who has consolidated power as a result, can appear even stronger when television news media illustrate him performing in the role of statesman during an election campaign. Conversely, an incumbent who has failed to consolidate power and whose political successes are few will almost certainly appear as an ineffective leader while engaging in a late and almost certainly futile effort to unite his own partisans. Television news media can enhance the growth of a previously existing consensus that supports the reelection of a strong incumbent and accelerate the fall of an already weak incumbent from power.

Television news media have influenced modern elections in other ways than simply through their illustrations of the strengths or weaknesses of various incumbents. As discussed in Chapter 3, they have contributed to the growth of the modern Vice Presidency as the most important vantage point from which a candidate can now seek the nomination of the presidential party when the incumbent retires. An important consequence of this recent development is that candidates whose political bases reside in other components of American government are virtually eliminated as viable contenders for that party's nomination. The influence of television news media is also important with respect to the definition of the nature of an incumbent's opposition. Television news media tend to illustrate the promises and performance of the opposition party and its leading personalities in a manner that is quite the reverse of how they depict the incumbent. When strong incumbents seek reelection, television news media tend to encourage the growth of dissensus within the opposition party and even help to extend the duration of that party's nomination campaigns far beyond the time that they should take. Conversely, they encourage the early—perhaps too early—resolution of the opposition's nomination in those years when the incumbent is in political trouble. These patterns of reporting contribute to the trivialization of modern campaigns by encouraging the development of a superficial consensus that either supports or opposes the reelection of an incumbent or succession by his surrogate without much regard to the consequences of an election outcome. As voters, many of us did not truly consider the potential troubles that such "statesmen" as Johnson and Nixon or such "presidential"-appearing challengers as Carter and Reagan might lead us into. Television news media, as the

CONCLUSIONS AND EPILOGUE

leading source of campaign information, failed to provide us with much of this needed information. These victors gave us lost wars, political scandals, policy confusion, and long-term economic disasters that we had to confront after they left office. The trivialization of election campaigns around stereotypical images will not help to improve these limitations in our public rhetoric either.

It is far too early at this time (1993) to make any realistic forecasts about the outcome of the campaign and election of 1996, except to say that Bill Clinton will be the central personality in that quadrennial endeavor and that television news media will illustrate the events of that year in ways that are predictable today. The fate of Clinton will already be cast by the outset of the televised coverage of the campaign that will begin in January of 1996. Clinton will either have consolidated political power by that time and will have developed a widespread following as a result of a number of significant policy and personal successes, or he will have failed and thereby will be yet another ineffective and unpopular one-term President. If he has succeeded, television news media will treat him as the American equivalent of European royalty and will illustrate him performing favorably in the unifying role of statesman. They will also enhance his electoral prospects by directing considerable attention during the first half of the election year to the most divisive features and personalities of the Republican nomination campaign. If Clinton is a weak and embattled incumbent, however, television news media will illustrate his most important failures while depicting the front-running Republican contender as a highly qualified President-in-waiting. This pattern of coverage will enable that front-runner to unite his party quite early during the year and then win the election. Beware the Ides of March. We should know the name of the next President of the United States by that day.

Selected Bibliography

Abramson, Paul R., John H. Aldrich, and David W. Rohde. *Change and Continuity in the 1980 Elections*. Washington, D.C.: Congressional Quarterly Press, 1982.
_____. Change and Continuity in the 1984 Elections. Washington, D.C.: Congressional Quarterly Press, 1986.
_____. Change and Continuity in the 1988 Elections. Washington, D.C.: Congressional Quarterly Press, 1990.
Agranoff, Robert. *The New Style in Election Campaigns*. Boston: Holbrook Press, 1972.
Aldrich, John H. *Before the Convention: Strategies and Choices in Presidential Nomination Campaigns*. Chicago: University of Chicago Press, 1980.
Asher, Herbert B. *Presidential Elections and American Politics: Voters, Candidates, and Campaigns since 1952*. 5th ed. Pacific Grove, Calif.: Brooks/Cole, 1992.
Atherton, F. Christopher. *Media Politics: The News Strategies of Presidential Campaigns*. Lexington, Mass.: Lexington Books, 1984.
Barber, James David, ed. *Race for the Presidency: The Media and the Nominating Process*. Englewood Cliffs, N.J.: Prentice-Hall, 1978.
Barilleaux, Ryan J. *The Post-Modern Presidency*. New York: Praeger, 1988.
Bartels, Larry M. *Presidential Primaries and the Dynamics of Public Choice*. Princeton: Princeton University Press, 1988.
Bass, Jack, and Walter DeVries. *The Transformation of Southern Politics: Social and Political Consequences since 1945*. New York: Times-Mirror, 1977.
Beck, Paul Allen, and Frank J. Sorauf. *Party Politics in America*. 7th ed. New York: Harper, Collins, 1992.
Bennett, W. Lance. *The Governing Crisis: Media, Money, and Marketing in American Elections*. New York: St. Martin's Press, 1992.
Berelson, Bernard R., Paul F. Lazersfeld, and William N. McPhee. *Voting*. Chicago: University of Chicago Press, 1954.

SELECTED BIBLIOGRAPHY

Black, Earl, and Merle Black. *The Vital South: How Presidents Are Elected.* Cambridge, Mass.: Harvard University Press, 1992.
Blumenthal, Sidney. *The Permanent Campaign.* 2nd ed. New York: Touchstone Books, 1982.
Buell, Emmett H. Jr., and Lee Sigelman. *Nominating the President.* Knoxville: University of Tennessee Press, 1991.
Burke, Kenneth. *Language as Symbolic Action.* Berkeley: University of California Press, 1966.
Burnham, Walter Dean. *Critical Elections and the Mainsprings of American Politics.* New York: Norton, 1970.
Burns, James MacGregor. *The Deadlock of Democracy.* Englewood Cliffs, N.J.: Prentice-Hall, 1963.
Caeser, James. *Presidential Selection.* Princeton: Princeton University Press, 1979.
———. *Reforming the Reforms.* Cambridge, Mass.: Ballinger, 1992.
Campbell, Angus. "A Classification of Presidential Elections." In *Elections and the Political Order,* by Angus Campbell, Philip E. Converse, Warren E. Miller, and Donald E. Stokes. New York: John Wiley and Sons, 1966, pp. 963–77.
Campbell, Angus, Philip E. Converse, Warren E. Miller, and Donald E. Stokes. *The American Voter.* New York: John Wiley and Sons, 1960.
Carmines, Edward G., John P. McIver, and James A. Stimson. "Unrealized Partisanship: A Theory of Dealignment." *Journal of Politics* 49 (May 1987): 376–400.
Chaffee, Steven H., ed. *Political Communication.* Beverly Hills: Sage Publications, 1975.
Clubb, Jerome M., William H. Flanigan, and Nancy H. Zingale. *Partisan Realignment: Voters, Parties, and Government in American History.* Beverly Hills: Sage Publications, 1980.
Converse, Philip E. "The Concept of a Normal Vote." In *Elections and the Political Order,* by Angus Campbell, Philip E. Converse, Warren E. Miller, and Donald E. Stokes. New York: John Wiley and Sons, 1966, pp. 9–39.
Converse, Philip E., Angus Campbell, Warren E. Miller, and Donald E. Stokes. "Stability and Change in 1960: A Reinstating Election." *American Political Science Review* 55, 2 (June 1961): 269–80.
Converse, Philip E., Aage R. Clausen, and Warren E. Miller. "Electoral Myth and Reality: The 1964 Election." *American Political Science Review* 59, 2 (June 1965): 321–36.
Converse, Philip E., Warren E. Miller, Jerrold G. Rusk, and Arthur C. Wolfe. "Continuity and Change in American Politics: Parties and Issues in the 1968 Election." In *American Political Science Review* 63, 4 (December 1969): 1083–1105.
Corrado, Anthony J. *Creative Campaigning: PAC's and the Presidential Selection Process.* Boulder, Colo.: Westview Press, 1992.
Cronin, Thomas E. *The State of the Presidency.* 2nd. ed. Boston: Little, Brown, 1980.
Crotty, William J. *Decision for the Democrats: Reforming the Party Structure.* Baltimore: Johns Hopkins University Press, 1978.
———, ed. *America's Choice: The Election of 1992.* Guilford, Conn.: Dushkin Publishing Group, 1992.

SELECTED BIBLIOGRAPHY

Crotty, William J., and John S. Jackson III. *Presidential Primaries and Nominations.* Washington, D.C.: Congressional Quarterly Press, 1985.

Crouse, Timothy. *The Boys on the Bus: Riding with the Campaign Press Corps.* New York: Ballantine, 1973.

Dalton, Russell J., Scott C. Flanagan, and Paul Allen Beck. *Electoral Change in Advanced Industrial Democracies: Realignment or Dealignment?* Princeton: Princeton University Press, 1984.

Davis, James W. *National Conventions in an Age of Party Reform.* Westport, Conn.: Greenwood Press, 1983.

Denton, Robert E. *The Symbolic Dimensions of American Politics.* Prospect Heights, Ill.: Waveland Press, 1982.

Denton, Robert E., and Gary C. Woodward. *Political Communication in America.* New York: Praeger, 1985.

DeVries, Walter, and Lance Tarrance. *The Ticket-Splitter: A New Force in American Politics.* Grand Rapids, Mich.: Eerdmans, 1972.

Diamond, Edwin, and Stephen Bates. *The Spot: The Rise of Political Advertising on Television.* Cambridge: MIT Press, 1984.

Dionne, E. J. *Why Americans Hate Politics.* New York: Simon and Schuster, 1991.

Donaldson, Sam. *Hold On, Mr. President.* New York: Random House, 1987.

Dover, E. D. "Presidential Elections in the Television Age: Realignment, Dealignment, and Incumbency." *Southeastern Political Review* 15 (1987): 27–43.

Dutton, Frederick G. *Changing Sources of Power.* New York: McGraw-Hill, 1971.

Ealy, Steven D. *Communication, Speech, and Politics: Habermas and Political Analysis.* Washington, D.C.: University Press of America, 1981.

Edelman, Murray. *The Symbolic Uses of Politics.* Urbana, Ill.: University of Illinois Press, 1964.

Edwards, George C. III. *The Public Presidency: The Pursuit of Popular Support.* New York: St. Martin's Press, 1983.

Eldersveld, Samuel J. *Political Parties: A Behavioral Analysis.* Skokie, Ill.: Rand-McNally, 1964.

Entman, Robert M. *Democracy without Citizens: Media and the Decay of American Politics.* New York: Oxford University Press, 1989.

———. "How the Media Affect What People Think: An Information Processing Approach." *Journal of Politics* 51 (May 1989): 347–70.

Epstein, Edward Jay. *News from Nowhere: Television and the News.* New York: Vintage, 1974.

Fenno, Richard F. *Home Style: House Members in Their Districts.* Boston: Little, Brown, 1978.

Fiorina, Morris. *Retrospective Voting in American National Elections.* New Haven: Yale University Press, 1981.

Fishel, Jeff, ed. *Parties and Elections in an Anti-Party Age.* Bloomington: Indiana University Press, 1978.

Galderisi, Peter, Michael S. Lyons, Randy T. Simmons, and John G. Francis, eds. *The Politics of Realignment: Party Change in the Mountain West.* Boulder, Colo: Westview Press, 1987.

Gans, Herbert J. *Deciding What's News.* New York: Vintage, 1980.

Germond, Jack W., and Jules Witcover. *Blue Smoke and Mirrors: How Reagan Won and Why Carter Lost the Election of 1980.* New York: Viking Press, 1981.

———. *Wake Us When It's Over: Presidential Politics of 1984.* New York: MacMillan, 1985.

———. *Whose Broad Stripes and Bright Stars: The Trivial Pursuit of the Presidency 1988.* New York: Warner Books, 1989.

Ginsberg, Benjamin. *The Captive Public: How Mass Opinion Promotes State Power.* New York: Basic Books, 1986.

Graber, Doris A. *Verbal Behavior and Politics.* Urbana, Ill.: University of Illinois Press, 1976.

———. *The President and the Public.* Philadelphia: Institute for the Study of Human Issues, 1982.

———. *Media Power in Politics.* 2nd ed. Washington, D.C.: Congressional Quarterly Press, 1990.

———. *Mass Media in American Politics.* 4th ed. Washington, D.C.: Congressional Quarterly Press, 1993.

Habermas, Jurgen. "On Systematically Distorted Communication." *Inquiry* 13 (1970): 205–18.

———. "Towards a Theory of Communicative Competence." *Inquiry* 13 (1970): 360–75.

Hart, Roderick P. *The Sound of Leadership: Presidential Communication in the Modern Age.* Chicago: University of Chicago Press, 1987.

Hertsgaard, Mark. *On Bended Knee: The Press and the Reagan Presidency.* New York: Farrar, Straus, and Giroux, 1988.

Hodgson, Godfrey. *All Things to All Men.* New York: Touchstone Books, 1980.

Hoffstetter, Richard. *Bias in the News: Network Television Coverage of the 1972 Election Campaign.* Columbus: Ohio State University Press, 1976.

Iyengar, Shanto. "Television News and Citizens' Explanations of National Affairs." *American Political Science Review* 81 (September 1987): 815–31.

Jamison, Kathleen Hall, *Packaging the Presidency.* New York: Oxford University Press, 1984.

———. *Eloquence in the Electronic Age: The Transformation of Political Speechmaking.* New York: Oxford University Press, 1988.

Keech, William R., and Donald R. Matthews. *The Party's Choice.* Washington, D.C.: Brookings Institution, 1977.

Keeter, Scott, and Cliff Zukin. *Uninformed Choice: The Failure of the New Presidential Nominating System.* New York: Praeger, 1983.

Kelley, Stanley. *Interpreting Elections.* Princeton: Princeton University Press, 1983.

Kernall, Samuel. *Going Public: New Strategies of Presidential Leadership.* Washington, D.C.: Congressional Quarterly Press, 1986.

Kessel, John H. *The Goldwater Coalition: Republican Strategies in 1964.* Indianapolis: Bobbs-Merrill, 1968.

———. *Presidential Campaign Politics: Coalition Strategies and Citizen Response.* 4th ed. Homewood, Ill.: Dorsey Press, 1992.

Key, V. O. *Southern Politics in State and Nation.* New York: Vintage, 1949.

———. "Secular Realignment and the Party System." *Journal of Politics* 21 (1959): 198.

———. "Toward a Theory of Critical Elections." *Journal of Politics* 17 (1955): 3–18.

———. *Politics, Parties, and Pressure Groups.* New York: Crowell, 1964.

———. *The Responsible Electorate.* Cambridge, Mass.: Belknap Press, 1966.

SELECTED BIBLIOGRAPHY

Kiewiet, D. Roderick. *Macroeconomics and Micropolitics: The Electoral Effects of Economic Issues.* Chicago: University of Chicago Press, 1983.

Ladd, Everett Carll Jr. *Where Have All the Voters Gone? The Fracturing of America's Political Parties.* 2nd ed. New York: Norton, 1982.

———. "Like Waiting for Godot: The Uselessness of Realignment for Understanding Change in Contemporary American Politics." *Polity* 22 (1990): 511–25.

Ladd, Everett Carll Jr., and Charles D. Hadley. *Transformations of the American Party System.* Rev. ed. New York: Norton, 1975.

Lamis, Alexander P. *The Two-Party South.* New York: Oxford University Press, 1984.

Lavrekas, Paul J., and Jack K. Holley, eds. *Polling and Presidential Election Coverage.* Newbury Park, Calif.: Sage, 1991.

Lazersfeld, Paul F., Bernard Berelson, and Hazel Gaudet. *The People's Choice: How the Voter Makes up His Mind in a Presidential Campaign.* New York: Columbia University Press, 1944.

Lewis-Beck, Michael S. *Economics and Elections: The Major Western Democracies.* Ann Arbor: University of Michigan Press, 1988.

Lowry, Dennis T. "Gresham's Law and Network TV News Selection." *Journal of Broadcasting* 15 (1971): 397–407.

McCartney, James. "The Triumph of Junk News." *Columbia Journalism Review* 15 (1977): 7–21.

McClure, Robert D., and Thomas E. Patterson. "Print vs. Network News." *Journal of Communication* 26 (Spring 1976): 18–22.

McCombs, Maxwell E., and Donald R. Shaw. "The Agenda-Setting Function of the Mass Media." *Public Opinion Quarterly* 36 (Summer 1972): 176–87.

McGinniss, Joe. *The Selling of the President 1968.* New York: Trident Press, 1969.

Miller, Arthur H., Warren E. Miller, Aldern S. Raine, and Thad E. Brown. "A Majority Party in Disarray: Policy Polarization in the 1972 Election." *American Political Science Review* 70 (1976): 753–78.

Miller, Arthur H., and Martin P. Wattenberg. "Throwing the Rascals Out: Policy and Performance Evaluations of Presidential Candidates, 1952–1980." *American Political Science Review* 79 (1985): 359–68.

Miller, Warren E. "Party Identification, Realignment, and Party Voting: Back to Basics." *American Political Science Review* 85 (1991): 557–68.

Miroff, Bruce. "Presidential Campaigns: Candidates, Managers and Reporters." *Polity* 12 (1980): 667.

Mueller, Claus. *The Politics of Communication.* New York: Oxford University Press, 1973.

Nelson, Michael, ed. *The Elections of 1984.* Washington, D.C.: Congressional Quarterly Press, 1985.

———. *The Elections of 1988.* Washington, D.C.: Congressional Quarterly Press, 1989.

———. *The Elections of 1992.* Washington, D.C.: Congressional Quarterly Press, 1993.

Neustadt, Richard. *Presidential Power.* New York: John Wiley and Sons, 1960.

Nie, Norman, Sidney Verba, and John Petrocik. *The Changing American Voter.* Enlarged ed. Cambridge, Mass.: Harvard University Press, 1979.

Nimmo, Dan. *The Political Persuaders*. Englewood Cliffs, N.J.: Prentice-Hall, 1970.

Nimmo, Dan, and James E. Combs. *Mediated Political Realities*. New York: Longman, 1983.

Nimmo, Dan, and Keith Sanders, ed. *Handbook of Political Communication*. Beverly Hills: Sage Publications, 1981.

Norpoth, Helmut. "Under Way and Here to Stay: Party Realignment in the 1980's?" *Public Opinion Quarterly* 51 (Fall 1987): 376–91.

Orren, Gary R., and Nelson W. Polsby. *Media and Momentum: The New Hampshire Primary and Nomination Politics*. Chatham, N.J.: Chatham House, 1987.

Page, Benjamin I., and Robert Y. Shapiro. *The Rational Public: Fifty Years of Trends in Americans' Policy Preferences*. Chicago: University of Chicago Press, 1991.

Parenti, Michael. *Make-Believe Media: The Politics of Entertainment*. New York: St. Martin's Press, 1992.

Patterson, Thomas E. *The Mass Media Election: How Americans Choose Their President*. New York: Praeger, 1980.

———. *The American Democracy*. New York: McGraw-Hill, 1990.

Patterson, Thomas E., and Robert D. McClure. *The Unseeing Eye: The Myth of Television Power in National Elections*. New York: G. P. Putnam's Sons, 1976.

Petrocik, John R. "Realignment: New Party Coalitions and the Nationalization of the South." *Journal of Politics* 49 (1987): 347.

Phillips, Kevin P. *The Emerging Republican Majority*. Garden City, N.J.: Doubleday, 1969.

———. *Mediacracy: American Parties and Politics in the Communications Age*. New York: Doubleday, 1975.

———. *The Politics of Rich and Poor: Wealth and the American Electorate in the Reagan Aftermath*. New York: Random House, 1990.

Polsby, Nelson, and Aaron Wildavsky. *Presidential Elections*. 8th ed. New York: Free Press, 1991.

Pomper, Gerald M. "Classification of Presidential Elections." *Journal of Politics* 29 (August 1967): 535–66.

———. *Voter's Choice: Varieties of American Electoral Behavior*. New York: Dodd, Mead, and Company, 1975.

———. *The Election of 1980: Reports and Interpretations*. Chatham, N.J.: Chatham House, 1981.

———. *The Election of 1984: Reports and Interpretations*. Chatham, N.J.: Chatham House, 1985.

———. *The Election of 1988: Reports and Interpretations*. Chatham, N.J.: Chatham House, 1989.

———. *The Election of 1992: Reports and Interpretations*. Chatham, N.J.: Chatham House, 1993.

Popkin, Samuel L. *The Reasoning Voter: Communication and Persuasion in Presidential Campaigns*. Chicago: University of Chicago Press, 1991.

Robinson, Michael J. "TV's Newest Program, the 'Presidential Nominations Game.'" *Public Opinion* 1 (May–June 1978) 41–45.

Robinson, Michael J., and Margaret A. Sheehan *Over the Wire and on TV: CBS and UPI in Campaign '80*. New York: Russell Sage, 1983.

Rubin, Bernard. *Political Television*. Belmont, Calif.: Wadsworth, 1967.

Rubin, Richard. *Press, Party, and Presidency*. New York: W. W. Norton, 1981.
Sabato, Larry. *The Rise of Political Consultants*. New York: Basic Books, 1981.
Salmore, Stephen A., and Barbara G. Salmore. *Candidates, Parties, and Campaigns*. Washington, D.C.: Congressional Quarterly Press, 1985.
Sandoz, Ellis, and Cecil V. Crabb, Jr., eds. *A Tide of Discontent*. Washington, D.C.: Congressional Quarterly Press, 1981.
Scammon, Richard M., and Ben J. Wattenberg. *The Real Majority*. New York: Coward-McCann, 1970.
Schramm, Martin. *The Great American Video Game: Presidential Politics in the Television Age*. New York: Morrow, 1987.
Shafer, Byron, and Richard Larson. "Did TV Create the 'Social Issue?'" *Columbia Journalism Review* 11 (Sept.–Oct. 1972): 10–17.
Smoller, Fred. "The Six O'clock Presidency: Patterns of Network News Coverage of the President." *Presidential Studies Quarterly* 16 (1986): 31–49.
Stanley, Howard W., William T. Biance, and Richard G. Niemi. "Partisanship and Group Support over Time: A Multivariate Analysis." *American Political Science Review* 80 (Sept. 1986): 969–76.
Stokes, Donald E. "Valence Politics." In *Electoral Politics*, ed. Dennis Kavanagh. Oxford: Clarendon Press, 1992.
Sundquist, James L. *Dynamics of the Party System: Alignment and Realignment of Political Parties in the United States*. Rev. ed. Washington D.C.: Brookings Institution, 1983.
Taylor, Paul. *See How They Run: Electing the President in an Age of Mediacracy*. New York: Knopf, 1990.
Tulis, Jeffrey. *The Rhetorical Presidency*. Princeton: Princeton University Press, 1988.
Wattenberg, Martin P. *The Decline of American Political Parties: 1952–1980*. Cambridge, Mass.: Harvard University Press, 1990.
Wayne, Stephen J. *The Road to the White House: The Politics of Presidential Elections*. 4th ed. New York: St. Martin's Press, 1992.
White, Theodore H. *The Making of the President 1960*. New York: Atheneum, 1961.
———. *The Making of the President 1964*. New York: Atheneum, 1965.
———. *The Making of the President 1968*. New York: Atheneum, 1969.
———. *The Making of the President 1972*. New York: Atheneum, 1973.
———. *America in Search of Itself: The Making of the President 1956–1980*. New York: Harper & Row, 1981.
Winebrenner, Hugh. "The Iowa Precinct Caucuses: The Making of a Media Event." *Southeastern Political Review* 13 (1985): 99–132.
Witcover, Jules. *Marathon: The Pursuit of the Presidency 1972–1976*. New York: Viking, 1977.

Index

American Broadcasting Company (ABC), 14, 125
Anderson, John, 5, 132; general election campaign of 1980, 156–57, 162–63; nomination campaign of 1980, 142, 150

Babbitt, Bruce, 100, 104
Baker, Howard, 142, 150
Bayh, Birch, 142, 147
Biden, Joseph, 100, 104
Brown, Edmund, Jr. (Jerry), 143, 147, 152, 155
Buchanan, Patrick, 121–22, 131–32, 163–64; candidacy in 1992, 123, 133–34, 137, 157
Bush, George, 31; election of 1980, 142, 149–52; general election campaign of 1988, 107, 111–19; general election campaign of 1992, 5, 7, 65, 156–57, 160, 163, 171; nomination campaign of 1988, 75–78, 87–92, 105; nomination campaign of 1992, 121–24, 129–34

Cable News Network (CNN), 14, 131
California primary, 52–53, 85, 87
Campbell, Angus, 3–4, 8

Carter, Jimmy: comparison of 1976 and 1980 elections, 149–50, 152, 154; context of 1980 election, 121–22, 125–29, 133; election of 1976, 1–2, 5, 20, 122, 124; election of 1980, 1–2, 7, 38,; general election campaign of 1976, 68–69, 156–57, 160–62, 165, 169; general election campaign of 1980, 156, 158–60, 162–66, 171; nomination campaign of 1976, 142, 144–48; nomination campaign of 1980, 135–37, 149, 151
Challengers: of strong incumbents, 8, 23, 25, 60; of surrogate incumbents, 74–75, 108, 118–19; of weak incumbents, 123, 130, 132
Checkers speech, 11, 80, 153–54
Church, Frank, 142, 147
Civil Rights disturbances, 35–36, 84
Civil Rights Movement, 32–33, 165
Clinton, Bill, 5, 66, 69, 117, 173; general election campaign of 1992, 158–59, 163–67, 169, 171; nomination campaign of 1992, 122–23, 138, 143, 152–57
Clinton, Hillary, 153–54
Columbia Broadcasting System (CBS), 14, 153–54

Congress, 4, 7, 16–19, 40, 97–98
Connally, John, 142, 150
Consolidation of power: reporting by television, 8, 140, 171; by strong incumbents, 25, 28, 69–70, 72, 123
Converse, Philip, 2–3, 5–8
Crane, Philip, 142, 150

Deaver, Michael, 14, 40
Debates, 19, 150, 160–64
Democratic party, 2–5, 7, 49–50; electoral performances 10–11, 20, 43, 93, 97–98, 163–64
Deviating election, 3–4
Dole, Robert, 27, 89–91, 142, 150, 161
Dukakis, Michael, 5, 68, 133, 152; general election campaign of 1988, 107, 109–114, 116–17; nomination campaign of 1988, 92–93, 98–106

Eisenhower, Dwight, 7, 11, 50, 66–68, 80–82, 95–97, 109, 116
Election of 1932, 3–4
Election of 1936, 24
Election of 1940, 65–67, 115
Election of 1944, 65–67, 115
Election of 1952, 3, 10–11, 67–68, 97
Election of 1956, 3, 11, 17, 68, 97
Election of 1960, 3–5, 9, 10–11, 21, 43, 48, 68, 73, 92; general election campaign, 108–116; nomination campaigns, 79–83, 98–104
Election of 1964, 1, 4, 8, 23–26, 43, 53–54, 95; general election campaign, 59–60, 63–64, 66, 68–70; nomination campaigns, 30–34, 50–54
Election of 1968, 1, 4–5, 9, 17, 26, 34, 43, 73, 92, 95; general election campaign, 113–14, 116, 119; nomination campaigns, 83–87, 100–103, 108–9
Election of 1972, 1, 5, 8, 20, 23–25, 27, 50, 95; general election campaign, 59–60, 63–64, 68–70; nomination campaigns, 34–38, 54–58
Election of 1976, 1, 2, 5, 8, 20, 27, 68–69, 95–96; general election campaign, 156–59, 161–62, 165; nomination campaigns, 124–25, 127–28, 130–31, 135–36, 142, 144–48
Election of 1980, 1, 5, 8, 27, 43, 95; general election campaign, 156–59, 162–63, 165–66; nomination campaigns, 125–26, 128–29, 130–31, 136–37, 142, 148–52
Election of 1984, 1, 5, 8, 10, 17, 20, 23–27, 38, 41, 95; general election campaign, 59–60, 63–64, 68; nomination campaigns, 38–42, 44–50
Election of 1988, 5, 9–10, 27, 73, 92; general election campaign, 108–9, 110–14, 116–17, 119; nomination campaigns, 100–101, 104–6
Election of 1992, 1–2, 5, 8, 10, 39; general election campaign, 156–59, 163–64, 166–67; nomination campaigns, 126–27, 129–32, 137–39, 143, 152–56
Election of 1996, 173
Elections with strong incumbents, 8, 22–72
Elections with surrogate incumbents, 9–10, 22, 73–119
Elections with weak incumbents, 8–9, 22, 121–69

Ford, Gerald, 2, 7, 76, 89; general election campaign of 1976, 147, 156–57, 160–63, 165, 171; nomination campaign of 1976, 121, 124, 127–28, 132–33, 135–36
Front-runner, 19–22; Jimmy Carter, 122–23, 144, 146–47; Bill Clinton, 122–23, 153–56; Michael Dukakis, 101–2, 104, 110; in elections with strong incumbents, 44, 54, 71–72; in elections with weak incumbents, 122, 134, 141–43; Barry Goldwater, 51–52; John Kennedy, 101, 103, 110; George McGovern, 57; Edmund Muskie, 55–56; Richard Nixon, 101, 110; Ronald Reagan, 122–23, 148–50

Gallup poll, 59–60, 108–9, 114, 156–57
Gephardt, Richard, 101, 105–6

INDEX

Goldwater, Barry, 18; campaign of 1960, 82, 96, 100; general election campaign of 1964, 23–24, 59–60, 63–64, 116; nomination campaign of 1964, 32–33, 50–54, 71
Gore, Albert, Jr., 101, 105–6, 166

Harkin, Tom, 143, 155
Harris, Fred, 142, 147
Hart, Gary, 25, 44, 46–49, 53, 72, 97, 100
Humphrey, Hubert, 5, 20, 31, 34, 54–58; general election campaign of 1968, 107, 109, 113–16, 119; nomination campaign of 1968, 75–76, 85–87, 90, 99, 101

Ideology, 2, 24–25, 51
Incumbency, 5–7, 16–17; strong, 23, 25–26, 28–29, 42, 70; weak, 122–23, 134–35, 140, 167–68
Iowa caucuses, 20, 45–46, 144, 148
Iranian hostage crisis, 1, 18, 62, 98, 125

Jackson, Henry, 55, 142, 146–47
Jackson, Jesse: election campaign of 1984, 20, 25, 45, 47, 54; election campaign of 1988, 100, 104–6
Johnson, Lyndon, 96–97, 124, 127, 130; election campaign of 1960, 66, 99, 103, 115, 166–67; election campaign of 1968, 7, 35, 54, 76, 83–87, 116, 121–22, 133; general election campaign of 1964, 5, 7, 23–24, 59–60, 113–14, 171; nomination campaign of 1964, 26, 30–34, 38, 51, 53

Kennedy, Edward, 49, 97, 151; election campaign of 1980, 121, 123, 130–31, 133, 135–37, 139
Kennedy, John, 10–11, 13, 23, 29–33, 79; election of 1960, 4, 11, 18–19, 48, 69, 71, 115, 165; general election campaign of 1960, 107–10, 112–16, 119, 159, 161; nomination campaign of 1960, 86, 92–93, 98–99, 101–3, 106
Kennedy, Robert, 5, 26, 30, 54, 83, 85–87, 121, 131–32

Kerrey, Robert, 143, 155
Key, V. O., 3

Leading adversary, 20–21, 54, 56–57, 72, 132; television coverage of, 43–44, 51, 142, 149, 151
Lodge, Henry Cabot, Jr., 51–52

Maintaining election, 3–4
Marginal viewers, 15–16, 142
McCarthy, Eugene, 5, 54, 85, 133
McGovern, George, 18, 45, 152; general election campaign of 1972, 23–25, 59, 63–64, 71; nomination campaign of 1972, 54–58
Midwestern states, 32, 66–69, 115, 117, 165–66
Mondale, Walter, 71–72, 76, 151; general election campaign of 1984, 23–25, 59–60, 62–64, 161; nomination campaign of 1984, 44–50, 54, 97
Muskie, Edmund, 54–57

National Broadcasting Company (NBC), 14
Nixon, Richard, 51, 89, 128, 131, 134, 158; general election campaign of 1960, 4–5, 10–11, 96, 100, 108–9, 112–13; general election campaign of 1968, 75–76, 107–110, 113–16, 119, 159, 172; general election campaign of 1972, 2, 7, 23, 27, 59–60, 171; nomination campaign of 1960, 17, 75, 79–83, 90, 96; nomination campaign of 1968, 92–93, 98, 101–4; nomination campaign of 1972, 34–38
New Hampshire primary: election of 1964, 51–52; election of 1968, 85, 101; election of 1972, 26, 55–57; election of 1976, 135, 146; election of 1980, 132, 135–36, 151; election of 1984, 45, 47; election of 1988, 90, 106; election of 1992, 155
News reporting (television), 16–22; coverage of incumbents, 27–28, 61–62, 84; coverage of nomination campaigns, 46, 48–49, 74–75, 109–110, 118, 153, 169

Northeastern states, 32, 66–68, 115–17, 165–67

Opposition party, 7–10, 21–22, 94; in elections with strong incumbents, 28–29, 42–58; in elections with surrogate incumbents, 92–106; in elections with weak incumbents,28–29, 140–156; television coverage of, 18, 25, 71–74, 112, 122

Partisanship, 2–3, 7–8, 58–59, 64–65, 69–70, 116
Perot, Ross, 5, 132, 134, 138–39, 156–58, 163–64, 167
Phillips, Kevin, 3–4, 35
Presidency, 6–7, 25–26, 31, 60, 73–74, 134, 139
Presidential party, 7–10, 21–22, 94; in elections with strong incumbents, 25–42; in elections with surrogate incumbents, 75–92; in elections with weak incumbents, 123–40; television coverage of, 16, 142, 168

Reagan, Ronald, 7, 14, 87–88, 117, 126, 139; general election campaign of 1980, 2, 5, 130–31, 142, 156–59, 162–63, 165–66, 169; general election campaign of 1984, 7, 23–25, 50, 59–60, 95, 171; nomination campaign of 1968, 39, 91, 94, 100, 104; nomination campaign of 1976, 121–23, 125, 132–33, 135–37, 144; nomination campaign of 1980, 148–52; nomination campaign of 1984, 27, 38–42, 44
Realigning election, 3–4
Republican party, 2–5, 7, 11; electoral performances 35, 43, 81–82, 93, 95–97
Rockefeller, Nelson, 36, 51–53, 72, 82, 97, 100–101, 103–4
Romney, George, 51, 100
Roosevelt, Franklin, 64–69, 81, 115–16
Rose Garden strategy, 34, 60, 64, 70, 111

Sanford, Terry, 55, 142
Scranton, William, 51, 53–54
Short-term factors, 3, 58–59, 115–16
Shriver, Sargent, 32, 142, 147
Simon, Paul, 100, 104–6
Southeastern states, 66, 68–69, 90, 115–16, 165–67
Stahl, Lesley, 14, 40
Statesman role, 25, 28, 43, 60, 70, 122–23, 172
Stevenson, Adlai, Jr., 11, 97, 99, 103, 115
Symington, Stuart, 99, 103

Taft, Robert, 80, 96
Television age, 10–12, 16
Television effects, 6, 12–19, 25, 28–29, 46, 69
Television news coverage: George Bush, 87–91, 129–30, 134, 139–40; Jimmy Carter, 128–29, 134, 139–40, 144–48; Bill Clinton, 152–56; Michael Dukakis, 104–6; election of 1996, 173; Gerald Ford, 127–28, 134, 139–40, 161; Barry Goldwater, 51–54; Gary Hart, 46–49, 104; Hubert Humphrey, 54–57, 83–86, 113; Lyndon Johnson, 31–34; John Kennedy, 29–30; George McGovern, 55–58, 63; Walter Mondale, 46–47, 49–50; Edmund Muskie, 55–57; Richard Nixon, 37–38, 76–82; Ross Perot, 138–39; Ronald Reagan, 42, 148–52; strong incumbents, 27–29, 60–62, 70–72; Vice Presidency, 77–79, 118–19; weak incumbents, 122, 139–40, 143, 157–58
Television news media: approaches and values, 8–10, 12–16, 19–21, 25; definition, 6
Truman, Harry, 11, 66, 97, 115, 172

Udall, Morris, 142, 146–47

Van Buren, Martin, 17, 76
Vice Presidency, 11, 16–17, 86, 97, 124–25; electoral role, 107–8; surrogate role, 7, 9, 30–31, 73–79, 91–92

Vietnam, 1, 33, 35–36, 57, 63, 83–84, 97, 109, 128

Wallace, George, 5, 26, 33, 54–56, 109, 116, 142

Watergate, 1, 35, 38, 128, 131
Western states, 66–67, 115–17, 165–67
White, Theodore, 19, 48, 71, 106
Winnowing processes, 19–22

About the Author

E. D. DOVER is Associate Professor of Political Science, Public Policy, and Administration at Western Oregon State College. He has taught at the University of Tennessee at Martin, the University of Colorado at Boulder, and the University of Wyoming. A long-time political and labor union activist, he is president of the Western Oregon State College Federation of Teachers.

ISBN 0-275-94840-4

HARDCOVER BAR CODE